Finding a Social Voice

# FINDING A SOCIAL VOICE

## The Church and Marxism in Africa

*by*

JOSEPH C. MCKENNA, S.J.

Fordham University Press
New York
1997

Library of Congress Cataloging-in-Publication Data

McKenna, Joseph C.
    Finding a social voice : the Church and Marxism in Africa / by
Joseph C. McKenna.
       p.   cm.
    Includes bibliographical references.
    ISBN 0-8232-1712-4 (hardcover : alk. paper).—ISBN 0-8232-1713-2
(pbk. : alk. paper)
    1. Communism and Christianity—Catholic Church—Africa, Sub-
Saharan—History.  I. Title.
BX1396.4M45   1997
261.2′1—dc21                                97-8013
                                                    CIP

For My Brothers and Sisters:
Lawrence, Helen, George, and Irene

# CONTENTS

# ACKNOWLEDGMENTS

Neither scholars nor journalists have written much about the subject of the present book. I therefore faced exceptional difficulties in becoming and staying informed about many events and developments which were virtually contemporaneous, bearing on the interaction between Church and State in the countries I was dealing with. For this reason I needed exceptional help, and I am grateful that so many people gave it so generously. It would be impractical to acknowledge them all by name, however, and in any case many of them preferred anonymity. So I express my thanks in general terms.

Something like sixty people gave me their time and shared their knowledge and perceptions with me in the course of extended conversations. In Rome and Lisbon, officials of religious and missionary congregations directed me to little-noticed sources of documentation and helped me obtain access to them. In Africa, several of my Jesuit confreres provided similar direction and assistance. They also put me in touch with the Church's local undertakings, arranged meetings with knowledgeable people, guided me over unfamiliar terrain, and brought me to places not easy to reach. I am particularly indebted on this account to Frs. Jean Verley in Madagascar, Richard Randolph in Zimbabwe, and Richard Cremins in Zambia.

The directors of five specialized libraries made available a number of items that I could not have found elsewhere: the libraries at the generalates of the Holy Ghost Fathers and the White Fathers (Missionaries of Africa) in Rome, of the IDOC Documentation Center in the same city, of the Institut Supérieur de Théologie in Antananarivo, and of the Maryknoll College of Theology in Maryknoll, New York. I also drew heavily on the resources of Fordham University's Duane Library. Its reference staff was especially helpful in tracking down material at Fordham and elsewhere.

Europa Publications, London, granted permission to reproduce the map of Africa (opposite page 1). The map appears on page 4 of their *Africa South of the Sahara 1995*, published in 1994.

Provincial Superiors of the Jesuits' New York Province allowed me time for research and writing and financed my travel and other expenses. The foundation, Kirche in Not/Ostpriesterhilfe, in Königstein, Germany, provided a generous grant to assist with publication.

An anonymous reader for the Fordham University Press suggested useful improvements of the manuscript. Dr. Mary Beatrice Schulte, the Press's Executive Editor, guided it to ultimate publication.

The responsibility for what I have written is, of course, exclusively my own.

# Finding a Social Voice

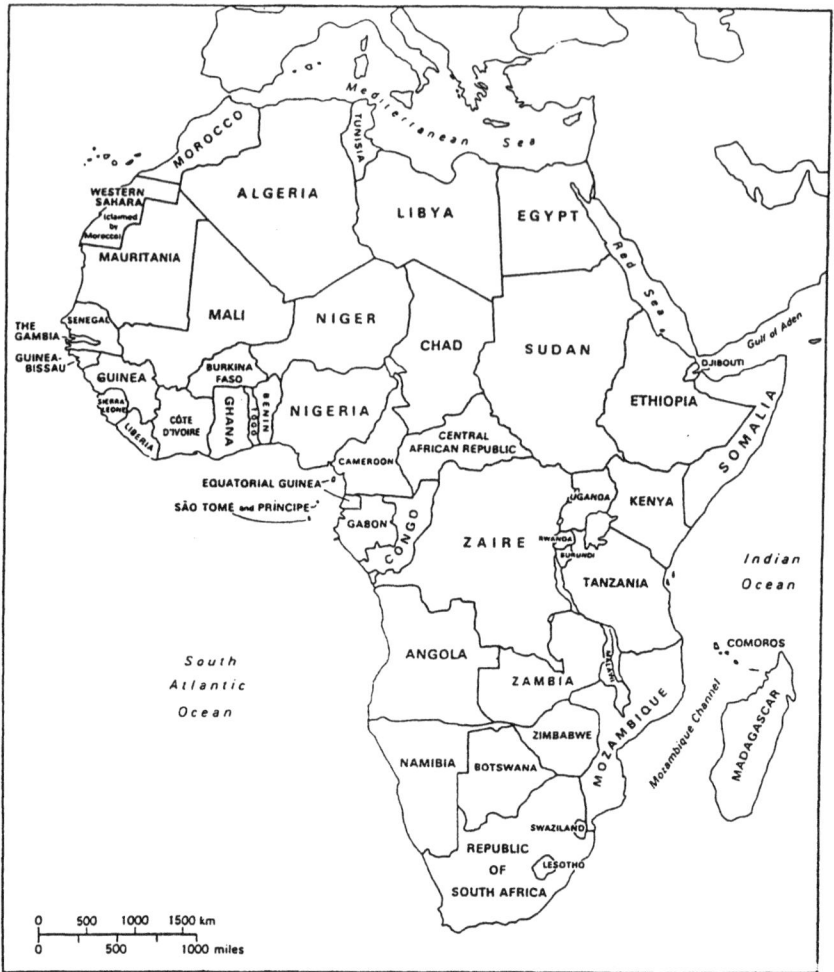

OUTLINE POLITICAL MAP OF CONTEMPORARY AFRICA

Source: *Africa South of the Sahara 1995* (London: Europa Publications, 1994), p. 4.

# 1

# Rationale, Approach

## RATIONALE

FROM THE LATE 1960s until the mid-1980s, the influence of Marxist ideas expanded in sub-Saharan Africa. The Catholic Church saw this influence as likely to affect the accomplishment of its mission. Its pastoral efforts accordingly sought to deal with the Marxist thrust. In the late 1980s, Marxist influence in Africa declined sharply as Marxist political dominance in Eastern Europe collapsed. The Church's concern with Marxism then became less intense. Nevertheless, the Church's encounter with Marxist influence in the earlier decades constituted an important chapter in both secular and ecclesiastical history. The present book tries to record and analyze some significant elements of this encounter.

On the secular side, for reasons arising out of colonial history, the Church's weight in many newly independent African states was often disproportionate to the number of its members. In consequence, "marxizing" governments could not disregard the Church's views. It seems likely, then, that these views had an impact, although it is not readily identifiable, on the structures, policies, and methods that such governments adopted.

On the ecclesiastical side, the Church's pastoral response to Marxist influence was part of its coming to maturity. These were the years in which the churches in Africa were passing from missionary tutelage to indigenous control. Pastoral theologians and religious sociologists were pressing for "inculturation"—the insertion of liturgy, sacramental life, moral norms, and systematic theology into traditional cultures. Equally urgent, however, was the need to bring the Church's social perspectives to bear on the processes of political, economic, and social modernization through which traditional cultures were passing. The encounter with Marxism compelled the Church to deal with this facet of its mission.

This ecclesiastical side of the encounter is the principal concern here. The focal issue is not the impact of the Church's response on the development of Marxism in Africa; it is the impact of this response on the Church itself.

The meeting between the Church and Marxism in Africa has not received much attention in scholarly or popular writing. Although a number of recent books have dealt with Marxism in Africa from social, political, and economic viewpoints, they have scarcely touched religion at all. Papal documents, from Pius IX to John Paul II, have treated Marxist theories, but only at the level of general principle. During the past fifteen years, the Vatican Secretariat for Non-Believers, the Union of Superiors General, and the missionary institute Servizio di Documentazione e Studi (SEDOS) have sponsored studies and consultations on the relationship between Christian faith and Marxist ideology.[1] Since 1966 the Secretariat for Non-Believers has been publishing a quarterly journal, *Ateismo e Dialogo*, which documents and studies current developments in Marxism as these relate to the problem of unbelief. In these undertakings, however, European, Asian, and Latin American perspectives have overshadowed the African perspective. *L'Afrique face au communisme*, by Roland Vezeau, W.F., did deal with ideological and political aspects of Marxist influence in Africa and Madagascar as they affected the Church. Though this is an informative book, it appeared thirty years ago, in 1967. More recently, Armand Guillaumin, W.F., published *La séduction marxiste*, which treats the intellectual encounter of Marxist and Christian thought in the African context.[2] A few articles in ecclesiastical periodicals have been concerned with Marxist influence as it touched particular Church interests in particular countries. It is partly because so relatively little has appeared on the topic that the present book was written.

## APPROACH

Although Marxism raises problems for other Christian bodies, for Islam, and for African traditional religions, this book's concern is with the Roman Catholic Church. Even then, the word "church" has many meanings. The focus here is primarily but not exclusively on the Church as an organization, because it is through organizational channels that the Church coordinates its responses to issues that affect its pastoral efforts.

The term "Marxism," too, has many meanings. Marxist scholars differ among themselves in their understanding of Karl Marx's ideas, and in the 1970s and 1980s Marxist political leaders around the world were no longer looking to the Soviet Union for authentic interpretation of the theory as they had earlier. Broadly, however, "Marxism" is here taken to mean social theorizing at least nominally based on the philosophy of Karl Marx and Friedrich Engels as this was developed in the thinking and practice of V. I. Lenin and the leaders of Eastern European countries. Imprecise equivalents are "Marxism-Leninism" and "Scientific Socialism."

This book looks at "sub-Saharan Africa." This comprises the forty-seven (less two) independent countries of the continent and its offshore islands which are south of the Sahara Desert. Excluded are Namibia, which became independent only in 1990, and the Republic of South Africa, where the context was totally different from anywhere else in the region. The study is concerned, generally speaking, with developments during the period from 1975 to 1988.

Essentially the book consists of narration, description, and explanation. But it draws upon information and other relevant materials collected from scattered sources: books and journals on theology, philosophy, history, and political science; government documents; the public press; files of Church organizations; people involved with the apostolate; and the author's brief personal observation in several countries.

The study begins, in chapter 2, with a review of Marxist theory and practice. This will help toward understanding why Marxism aroused concern in the Church. Chapter 3 will offer a summary account of how Marxist influence expanded in Africa. Chapter 4 will present an overall view of the Church in Africa and its meeting with Marxism. Chapters 5 through 8 are detailed narratives of how Marxist influence affected the Church and of how the Church responded in four particular countries: Mozambique, Madagascar, Zimbabwe, and Zambia. These were chosen with several considerations in mind. In all of them Marxism had a significant impact, but the impact differed in its consequences. All of them had relatively large populations, ranging from six to ten million. This and other factors made them potentially important actors in the politics and economics of the continent. In all four countries, too, the Catholic Church was a notable presence; its members constituted between 8.5 and 26 percent of the total population. Although the four countries were similar on these counts, they also showed important diversities. These stemmed especially from their varied colonial backgrounds: Portuguese, French, and English. Zimbabwe and Zambia differed inasmuch as a professedly Marxist government controlled Zimbabwe, whereas in Zambia there was merely a perceptible inclination to transform a non-Marxist to a Marxist regime. Each chapter sketches the country's background, the rise of Marxist influence, the history and operations of the Church, how Marxism affected these operations, and how the Church dealt with these developments. Finally, chapter 9 looks for generalizations about the Church's response to Marxist influence, especially as related to the assumption of its social mission and the maturing of the "young" churches.

## NOTES

1. See Secretariat for Non-Believers, Circular letter from Cardinal König to the Presidents of Episcopal Conferences, November 24, 1974, Prot. n. 003465/74; and enclosure, "Conclusions of the Plenary Assembly, March 12–15, 1974. Theme 1: Relationship between Christian Faith and Marxist ideologies today. Theme II: Evangelization of the World Today, Confronting Atheism and Secularization," Prot. n. 003340/74, mimeographed. *SEDOS Bulletin*, 77/8 (1 May 1977), 181–203, and bibliographical appendix by J. Sommet, S.J. et al., mimeographed. This issue of the Bulletin contains material for the SEDOS General Assembly of May 30 on the topic: "New Insertions in Developing Societies Where There Is Marxist Influence." In January 1976, a commission of the Union of Superiors General discussed the position of the Church in Communist countries; confidential informant.

2. Roland Vezeau, *L'Afrique face au communisme* (Paris: Éditions Edimpra, 1967); Armand Guillaumin, *La séduction marxiste: Un prêtre médite Marx* (Bologna: E.M.I., 1987).

# 2

# Marxism: Theory and Practice

PEOPLE OFTEN USE THE WORDS "Marxism" and "Marxist" carelessly in political discussion. The Church's concern was not with concepts inaccurately labeled in this way but with the elaborate system of ideas first shaped by Karl Marx and Friedrich Engels and then developed by V. I. Lenin and others into the "Marxist-Leninist" theories underlying the governance of the Soviet Union. These were the theories that some people were trying to advance in Africa. Especially for readers whose knowledge of Marxism-Leninism is somewhat casual, a review of the system's major concepts will help toward an understanding of both the Church's concern and its response.

## MARX, ENGELS, BACKGROUNDS

Marx[1] lived from 1818 to 1883. He was born in Germany. Although he planned a career as a professor of philosophy and took his doctorate in that field, he involved himself instead in political journalism and revolutionary activism in his own country and in France and Belgium. Among other things, he perceived that economic changes in the Rhineland and Westphalia were devastating the lives of the poor, and so he began serious study of economics. He took part in the revolution of 1848 in Germany; when it failed, he was forced into exile and settled in London. There he mainly devoted himself to producing his monumental book, *Das Kapital*. He published its first volume in 1867; the second and third volumes were published after his death. Even apart from *Das Kapital* he was a prolific writer.

Marx did not work alone. In 1844 Friedrich Engels became his lifelong friend and collaborator. Engels[2] was likewise German, born in 1820. His family were manufacturers—capitalists. From 1842 to 1844 and again from 1850 to 1870, he worked in his family's business in Manchester, England. After the first of these periods, he published *The Condition of the Working Class in England*, in which he powerfully described urban poverty and predicted a socialist revolution. From 1844 to 1849, Engels associated himself with Marx's writing and revolutionary activities on the continent, and took part in the unsuccessful uprising of 1848. During his second stay in Manchester, Engels provided Marx with financial support for the writing which he regarded as vital for the revolution. He prospered in business and retired comfortably to London in 1870. There he wrote several more books of his own and helped with Marx's work while the latter lived. After Marx died, Engels edited and published volumes 2 and 3 of *Das Kapital* and arranged for posthumous publication of other writings by Marx. Engels died in 1895. Although differences of understanding sometimes show between the respective writings of Marx and of Engels, their works serve as the basic documents of "Marxism."

Marx himself stressed that men's thinking is powerfully influenced by the circumstances in which they live, and this was true in his own case. One of the most far-reaching social developments of nineteenth-century Europe presented him with a focal preoccupation. This was the mass production of consumer goods by semi-skilled workmen using power-driven machinery. A new structure of social classes was taking shape; especially notable was the rise of a moneyed middle class, the upper "bourgeoisie"—the capitalists who owned the factories and machines and controlled the big commercial ventures—and of a burgeoning class of factory workers who could sustain themselves only by the work of their hands. Marx called these people the "proletariat."

Marx's thinking was affected, as well, by general tendencies that pervaded Europe's intellectual climate. He was a Rationalist; he shared the conviction that man's reason, unaided by religious faith, could solve all the mysteries of the universe. He was a Materialist; he took it for granted that only material beings, beings that man's senses experienced, really existed. He rejected religious belief; during his secondary studies he was still a Christian of sorts, but the contemporary criticism of religion by David Strauss, Bruno Bauer, and others soon drew him to atheism. He was also attracted to the widely accepted Idealist philosophy of G. W. F. Hegel—but with a difference. Although in principle Hegel's Idealism eschewed materialism, Marx aligned himself with the "Young Hegelians," who rejected a theological strain perceptible in Hegel's thought; ultimately he substituted a materialist base for Hegel's system. Engels's youthful development followed a different course, but he, too, joined the

Young Hegelians. Despite his strict Protestant upbringing, he became an atheist. He was drawn to socialism before Marx was.[3]

## MARX'S GENERAL PHILOSOPHIC CONCEPTS

When we turn from the historical background of Marx and Engels to their theories, we find that they did not set forth a systematic general philosophy.[4] Their general concepts were only incidental to their social and revolutionary ideas. Some of these concepts, however, help toward understanding their social thought.

Marx's epistemology takes it for granted that the human mind can have valid knowledge of outside reality. For him, however, the social circumstances of the knower—specifically, the material interests of his social class—will distort his mental vision. People, notably the bourgeoisie, suffer "false consciousness," which clouds their thinking. This makes history's march toward revolution inexorable, because the dominant social class cannot change its thinking in order to change history's direction.[5]

Although Marx did not study the makeup of human beings very closely, he clearly placed a high value, even the highest value, on "man." He believed that men should fully develop their specifically human qualities; here he apparently had in mind artistic and scientific pursuits. At the same time, he decried self-regarding individualism and stressed the social character of personal growth; man "will develop his true nature only in society." He severely criticized forces that dehumanized man and bemoaned what he called "alienation." What he had in mind was that in developing himself and the universe, man should be master of himself and of whatever he accomplishes. Sometimes, instead, man's efforts put both his activity and its product outside his own control, even making them hostile, "alien," to himself.[6]

The Marxist philosophy of history is commonly called "dialectical materialism."[7] Marx took over the "dialectic" from Hegel but put it on an entirely different basis. According to Hegel, objective happenings were some kind of limited projection of the Absolute Mind. Their reality was "idea-l" or "spiritual." Because these events were the reflections of a Mind, the march of history necessarily followed some controlling rule or law. Hegel decided that the law worked this way: the succession of historical events was like a conversational dialogue. A particular event was like a statement. The built-in limitations of the event were like a negation or contradiction of the statement. From the statement and its contradiction there came a new event, a synthesis, which was a corrected and improved restatement. As events followed events in this dialectical process, limited "idea-l" realities became fuller, better, and truer expressions of the Absolute Mind. For Marx as a materialist, however, there was no Absolute Mind, and so external events could not be ideas emanating from it. In the march of history, it was matter that passed through the stages that Hegel described, and the process was following a necessity that was somehow built into the nature of things. We will discuss later Marx's actual use of dialectical materialism to interpret human history.[8]

Even though Marx used the language of morality, he did not work out any general principles of ethics. He spoke about moral and immoral conduct, obligation, and conscience. He detested human alienation and social practices that exploited workers. He denounced certain activities, situations, and policies as contrary to humanity. Yet even in his criticism of capitalist society he was not directly condemning its injustices; he was analyzing its dynamics and foretelling its collapse. His point was not that a new social system *ought* to be established to bring justice for the oppressed but that a new social system *will in fact* be established and will in fact bring justice for the oppressed.[9]

Marx gave little attention to "rights" as a category of morality, but he did deal sometimes with particular rights. In his early journalism, he vigorously defended freedom of the press against government restrictions in Prussia. He took exception, however, to the view that the right to private property was one of the "rights of man." He saw these "rights" as individualistic and harmful to social cohesion. He looked instead toward overcoming the split between private and community interests. Every man could develop his personal aptitudes, but he would do so as an integrated human being who saw himself as a bearer of community. Unfortunately, this view opened the way to society's absorbing the individual and to the individual's having no claims against society.[10]

We come finally to Marxist philosophy on God and religion. In the materialist view, as Engels put it: "Nothing exists outside nature and man, and the higher beings our religious fantasies have created are only the fantastic [i.e., imaginary] effects of our own essence."[11] For Marx and Engels, the existence of God was not credible. Primitive people had "created" God to explain natural phenomena they did not understand, and they projected their own human qualities onto their concept of God. Later on, dominant classes in society preserved the notion of God and religion in order to protect their worldly interests against challenge. Whereas Marx's atheism followed logically upon his materialism, he rooted his rejection of God more emphatically in his humanism—his esteem for man. As he saw it, a man subjected to God was less a man; he was "alienated"; his morality followed laws made by someone else who was, moreover, a mere figment of the person's own imagination. In Marx's mind, man belonged to himself; he was free to develop his own natural powers; he was autonomous; "human self-consciousness [was] the highest divinity."[12]

Because there was no God, religious organizations and observances had no meaning. But Marx opposed religion for more specific reasons. In his view, religion made men and women passive and submissive. It led them to wait for other-worldly solutions of social problems instead of actively seeking this-worldly answers. Religion was the "opium of the people," in the sense that people used its illusions to forget their pain. In the 1840s, Marx's atheism was militant. Later, he seldom spoke out on religious issues, but, according to his dialectical theory, religion would fade away and die when classless society took the place of bourgeois society.[13] Engels, by contrast, studied and wrote about religious questions all his life, arguing especially that new findings both of natural science and of biblical scholarship confirmed the Marxist position. Still, in 1874 he warned that persecution would strengthen religion; "the only service that can still be rendered to God is to make atheism a compulsory dogma."[14]

## MARX'S SOCIAL PHILOSOPHY

It was not Marx's general philosophy but his social theory that gave his system its political impact. Parts of this appeared in *Das Kapital*, parts in his many writings from 1844 onward. But he never did complete a comprehensive statement of it.[15]

His theory had a twofold thrust. First, he contended that capitalist production in the Europe of his era exploited the working class and dehumanized both the worker and the capitalist. Second, he predicted that this situation would inevitably provoke revolution, put socialist production in place of capitalist, end exploitation, and promote humanization.[16]

The supporting argument for this theory was very complex. Central to it was a supposed law of social evolution. From earliest historical times, society's structures passed through systematic changes from one period to the next. Each change arose out of the development of particular classes and the conflict between them. Every such change in turn started the next one. The decisive factor shaping the classes and their conflict was the method of producing goods that was characteristic of the particular period.

In primitive society, property and labor were communal; families worked together for their subsistence. There was no surplus production; there were no social classes. Then new methods of production emerged and led to specialization and division of labor. They produced surplus goods and gave rise to rivalry over control of the surplus. Thus, European history saw an era of masters and slaves in antiquity, of lords and serfs in the Middle Ages, and of aristocracy and bourgeoisie in the Renaissance. The bourgeoisie then became dominant through the French Revolution and industrialization. In this new era, according to Marx, technology and the capitalist mode of production were forming a capitalist bourgeoisie and a proletarian class, and were enkindling conflict between them. Proletarian revolution would overthrow the capitalists. During a transitional period, private ownership of capital would be abolished and capitalists would disappear. Then a new classless, harmonious society would emerge and would last forevermore.[17]

Marx's analysis was linked with his theory of dialectical materialism. The "contradictions" of capitalism, its own destructive operations, were the very things causing its downfall. Under capitalism, the workers depended completely on the owners for access to the tools of production, the machines. Owners could therefore hire the workers on their own exploitative terms. To explain the exploitation, Marx used the notion of "surplus value." Although his full argument was complicated, essentially he said that the worker, laboring for a wage that provided him with mere subsistence, produced more value than he was paid for, and that the employer was appropriating the "surplus" for himself. Driven, moreover, by his desire for more and more surplus value, the capitalist kept introducing new techniques to make the worker's labor more productive. Using the new techniques, workers turned out more goods more cheaply, but this led to overproduction. Workers were then dismissed, the level of wages went down, and the masses' purchasing power fell. The contradiction lay in the fact that greed for profit increased the availability of goods at the very time it reduced the demand for them. There was a built-in barrier to expanding production. Economic chaos would finally force the replacement of capitalism with a better system.[18]

The capitalist system, further, gave rise to psychological phenomena that dehumanized both worker and capitalist. Detailed explanation of this point is not necessary here. Briefly, the worker came to see his labor merely as a commodity and himself as a thing instead of a person; and his animal concern just to keep alive spawned a self-regarding individualism that undermined the establishment of any real community.[19] Meanwhile the capitalist's drive to create surplus value made him act in a certain way. His own character and personal good intentions played no part in his economic activities. He became "capital personified." It was pointless for the social reformer to appeal to his humanity and good will.[20]

These, then, were the social dynamics that were simultaneously building and destroying the capitalist system. Capitalism was giving rise to two antagonistic social classes: capitalists and proletariat. The proletariat was growing bigger as recurring economic crises squeezed weaker entrepreneurs out of the capitalist ranks, downward. The proletariat was also becoming more class conscious. Industrial urbanization was drawing the masses into denser concentrations and intensifying communication among them. Above all, their resentment over exploitation, their mounting feeling of alienation and dehumanization, and the increasing economic chaos were rousing their revolutionary consciousness.[21]

Marx did not say clearly when or how the proletariat's revolutionary consciousness would pass into action. In 1850 he conceded that the workers might have to struggle for fifty years before they could seize power. Generally, he saw the revolution as violent, but late in life he thought revolutionaries might take power by parliamentary means in some places. In countries marked by traces of feudalism he foresaw a two-step revolution. First, the liberal bourgeoisie would overthrow the aristocracy; then the proletariat would overthrow the bourgeoisie.[22]

Regardless of how the revolution came about, Marx saw it as passing through two phases. In the first phase, the revolutionaries would exercise their power as a "dictatorship of the proletariat." He did not say how long the dictatorship would last or what its structure would be. According to the *Communist Manifesto*, which he wrote in 1848, the Communists would play a leading role. They were the most advanced sector of the proletarian party and represented the interests of the entire proletariat. They had the best knowledge of what was going on. But the *Manifesto* left room for the enlightened bourgeoisie to join the proletariat, "in particular, . . . bourgeois ideologists who . . . [comprehend] the historical movement as a whole." It thus left room for men of Marx's and Engels's social background to take part and even to play a dominant role.[23]

The dictatorship of the proletariat would use ruthless coercion. It would dismantle the capitalist system. It would abolish private ownership of capital property and take public ownership of this property in the name "of the proletariat, organized as the ruling class." The new rulers would aim to revolutionize the means of production. As typical measures, they might abolish land ownership and inheritance, impose heavy progressive taxes, centralize credit in government banks, set up a government monopoly of transport and communications, and make everyone equally liable to labor. Although some steps might initially be economically inefficient, the process would expand the forces of production and establish an economy of abundance. The dictatorship would plan production.[24]

The very dynamics of the revolution's first phase would lead to its second phase. The dismantling of the capitalist system would eliminate capitalists as a class. The proletariat would also disappear as a class, because the reason for its class-consciousness would be no more. The state or government would "wither away," too, because laws and other governmental institutions were merely the instruments the dominant class used to protect its own interest; they would no longer be needed. Only the administrative functions of government would continue. So the dictatorship of the proletariat would likewise vanish.[25]

The society that emerged would accordingly be not just a society without conflict but also a society of positive harmony. Labor would no longer be alienating. People would see their work in interpersonal terms— producing objects useful for other people. From one phase of the revolution to the next, in Marx's view, the arrangements for work would change. During the first phase, the workman would be compensated in proportion to the time he worked, but he would be *fully* compensated. Part of what he produced would be set aside for social needs; the rest would be his. During the second phase, however, goods would be abundant and a new principle would operate: "From each according to his ability, to each according to his needs."[26]

Even though this slogan was egalitarian, and even though Marx so fiercely criticized the harsh living conditions imposed on the working class, his expectation was not mainly that the revolution would conquer poverty and establish equality. He expected that it would also overcome alienation and restore people's humanity. It would create an atmosphere in which people felt that they were masters of their social institutions, their machines, their toil, and their lives. People would also have more free time for creative activity, for developing their personal abilities through education, art, and science. They would recapture the positive social relationships that were part of being human.[27]

The main lines of Marx's theory did not touch colonialism, but he did deal with this topic, mostly in his journalistic pieces. In the *New York Tribune* he often wrote about Great Britain's treatment of four or five issues in China and India. He castigated Britain's promotion of the opium trade, its imposition of many taxes on local peoples, and its high-handed diplomacy. What drove Britain to these injustices was its eagerness to extract surplus value from subject populations overseas. Colonialism was an extension of capitalism and carried the same kind of "contradiction." It was undermining Britain's own economy and raising the consciousness of the subject nations. On the other hand, Marx also showed blunt disdain for Asian cultures. Britain's oppressive administration in India, he argued, was working as an instrument of history; it was breaking down backward elements of local culture so as to open the way for the country's march toward a new age.[28]

A final feature of Marx's social theory was his insistence that it was "scientific." He wrote: "We established . . . the scientific understanding of society as the only tenable theoretical foundation" for socialism. Although he did not make clear what he meant by "scientific," his main point seemed to be that he based his theories on empirical study of people's social interaction. In effect, he was reacting against certain intellectual tendencies of his era, among them the Utopian socialism which drew enchanting but impractical blueprints of the new order; this was one reason why he refrained from painting his own pictures of postrevolutionary society.[29]

Marx greatly respected the achievements of natural science which marked the late nineteenth century, and he expected that social science would someday be integrated with it.[30] But he himself did not explicitly use the special methodologies that were bringing about such marvelous discoveries. Even so, in the minds of many people, the claim that his theories were scientific gave them the same prestige that natural science enjoyed.

## LENINISM: LENIN AND THE OCTOBER REVOLUTION

Such were the social theories of Karl Marx and Friedrich Engels. But they do not constitute a complete picture of present-day Marxism. In 1917, a revolutionary movement that claimed to be guided by Marx's thought seized political control in Russia. The revolution itself and the subsequent governance of that country gave rise to Marxism-Leninism, the version of Marx's theories that was most relevant to political life in sub-Saharan Africa. To help toward understanding this elaboration of Marx's ideas, it will be useful to present a brief account of the revolution and what followed, and to outline the thinking of the two men who most influenced these developments, V. I. Lenin and Joseph Stalin.

In the early twentieth century, the Russian Empire reached from Europe across Asia, embracing Asian as well as European peoples. It was far less developed than other European countries, however; industry was only beginning to grow. Class division was marked, especially between the landed gentry and the peasants. Frictions of class, ethnicity, and religion made for serious social unrest. The czar ruled the country as an absolute, reactionary, and widely detested monarch. Countless revolutionary organizations, many of them Marxist, aimed at radical change of one kind or another. World War I aggravated the tensions within the country. Military defeats, heavy casualties, shortages of basic goods, and other hardships demoralized both soldiers and civilians. This set the stage for two fateful revolutions in 1917.

Success in these revolutions ultimately went to a group called the Bolsheviks, a faction of the Russian Social Democratic Party led by Lenin. Lenin, whose real name was Vladimir Ilyich Ulanov, was born in 1870 in eastern Russia. He became a revolutionary in 1887 and then a Marxist. After a period of imprisonment and internal exile, he went abroad to organize émigré Social Democrats into a coherent movement. There he became the leader of the party's Bolshevik wing.[31]

In February 1917 civilian discontent broke out in public demonstrations, followed by a bloodless coup in which the czar surrendered power to a Provisional Government. Lenin returned home and organized opposition to this regime. Public discontent continued, and in October a second coup replaced the Provisional Government. A Council of People's Commissars took power, with Bolsheviks holding a majority of the seats. The council made Lenin prime minister. He ruled the new Russia thenceforward until he died seven years later—a forceful, domineering personality with iron determination.[32]

## Lenin's Regime

His policies varied, however, as the circumstances varied. When he came to power, he had to deal with the very same public discontents he had exploited to overthrow the Provisional Government. He had promised "peace." He quickly negotiated a treaty with Germany; this required Russia to grant independence to some non-Russian nationalities in its borderlands: the Poles, the Ukrainians, and others. He had promised "land" to the peasants' party to win its support for the Bolsheviks' maneuvers. So his government decreed that land belonged to those who worked it. He had also promised "bread" to the city dwellers; but his draconian efforts to deliver bread brought him into conflict with the peasants, who were unwilling to ship food to the cities when the cities were shipping nothing to them. His regime reacted vigorously, too, against the efforts of other groups to regain power. In December 1917, the government organized the CHEKA, secret police, to combat counterrevolution. It established forced labor camps at about the same time. Following an attempt on Lenin's life in April 1918, it began a campaign of terror against intellectuals, bourgeoisie, and opposition socialists.[33] From 1917 to 1921, Lenin's government also faced civil war. Old-line officers (the "Whites") led military forces against the regime in various parts of the country, but a new Red Army defeated them.

This period came to be called the "years of War Communism." From its very beginning, Lenin's regime took radical steps to make the economy socialist; and to pursue the civil war, it imposed even more drastic discipline. It nationalized industries, banks, and lands. It forced workers to join labor unions controlled by government. It forbade workers to strike. It rationed food and other commodities in the cities. It seized all the peasants' surplus production. Private trading disappeared. The results were disastrous. Peasants cut their production; food stocks declined; drought in 1921 made the shortages worse. Peasants and workers rioted.[34]

Faced with these problems, Lenin retreated from socialism. He introduced his New Economic Policy (NEP). Government reorganized banks along semi-capitalist lines. It allowed small private firms to operate. It stopped requisitioning the peasants' produce and substituted a limited "grain tax." Private traders began bringing basic supplies from the cities to the villages and food from the villages to the cities. Recovery was rapid. The NEP lasted from 1921 to 1928.[35]

Restlessness continued, meanwhile, among the subject peoples, and some of them managed to assert their independence. Lenin's regime dealt with this development in two ways. The Red Army reconquered the Ukraine; it tried this also with Poland but was turned back. And the regime introduced a new, federal constitution which gave nominal autonomy to some nationalities.[36]

The same constitution, adopted in 1918, set up the structure of political power. Lenin was explicit in wanting to abolish the separation of legislative and executive powers. At the top of the new system was a national congress which was elected indirectly and by non-secret ballot. The congress, in turn, elected a permanent executive committee and an even smaller Council of People's Commissars to run public business during the long intervals between congressional sessions. Real control of these government bodies, however, lay with the parallel organs of the Communist Party (the new name for the Bolsheviks). The party had a central committee, and the committee had a small political bureau, the Politburo. It was the Politburo that exercised dictatorship. And in the Politburo Lenin was supreme.[37]

Lenin established one other agency that merits special mention. This was the Third (Communist) International. He saw this as replacing the Second (Socialist) International, which had collapsed in 1914. The members of the new body were Communist parties all over the world, but the conditions of membership ensured control by the Soviet Union's party. Lenin used the Comintern to orchestrate the positions of the other parties on domestic and international affairs in their own countries—always in the interest of the Soviet Union. It became a novel instrument of foreign policy.[38]

## STALIN'S REGIME

Lenin died in 1924. After several years of infighting among the Bolshevik leaders, Joseph V. Stalin[39] became heir to his power and held it until he died in 1953. Stalin, whose real name was Joseph (Yosif) Dzugashvili, was born at Gori, Georgia, in 1879. By 1899 he was a Marxist. He soon became an active Bolshevik, and he served several terms of imprisonment and exile. At Lenin's urging, the party made him a member of its Central Committee in 1912 and appointed him its General Secretary in 1922. This post controlled arrangements for party congresses and for appointments inside the party. It thus became the source of enormous influence. By 1929, Stalin's shrewd maneuvers vanquished all his rivals for power; he definitively liquidated most of them in a series of "show trials" in the 1930s. He thus acquired complete control of the party, the government, and the country. Even though he held no government post from 1922 to 1941, he was the actual ruler of Soviet Russia.

As ruler, Stalin began centralized planning of the economy in 1928, with a series of "five-year plans." These established tight control of the economy and ended the NEP. They favored expanding heavy industry over providing consumer goods, which were scarce, poor in quality, and rationed. The purpose was to overtake in ten years' time the Western countries' fifty- or hundred-year lead in industrial development.[40]

Meanwhile, the cities had to be fed, and Russia was selling grain abroad to earn foreign exchange. In the absence of consumer goods, however, the peasants had no incentive to raise cash crops. Stalin brought agricultural lands together into large collective and state farms, and coerced the peasants into joining these. He aimed thus both to make agriculture more productive by using heavy machinery and to break the peasants' resistance to planning. Once again, government forcibly seized farm produce. Even in the midst of drought, the government kept up deliveries of grain abroad while it starved its own citizens at home. It directed its pressures especially against the "kulaks"—the most skilled and prosperous peasants—because they had the most independent attitudes. Sadly, collectivization brought death to millions of the people who worked the land. It also led to destroying half the country's livestock.[41]

Stalin organized the state's coercive resources, the police and the forced-labor camps, to serve his own absolute and arbitrary power. Although the CHEKA's name changed successively to OGPU, NKVD, and KGB, its role and style of operation remained the same. The police could arrest, interrogate (even by torture), convict, and punish. Administrative judgments supplanted public trials. The trials that did take place were "show trials," at which the accused abjectly confessed their guilt. Offenders who were not executed were sent to labor camps located in Russia's most inhospitable terrain and climate. Food, clothing, and shelter there were barely sufficient. Discipline was ruthless. The prisoners worked without adequate tools in exhausting tasks such as mining, lumbering, and construction. Stalin thus built much of the country's industrial infrastructure: dams, railways, canals, ports, steel plants, and chemical factories. The estimated death toll in the camps from 1917 to 1959 was 66 million.[42]

Stalin consolidated his control by a maneuver in the realm of ideology. Shortly after Lenin's death, he gave a series of lectures entitled "Foundations of Leninism." These justified Lenin's application of Marx's theories, gave Lenin the same eminence as Marx, and created "Marxism-Leninism." At the same time, Stalin also placed on his own shoulders the mantles of both men and set himself up as their sole interpreter. Henceforth, authentic Marxism-Leninism meant whatever Stalin said it meant *at any given time*. He also gave his name to a book called *The History of the Communist Party of the Soviet Union*. This included a simplified explanation of Marxism. It was used in training programs everywhere in Russia, thus imprinting a mindset on the whole nation.[43]

Stalin's foreign policy followed many turns. When radical revolutions did not break out in nearby countries as the Bolsheviks expected, he began to portray the Soviet Union as the "socialist motherland," "encircled" by hostile capitalist powers. He continued to use the Comintern to direct Communist parties in other countries, thus aggravating international friction. When World War II began to loom in 1933, he sought support against Germany in friendly relations with France and Britain. In 1938 he shifted to a non-aggression pact with Hitler, but in 1941 returned to cooperation with the Western Allies. After Germany's defeat in 1945, the Soviet Union won political hegemony over Eastern Europe. It annexed Lithuania, Latvia, Estonia, and parts of other countries. It backed local Communists in taking over the governments of Poland, East Germany, Hungary, Czechoslovakia, Bulgaria, and Rumania. It thus created "the Communist bloc," and the "cold war" with the Western powers began.[44]

A pervasive feature of Stalin's activities, finally, was this: during his regime he inspired an ever more servile cult of his own personality. By controlling education, scholarship, and the public media, he rewrote history to magnify his own achievements. By controlling the police, he suppressed all criticism. He portrayed himself as supreme social theorist, sage economist, scientific genius, shrewd and courageous military strategist, and far-seeing statesman. This myth increased his power.[45]

## The Soviet Union after Stalin

Nikita Khrushchev succeeded Stalin. Speaking to the Twentieth Congress of the Russian Communist Party in 1956, he shocked the entire Marxist world. He denounced Stalin as a cruel, egotistical paranoiac who had almost destroyed Russia. He thus began the process of "de-Stalinization" among Communists. Some observers claim, however, that this occasioned no fundamental change in the Soviet system. Khrushchev did not attack the theory that spawned the dictatorship. The oligarchy that replaced one-man rule was still absolute. Marxist-Leninist ideology remained in place.[46] The Soviet Union continued to struggle with problems of industrial and agricultural productivity. East–West hostility in international relations persisted. Soviet troops put down popular uprisings in East Germany, Hungary, Poland, and Czechoslovakia. Russia incorporated the armed forces and the national economies of the Communist bloc into its military and economic planning. It also supported revolutions in Third World countries, often with military aid.

The Soviet scene changed surprisingly, however, in 1985. Mikhail Gorbachev, the party's new General Secretary, sought to promote readier access to information, greater freedom in discussing public issues, restructuring of the country's economy, and friendlier relations with the Western powers. By 1991, the process that he began led to the dissolution of the Communist bloc, the democratization of its members, and the breakup of the Soviet Union itself into a "Commonwealth of Independent States." The cold war came to an end, and diplomatic cooperation between the Soviet Union and the United States achieved peaceful resolution of conflicts which their rivalry had sustained in the Third World.

## LENIN'S THEORY

This account of the Bolshevik Revolution and what followed in the Soviet Union makes it possible to see how Marx's theory evolved into Marxism-Leninism. How did Lenin and Stalin develop Marx's ideas?

Lenin did not write much that is relevant by way of general theory. He wrote mostly short tracts and journalistic pieces dealing with specific issues of strategy and tactics. Because he did not have much guidance from Marx on how to make a revolution or how to rule thereafter, his writings were often attempts to justify his practical decisions as applications of Marx's principles. For him, the key to making such applications was simply any given principle's usefulness for promoting the revolution. As one commentator put it, "All theoretical questions were merely instruments of a single aim, the revolution; and the meaning of all human affairs, ideas, institutions and values resided exclusively in their bearing on the class struggle."[47]

Lenin accordingly rejected the idea that imperial Russia had to have a more mature capitalist economy and a numerous proletariat before the revolution could happen. If he accepted this opinion, he could never hope to bid for power. Accordingly, his interpretation of dialectical materialism stressed the functioning of human will rather than of historical development in preparing the way for revolution. So he worked to create and exploit the political tensions that would effect the Bolshevik takeover.[48]

Lenin likewise adjusted his interpretation of class warfare to existing circumstances. The industrial proletariat in Russia was only 1.5 percent of the population, far too small to overturn the government. To meet this difficulty in 1917, Lenin first sought the peasant party's support by promising "land to those who worked it." Then, after he had consolidated Bolshevik power, he met the peasants' resistance to his policies by treating them as class enemies.[49] He took similar liberties with Marx's idea that the proletariat should not go on with the second stage of revolution until the bourgeoisie had organized a productive economy for them. Far from letting the Provisional Government organize anything, Lenin sought its immediate destruction. Marx, moreover, had not said clearly how classes would disappear. But Lenin quickly set about destroying the bourgeois state and replacing it with a proletarian state—which could crush the resistance of exploiters and guide the masses to a socialist economy. For him, this state *was* the dictatorship of the proletariat. Coercive violence was one of its characteristics. He had written in 1906, "The scientific term 'dictatorship' means nothing more or less than activity untrammeled by any law, absolutely unrestricted by any rules whatever, and based directly on violence." In 1920, he described dictatorship as the exercise of force by the proletariat against the exploiters it had overthrown.[50]

While the regime warred against class enemies, moreover, there could be no question of representative institutions, civil rights, or popular control over government. Law was nothing but an instrument by which one class oppressed another. Terror should not be banned, but legalized "without any make-believe." Lenin proposed a clause for the Criminal Code providing as follows: "Propaganda or agitation that objectively serves . . . the interests of the international bourgeoisie . . . is an offense punishable by death, which . . . may be commuted to deprivation of liberty, or deportation." The phrase "objectively serves" gave government unlimited discretion to execute, imprison, or exile whomever it wished. Calculated vagueness became characteristic of criminal legislation. As one critic observed: "It is not that the criminal code is severe, but that it has no existence except in name."[51]

In Lenin's view, further, the dictatorship of the proletariat was a form of minority rule, connected with his concept of the "party." In 1920 he ridiculed the idea that workers could directly manage industry or the state. "We know," he said, "that workers in touch with the peasants are liable to fall for non-proletarian slogans." The dictatorship, accordingly, was not rule *by* the proletariat; it was rule *in the name of* the proletariat—by the party.[52]

The party's function was first to seize power and then to use it. Lenin's ideas on the party as ruler of the revolutionary state followed his ideas on the party as maker of the revolution. For both tasks it had to be selective in membership and under centralized control. Members had to be tightly disciplined. They need not be proletarians; they could be intellectuals. But they all had to be professional, dedicated revolutionaries. They were a "vanguard." And this vanguard had the right to rule because it had superior knowledge; scientific socialism gave it the understanding of where history was going and how the new society should move with it. Even though the party ruled in the name of the proletariat, this did not mean that the proletariat had to choose the leaders or give them their mandate. The leaders, whatever their class origin, somehow identified themselves with the proletariat's outlook and interests. The discipline Lenin spoke of applied even to internal debate. He was convinced that he had the right answers, and he insisted that the party could not afford "the luxury of studying shades of opinion"; it had to stop "all arguments about deviations." An incidental effect of Lenin's concept was to make party members a new elite. The revolution meant to bring about a classless society thus gave birth instead to a "new class" of highly privileged citizens.[53]

In determining the economic policies of his new regime, Lenin again interpreted Marx in pragmatic fashion. The Bolsheviks' initial policies were faithful to Marxism's general inspiration in a doctrinaire way. They tried to make a clean sweep of capitalist structures, and gave their action an egalitarian flavor. Government took over major enterprises, initiated worker participation in management, and eliminated commercial middlemen. But when production and distribution of basic commodities then failed, the regime tried coercion, and coercion made things worse. Whereupon Lenin cited Marx's *Critique of the Gotha Programme* to justify *gradual* movement toward socialism. He found grounds for giving greater compensation to people who had technical and managerial skills. He saw the need for *authoritative* administration of complex enterprises. He recognized that material incentives for peasants and modest opportunities for middlemen promoted prosperity more effectively than coercion. And so he developed his NEP.[54]

Because so many ethnic groups resided in Russia's vast territory, Lenin had to think hard about questions of "nationality." For decades, ethnic minorities all over Europe had complained that the majorities were oppressing them, and they sought independence or autonomy, and Marxists had joined the debate about "national self-determination." In two essays published in 1913 and 1914, Lenin agreed that nationalism was a bourgeois ideology that would disappear when capitalism died. He nevertheless supported national self-determination. This doctrine was useful for fomenting unrest in czarist Russia. But he limited his support with key conditions: The right to national self-determination was subordinate to the success of the party and the revolution, and only the party could make decisions on national aspirations in particular cases. When his new regime faced civil war, then, he made concessions to Russia's ethnic minorities in order to weaken their nationalist sentiment. His 1918 constitution gave some of them autonomy and the legal right to secede—although control by local vanguard parties would make the right unreal. Then when the military situation became more favorable, the Red Army overran two areas that had, in fact, seceded and even tried, unsuccessfully, to reconquer Poland.[55]

Lenin showed little interest in colonialism. But in 1916 he published *Imperialism: The Highest Stage of Capitalism*, which later contributed powerfully to the influence of Marxism-Leninism in the Third World. According to Lenin, three factors had postponed the collapse of capitalist society that Marx predicted. One of these was the fact that, because capitalistic investment had reached its maximum profitability at home, the financial oligarchy was investing in less-developed parts of the world, seeking higher profits. This new investment abroad prevented the economy from coming to a standstill and thus stimulating social unrest. So it was delaying the revolution. But the capitalist countries' share-out of the world was now complete. Their quest for further opportunities was leading inevitably to collisions among them, war, and the collapse that Marx had prophesied.

Lenin was concerned mainly with the impact of "imperialist" investment in the less-developed countries of Eastern Europe, including Russia. Nevertheless, he also cited investment in colonies and "semicolonies" such as Turkey, China, and Persia. The investors were looking for cheap land, cheap labor, and abundant raw materials. They were extracting surplus value from a new source: the toil of the colonial and semicolonial masses. They were also establishing the permanent dependence of these areas on foreign capital. But the Marxian dialectic was at work; exploitation was building revolution among the dependent peoples abroad just as it was among the proletariat at home. *Imperialism*, understandably, drew many nationalist leaders in the colonies to Marxism-Leninism.[56]

## STALIN'S THEORIES

So much for Lenin's theories; what of Stalin's? Stalin had done some pamphleteering before the October Revolution. After he succeeded

Lenin, he published his *Foundations of Leninism* and his *Short Course*. He also made many official speeches and issued numerous official documents. His interpretations of Marxism, for the most part, touched on issues that were of immediate practical concern. Several of these had a big place in the Bolshevik leaders' struggle for power after Lenin died. During this struggle, Stalin allied himself first with one rival, then with another, until he managed to eliminate them all. And as he changed his alliances, he correspondingly changed his views.

One such issue was the New Economic Policy. In order to encourage productivity, its supporters were willing to allow some folk to be better off than others, since their activity improved conditions for everyone. The policy's opponents argued that this would increase the peasants' power of resistance and slow down industrialization. Stalin agreed with NEP's supporters until 1929; then he switched to the opponents' view. He collectivized agriculture, began his brutal campaign against the kulaks, and, to accelerate industrial growth, again brought the entire economy under centralized control. Meanwhile, he put forth the theory that the proletarian state had to become stronger before it withered away, and that the class struggle had to become more intense before it was completed. These ideas justified his ruthless style of governing.[57]

Stalin's views on national self-determination echoed Lenin's. In 1913 he wrote for Lenin a long article entitled "Marxism and the National Question." He favored national self-determination for the proletariat, not for the bourgeoisie; but even the proletariat enjoyed the right only if this did not hinder the revolution. He became Commissar for Nationalities in the first Bolshevik government, and was instrumental in the constitutional recognition of secession. But he also sent the Red Army to re-annex his native Georgia, which had declared its independence. During World War II, he dissolved four of the Soviet Union's autonomous nationalities and resettled eight of its minority peoples en masse in Siberia or Central Asia, because he felt unsure of their loyalty to Russia.[58]

The Bolsheviks initially believed that their revolution could not succeed unless other revolutions took place in countries around them. When these revolutions did not develop, some leaders insisted that the Soviet Union must press to make them happen. According to Stalin, however, it was possible for Russia to build "socialism in one country." He would build Russia's strength without the help of like-minded governments. Nevertheless, Allied support for counterrevolutionaries in the civil war made plain the danger of "capitalist encirclement." It was therefore imperative for Marxists everywhere to defend the "socialist homeland."

With this theory, Stalin made the interests of world revolution identical with the interests of the Soviet Union and his own dictatorship. The theory also justified an exception to strict respect for "sovereignty" in international law. The principle of noninterference in the internal affairs of other countries did not hold in "wars of liberation." The Soviet Union could and should advance the cause of revolution by helping people everywhere who, in its view, were fighting "oppressive" and "reactionary" governments.[59]

Stalin also extended the primacy of world revolution explicitly to issues of colonialism. According to *Foundations of Leninism*, the proletariat in developed countries and the oppressed peoples in the colonies had an identical interest in revolution. For this reason, the proletariat must support liberation movements even in the colonies of their own countries. They would thus transform colonial populations from a strategic reserve of the bourgeoisie into an ally of the revolutionary proletariat. This did not mean, however, that the proletariat must support *every* national movement; it meant that "support must be given to such national movements as tend to weaken, to overthrow imperialism. . . . Cases occur when the national movements come into conflict with the interests of the proletarian movement. In such cases support is entirely out of the question." The issue, then, was not one of colonial populations' right but one of usefulness for the revolution. Soviet leaders were therefore free to support liberation movements in the colonial world or not, depending on whether they judged that support would help or hinder the revolution—which meant, for practical purposes, helping or hindering the interests of the Soviet Union.[60]

## LENIN ON RELIGION

The Marxist-Leninist view of religion is obviously a central issue in a study of the Church's response to Marxism. In the interest of clarity, we have left it for separate discussion.

Lenin was an atheist. For him, Marxist materialism was "absolutely atheistic and positively hostile to all religion." Religious beliefs grew out of social conditions; they would wither and die when conditions changed. "Marxism has always regarded all modern religion and churches . . . as an instrument of bourgeois reaction . . . to defend exploitation and befuddle the working class." Religion teaches the masses to be patient on earth in hope of a reward in heaven. Religion is "spiritual booze"; those who suffer misery in the capitalist system use it to drown their sorrows. Rejecting God, Lenin also rejected any morality founded on divine commandments or any other "idealist" or "extra-class" base. "Our morality is entirely subordinated to the interests of the proletariat's struggle." In 1913 Lenin wrote to the Russian writer Maxim Gorky: ". . . any idea of God at all . . . is the most dangerous foulness, the most shameful 'infection.'" "God is the complex of ideas generated by . . . the class-yoke— . . . ideas . . . which *lull* to sleep the class struggle."[61]

Struggle against religion was therefore an important function of the party. Lenin explained that "we founded the Russian Social Democratic Labour Party precisely for a struggle against any religious bamboozling of the workers." "The party must not be indifferent to . . . ignorance or obscurantism in the shape of religious belief." In pre-Revolutionary days, however, he advocated freedom of religion against the czarist government's granting privileges to the established Orthodox Church, and he opposed discrimination based on religious belief. Support for religious liberty was a form of political agitation, rousing public discontent against the government. At that time, then, he did not make atheism part of the party's program and he did not exclude believers from membership; the class struggle itself would ultimately undermine their religious convictions. After the Bolshevik Revolution, however, Lenin no longer relied on the class struggle. He launched a ruthless attack on religion.[62]

### SOVIET POLICY ON RELIGION

Stalin added nothing significant to Lenin's theories about religion. But he and his successors relentlessly continued the persecution Lenin had begun.[63]

The main target of the Soviet regime's antireligious campaign was the Russian Orthodox Church, which was the state church under the czars and counted far more members than any other. But the campaign also aimed at Latin and Eastern Rite Catholics, Jews, Muslims, and Protestants. Government harassed the churches with a multitude of laws and regulations. The Provisional Government had disestablished the Orthodox Church. But the Bolsheviks went one step further, decreeing that every citizen could profess any religious belief or none at all. While this decree, in theory, put belief and nonbelief on an equal footing, the practical administrative follow-up was antireligious. Government deprived the Church of its standing as a legal person. The Church lost its right to own property. The state nationalized the property it owned. Church buildings could be used for nonreligious and antireligious purposes.

Churches had to pay rent in order to use buildings for worship. Government disfranchised the clergy and barred their children from postprimary education. At first it was permissible to teach religion in primary schools; later, religious education for people under the age of eighteen was restricted. Subsequently, such instruction in churches was forbidden, religious holidays were banned, and organizations such as church youth clubs were prohibited.[64]

A constitutional amendment in 1929 authorized officials to punish "acts of deceit, with the purpose of encouraging superstition . . . and with a view to deriving profit therefrom." Other decrees set guidelines for the regulation and supervision of religious groups. Authorities used these vaguely worded laws obstructively. They refused or delayed permission to use particular places of worship; they withdrew permissions previously granted and closed such places. They restricted the publication of bibles and liturgical books. They limited the number of seminaries and controlled their enrollments. They kept the clergy under close watch, looking especially for statements that could be regarded as social or political commentary.[65]

The regime backed its restrictions with severe penalties, including jail, forced labor, and death. From 1919 to 1924, it tried, imprisoned, and killed at least twenty-three Orthodox bishops and one thousand priests. Stalin's purges liquidated still more. Among Roman Catholics of the "captive nations," fifty-five bishops, thirteen thousand priests, and 2.5 million layfolk, reportedly, were killed between 1917 and 1959. Large numbers of Protestants also suffered imprisonment in the labor camps.[66]

Government also discouraged religious practice by discriminatory treatment of believers. Authorities blocked access to higher education both for persons suspected of believing and for their children. The government similarly barred the way to better jobs, better housing, and other amenities. It made it dangerous for people to manifest belief even within the family circle, because it used small children as unwitting informers against their elders.

Beyond trying to eradicate religious belief and religious organizations, the Soviet government mounted a vigorous campaign to promote atheism. In 1922 the party founded a magazine, *Under the Banner of Marxism*, to propagate materialism; Lenin explicitly stated that its objective was antireligious. In 1923 the League of the Militant Godless was organized; its youth section was called the Young Godless. The schools introduced antireligious education in 1930. Antireligious universities provided special training for teachers of atheism. The government, in 1924, set up the

State Publishing House for Anti-Religious Literature. Beginning in 1964, the Academy of Social Sciences of the Central Party Committee included an Institute of Scientific Atheism, dedicated to research, training, and publication. The All-Union Society for the Dissemination of Political and Scientific Knowledge, established in 1972, took over the functions of the Militant Godless. Atheism Clubs and Houses of Atheism carried on the campaign at the local level.[67]

As part of this campaign, too, the party promoted the Marxist "new man" as a moral ideal; it urged the propagators of atheistic doctrine to live exemplary Communist lives in order to make their message persuasive. Government also sought to back the teaching of atheism with esthetic and emotional appeal. It surrounded events such as the registration of births and the issuance of passports with civic solemnity that would rival the attraction of religious ritual.[68]

In their efforts to destroy religion and promote atheism, it can then be said, government and party used every medium to achieve their purposes: newspapers, magazines, pamphlets, books, lectures, radio, cinema, television, museums, displays, classroom instruction, competitions, cartoons, posters, plays, parades, and person-to-person persuasion. The investment of manpower and money was enormous. This was an important issue for Marxist-Leninists in the Soviet Union.[69]

The campaigners for atheism often expressed an evangelistic eagerness to free the minds of believers from superstition and irrational fears. But Marxist atheism was not the only reason for the Soviet Union's stance on religious belief. The party's thrust toward absolute, totalitarian government logically required hostility to religion. The dictatorship of the proletariat could not tolerate any rival influence over the minds, attitudes, and activities of its subjects. It therefore had to counter the influence of the churches.[70]

In some cases, authorities saw this religious influence as the focal point of resistance to government actions. Conservative Orthodox churchmen opposed the whole revolutionary movement. Catholics in the Ukraine and elsewhere linked their religion with their national culture, so that it became part of their nationalistic resentment of Russian rule. Islam had something of the same effect in the southeast and in Central Asia.[71]

Government's religious repression, then, was part of its political repression. Its occasional relaxation of hostility was also political. Initially, Lenin and Stalin prescribed restraint in the treatment of Islam in order not to antagonize the large Muslim populations of Asia. But in 1927, government began to deal as rigorously with Muslims as with other believers. With World War II coming on, Stalin made concessions to the churches in the western borderlands in order to counter Germany's courtship of their favor. At the same time, he eased government's relationship with Orthodoxy, to present a better image to the liberal democratic governments whose friendship he was then seeking. He was also trying to enlist the emotional power of Russia's religious tradition in awakening patriotism. When the war was over, he resumed his old policies.[72]

## RELIGIOUS POLICIES OF OTHER COMMUNIST STATES

The Soviet Union was not alone in its hostility to religion. The same phenomenon appeared under other Marxist governments. A detailed account would be repetitious. But every country in the Soviet bloc—and Albania and Yugoslavia as well—warred ruthlessly against religion. They exiled, imprisoned, and killed believers. They used "show trials" to discredit effective churchmen. They dissolved Catholic religious orders. They interfered with the running of seminaries. They forbade religious instruction of youth and substituted atheistic indoctrination. They obstructed communications of Catholics with the Holy See. They tried to control the appointment of bishops and parish priests. They kept religious ministers under government surveillance. They encouraged division in the Church by setting up "patriotic associations" of clergy and faithful, subservient to government. The Marxist government of China pursued similar policies.[73]

## MARXISM'S APPEAL IN AFRICA

These, then, were the theories of Karl Marx and the theories of the men who invoked his ideas to engineer Russia's October Revolution and to shape the political, economic, and social life of the Soviet Union. Some features of these theories had special appeal for politicians and intellectuals in the newly independent countries of Africa, because they seemed to offer promising formulas for confirming their independence, for developing their economies rapidly, and for establishing more equitable societies. Inasmuch as the theories themselves called for remaking the world on the Marxist model, the Soviet and other Marxist governments, for their part, undertook a multitude of varied steps to propagate Marxism-Leninism in the sub-Saharan region, especially from 1960 onward. The following chapter will give an account of these efforts.

NOTES

1. For Marx's biography and the development of his thought I have relied mainly on David McLellan, *Karl Marx: His Life and Thought* (New York: Harper Colophon Books, 1977); and Leszek Kolakowski, *Main Currents of Marxism*, 3 vols. (Oxford: Clarendon, 1978), vol. 1.

2. On Engels, see William C. Henderson, *The Life of Friedrich Engels*, 2 vols. (London: Frank Cass, 1976), especially chaps. 1–3, 6, and pp. 200–201, 225–26; Kolakowski, *Main Currents of Marxism*, 1:144–46.

3. For some of these points about Marx's intellectual background, see Nicholas Lobkowicz, "Karl Marx's Attitude Toward Religion," *Review of Politics*, 26 (July 1964), 329–35. See also McLellan, *Karl Marx*, pp. 28–32. On Engels's loss of religious faith, see J. D. Hunley, *The Life and Thought of Friedrich Engels* (New Haven, Conn.: Yale University Press, 1991), pp. 9–11.

4. Marxist-Leninist indoctrination in the Soviet Union did include systematic general philosophy. Some standard textbooks were published in English. See, for example, A. P. Sheptulin, *Marxist-Leninist Philosophy* (Moscow: Progress Publishers, 1978). This discernibly relied on Lenin.

5. See Karl Marx, *The German Ideology*, reprinted in Karl Marx and Friedrich Engels, *On Religion*, rev. ed. (Moscow: Progress Publishers, 1975), pp. 66–67; Friedrich Engels, *Socialism: Utopian and Scientific*, ibid., pp. 258–59; Kolakowski, *Main Currents of Marxism*, 1:154–55.

6. See McLellan, *Karl Marx*, pp. 114–16; Kolakowski, *Main Currents of Marxism*, 1:265; Marx and Engels, *The Holy Family*, in *On Religion*, p. 60.

7. The phrase "dialectical materialism" was devised by the Russian Marxist G. V. Plekhanov (1856–1918). Engels spoke of "historical materialism." Marx did not use either phrase. See T. B. Bottomore and Maximilian Rubel, eds., *Karl Marx: Selected Writings on Sociology and Social Philosophy* (New York: McGraw-Hill, 1964), p. 20n5; Arthur McGovern, *Marxism: An American Catholic Perspective* (Maryknoll, N.Y.: Orbis Books, 1980), p. 51n6.

8. See Kolakowski, *Main Currents of Marxism*, 1:57–74, 387–88, 392, 403; McGovern, *Marxism*, pp. 51–52; Engels, *Ludwig Feuerbach*, in Marx and Engels, *On Religion*, pp. 217–19, 222–25.

9. See Kolakowski, *Main Currents of Marxism*, 1:323–25; Richard DeGeorge, *Soviet Ethics and Morality* (Ann Arbor: University of Michigan Press, 1969), pp. 1–4. R. G. Peffer draws upon what he calls Marx's "moral perspectives" to develop an "implicit" Marxist ethical theory directed toward effectuating social justice—an objective that would best be realized through "democratic, self-managing socialism." See his *Marxism, Morality, and Social Justice* (Princeton, N.J.: Princeton University Press, 1988). He outlines his argument in the Introduction, pp. 3–32.

10. See Kolakowski, *Main Currents of Marxism*, 1:127, 131, 161–62, 168–71; McLellan, *Karl Marx*, pp. 43–44, 83.

11. Friedrich Engels, *Ludwig Feuerbach* and *Dialectics of Nature*, in Marx and Engels, *On Religion*, pp. 197, 144–46, 164. Kolakowski comments generally on Engels's materialism, *Main Currents of Marxism*, 1:371–81, 406.

12. See Engels, *Ludwig Feuerbach*, in *On Religion*, pp. 229–32; Engels, *Anti-Dühring*, in ibid., pp. 128–30; McLellan, *Karl Marx*, pp. 37, 41, 89–90, 92; Lobkowicz, "Karl Marx's Attitude Toward Religion," 350–52; Kolakowski, *Main Currents of Marxism*, 1:128–29; McGovern, *Marxism*, p. 274n18. On Marx's religion in general, see Lobkowicz, "Karl Marx's Attitude Toward Religion," passim; Karl Marx, *Karl Marx: On Religion*, ed. Saul K. Padover (New York: McGraw-Hill, 1974), pp. xi–xxvii.

13. See McLellan, *Karl Marx*, pp. 88–90; Marx, *Contribution to the Critique of Hegel's Philosophy of Law*, in Marx and Engels, *On Religion*, pp. 38–39; Lobkowicz, "Karl Marx's Attitude Toward Religion," 319–29, 350–52; McGovern, *Marxism*, pp. 250–53.

14. Engels, "Emigrant Literature," in Marx and Engels, *On Religion*, p. 124. See also *Anti-Dühring*, in ibid., p. 130; *The Dialectics of Nature*, in ibid., pp. 143–51; *The Book of Revelation*, in ibid., pp. 180–86; *On the History of Early Christianity*, in ibid., pp. 275–300; McGovern, *Marxism*, pp. 255–58.

15. See Kolakowski, *Main Currents of Marxism*, 1:236–37; McLellan, *Karl Marx*, pp. 290–94. Marx's project was sketched in *Grundrisse der politischen Ökonomie*.

16. See Kolakowski, *Main Currents of Marxism*, 1:222–24, 305–306.

17. On the workings of the dialectic in history, see ibid., 1:335–38; Engels, *Ludwig Feuerbach*, in *On Religion*, pp. 225–27; Karl Marx and Friedrich Engels, *The Communist Manifesto* (Harmondsworth, U.K.: Penguin Books, 1984), pp. 79–82, 88–94, 105; Karl Marx, *Critique of the Gotha Program*, cited in McLellan, *Karl Marx*, pp. 432–35; Karl Marx, *Capital*, cited in Bottomore and Rubel, eds., *Selected Writings*, pp. 106–107.

18. See Marx and Engels, *Communist Manifesto*, pp. 84–94; Kolakowski, *Main Currents of Marxism*, 1:291–94, 297–301. Specifically on "surplus value," see Kolakowski, *Main Currents of Marxism*, 1:271–75, 279–81; McLellan, *Karl Marx*, p. 345.

19. See Kolakowski, *Main Currents of Marxism*, 1:281–86; McLellan, *Karl Marx*, pp. 110–12.

20. See Kolakowski, *Main Currents of Marxism*, 1:286–87.

21. See Marx and Engels, *Communist Manifesto*, pp. 88–90. For the concept of "class" and the role of classes other than capitalist and proletariat, see Kolakowski, *Main Currents of Marxism*, 1:352–58.

22. See Kolakowski, *Main Currents of Marxism*, 1:309–11, 361–62; McLellan, *Karl Marx*, pp. 203, 224, 233, 248–49, 281–82; Marx and Engels, *Communist Manifesto*, p. 120; *Karl Marx: On Revolution*, ed. Saul K. Padover (New York: McGraw-Hill, 1971), p. 64.

23. See Marx and Engels, *Communist Manifesto*, pp. 91, 95; McLellan, *Karl Marx*, pp. 432–34; Kolakowski, *Main Currents of Marxism*, 1:310–11, 361–62.

24. See Marx and Engels, *Communist Manifesto*, pp. 104–105; Friedrich Engels, *Anti-Dühring*, in Karl Marx and Friedrich Engels, *Collected Works*, vol. 25 (New York: International Publishers, 1987), pp. 279–80, 282, 295.

25. See McLellan, *Karl Marx*, pp. 187n4, 433–34; Kolakowski, *Main Currents of Marxism*, 1:359–63; Marx and Engels, *Communist Manifesto*, p. 105.

26. See McLellan, *Karl Marx*, pp. 432–33; Kolakowski, *Main Currents of Marxism*, 1:178–81, 307–308.

27. See McLellan, *Karl Marx*, pp. 120–21; Kolakowski, *Main Currents of Marxism*, 1:410–12.

28. See the texts collected in Karl Marx and Friedrich Engels, *On Colonialism: Articles from the New York Tribune and Other Writings* (New York: International Publishers, 1972). See especially "British Incomes in India," pp. 168–72; "The Approaching Indian Loan," pp. 174, 176; "The Opium Trade in China," pp. 215–20; "The Anglo-Chinese Treaty," pp. 221–25; "British Rule in India," pp. 40–45; "The Future Results of British Rule in India," pp. 81–85.

29. For the citation (from *Herr Vogt*), see McLellan, *Karl Marx*, p. 158. The term "scientific socialism" comes from Engels, not Marx; see Bottomore and Rubel, eds., *Karl Marx: Selected Writings*, pp. 14–16, 20. See also Kolakowski, *Main Currents of Marxism*, 1:225–26, 376–77; Tom Bottomore, ed., *Karl Marx: Early Writings* (New York: McGraw-Hill, 1964), pp. xiii–xiv; Marx and Engels, *Communist Manifesto*, pp. 117–18.

30. See McLellan, *Karl Marx*, p. 122; Kolakowski, *Main Currents of Marxism*, 1:414–16.

31. On Lenin, see David Shub, *Lenin: A Biography* (Garden City, N.Y.: Doubleday, 1948); Leonard Schapiro and Peter Reddaway, eds., *Lenin: The Man, the Theorist, the Leader* (London: Pall Mall Press, 1967); Kolakowski, *Main Currents of Marxism*, 2:356–62.

32. For brief accounts of the two revolutions, see Leonard Schapiro, *The Russian Revolutions of 1917: The Origins of Modern Communism* (New York: Basic Books, 1984); David Footman, *The Russian Revolutions* (London: Faber & Faber; New York: Putnam, 1962). Apparent discrepancies of dates connected with the revolutions arise from a change in Russia's official calendar: Imperial Russia used the Julian calendar, but in February 1918 the new Soviet government adopted the Gregorian calendar. I have used the old-style dates. On the October Revolution see Footman, *Russian Revolutions*, chap. 6. On Lenin's own moves during this period, see Kolakowski, *Main Currents of Marxism*, 2:473–75.

33. See Kolakowski, *Main Currents of Marxism*, 2:479–81, 486-88; Ivo Lapenna, "Lenin, Law and Legality," in Schapiro and Reddaway, eds., *Lenin*, pp. 253–55.

34. See Kolakowski, *Main Currents of Marxism*, 2:481–83; Footman, *Russian Revolutions*, pp. 125–29; Schapiro, *Russian Revolutions of 1917*, pp. 188–89.

35. See Kolakowski, *Main Currents of Marxism*, 2:481–85.

36. See Schapiro, *Russian Revolutions of 1917*, pp. 163–65, 170–80, 207. The

official name of the new Russia ultimately evolved from these events: the Union of Soviet Socialist Republics. The new regime moved the capital from Petrograd to Moscow in 1918.

37. See Robert Conquest, *The Soviet Political System* (New York: Frederick A. Praeger, 1968), pp. 13–19.

38. See Gunther Nollau, *International Communism and World Revolution: History and Methods* (New York: Frederick A. Praeger, 1961). Appendix IV gives the statutes of the Third International; Appendix V gives the twenty-one conditions for membership. These two documents ensured control by the Russian Communist Party.

39. Kolakowski briefly sketches Stalin's career in *Main Currents of Marxism*, 3:9–21. For fuller treatments see Isaac Deutscher, *Stalin: A Political Biography*, 2nd ed. (New York: Oxford University Press, 1974); Adam B. Ulam, *Stalin: The Man and His Era* (New York: Viking Press, 1973); Robert C. Tucker, *Stalin as Revolutionary, 1879–1929* (New York: W. W. Norton, 1973).

40. See Kolakowski, *Main Currents of Marxism*, 3:77–79; Deutscher, *Stalin*, pp. 328, 335–36. The plans also entailed immense use of forced labor in prison camps. The classic description and analysis of the camps is in Alexandr Solzhenitsyn, *The Gulag Archipelago, 1918–1936*, 2 vols. (New York: Harper & Row, 1973). Part IV, chap. 22 highlights the exploitation of the inmates' labor power, but also argues that the real costs (through sabotage, shoddy work, and administrative corruption) were much higher than the apparent costs of the system. Robert C. Conquest briefly recounts Stalin's defeat of his rivals in *The Great Terror: A Reassessment* (New York: Oxford University Press, 1990), pp. 7–28. Conquest's book is a history of the ways in which Stalin used "terror" to establish and maintain his dictatorship.

41. See Kolakowski, *Main Currents of Marxism*, 3:37–41; Deutscher, *Stalin*, pp. 317–44; Robert G. Wesson, *Why Marxism? The Continuing Success of a Failed Theory* (New York: Basic Books, 1976), pp. 76–77. See also Stalin's own roseate picture of the peasants' cooperation with the government in Joseph Stalin, *Foundations of Leninism* (New York: International Publishers, 1939), pp. 70–74.

42. See Kolakowski, *Main Currents of Marxism*, 3:54–56; Deutscher, *Stalin*, pp. 377–85; Solzhenitsyn, *Gulag Archipelago*, 1:10; vol. 1, part I, chaps. 1, 3, 4, 6, 8, 9; and part II, passim and pp. 591-93; vol. 2, part III, passim.

43. See Kolakowski, *Main Currents of Marxism*, 3:3–5, 93–101, 117; Stalin, *Foundations of Leninism*, pp. 5, 9–11, 13–14.

44. See Deutscher, *Stalin*, pp. 414–60.

45. See Kolakowski, *Main Currents of Marxism*, 3:147–48. For the beginning of Stalin's personality cult in 1929, see Tucker, *Stalin as Revolutionary*, chap. 13.

46. See Kolakowski, *Main Currents of Marxism*, 3:451–56. Khrushchev's speech has been published in many places; see, for example, Nikita Khrushchev, *The Anatomy of Terror: Khrushchev's Revelations about Stalin's Regime*, with an introduction by Nathanael Weyl (Washington, D.C.: Public Affairs Press, 1956), pp. 19–73.

47. Kolakowski, *Main Currents of Marxism*, 2:383; see also 2:381–84.

48. See ibid., 2:396–98, 494–95; McLellan, *Karl Marx*, pp. 439–42; Henderson, *Life of Friedrich Engels*, pp. 702–703.

49. See Kolakowski, *Main Currents of Marxism*, 2:384, 474, 480–81, 502–503; Footman, *Russian Revolutions*, p. 26.

50. See Kolakowski, *Main Currents of Marxism*, 2:473–75, 498–99.

51. See ibid., 2:507–508.

52. See ibid., 2:503–505.

53. See ibid., 2:387–96, 480, 489, 505, 513–14, 526–27, 3:161–66; Wesson, *Why Marxism?* p. 66; Stalin, *Foundations of Leninism*, pp. 109–11, 119–21. On the structure of the party and how it developed, see Ronald J. Hill and Peter Frank, *The Soviet Communist Party* (London: George Allen & Unwin, 1981), esp. chap. 3; Leonard Schapiro, *The Government and Politics of the Soviet Union* (New York: Vintage Books, 1967), esp. chaps. 3 and 6; John Hazard, *The Soviet System of Government*, 5th ed (Chicago: The University of Chicago Press, 1980), esp. chaps. 2 and 3.

54. See Kolakowski, *Main Currents of Marxism*, 2:482–86, 503–505.

55. See ibid., 2:399–405; R. N. Ismaligova, *Ethnic Problems of Tropical Africa: Can They Be Solved?* (Moscow: Progress Publishers, 1978), p. 15; Schapiro, *Russian Revolutions of 1917*, pp. 163–65, 178–80, 206–207.

56. V. I. Lenin, *Imperialism: The Highest Stage of Capitalism* (New York: International Publishers, 1939), see esp. pp. 47–67, 76–108. See also Kolakowski, *Main Currents of Marxism*, 2:471–72, 491–93; Alec Nove, "Lenin and the Economy," in Schapiro and Reddaway, eds., *Lenin*, pp. 198–203.

57. See Kolakowski, *Main Currents of Marxism*, 3:29–41, 100–101.

58. See ibid., 3:119; Robert Conquest, *The Nation-Killers: The Soviet Deportation of Nationalities* (London: Macmillan, 1970), pp. 64–66; Ismaligova, *Ethnic Problems of Africa*, pp. 243–46; Deutscher, *Stalin*, pp. 181–85; Hazard, *Soviet System of Government*, pp. 106–107; Schapiro, *Government*, pp. 82–83, 89, 104.

59. See Stalin, *Foundations of Leninism*, pp. 18–19, 44–46, 90–91; Kolakowski, *Main Currents of Marxism*, 1:160–61, 2:476–79, 3:21–24; Nollau, *International Communism*, pp. 162–67, 177–83.

60. See Stalin, *Foundations of Leninism*, pp. 33–37, 45–46, 76–87.

61. See Kolakowski, *Main Currents of Marxism*, 2:459–61; Bohdan Bociurkiw, "Lenin and Religion," in Schapiro and Reddaway, eds., *Lenin*, p. 108. See also V. I. Lenin, "The Attitude of the Workers' Party," in Lenin, *On Religion*, 3rd rev. ed. (Moscow: Progress Publishers, 1969), pp. 18–19, 21–22; and "Socialism and Religion," ibid., p. 7; "Task of the Youth League," ibid., p. 58; Letters from Lenin to Maxim Gorky, November 13 or 14, and "the second half of November," 1913, ibid., pp. 40, 44.

62. See Lenin, "Socialism and Religion," in Lenin, *On Religion*, pp. 6–11; "The Attitude of the Workers' Party Toward Religion," ibid., pp. 19–25; "From the Draft Program of the R.C.P. (B.). Section of the Program Dealing with

Religion," ibid., p. 99; David E. Powell, *Anti-Religious Propaganda in the Soviet Union: A Study in Mass Persuasion* (Cambridge, Mass.: The MIT Press, 1975), p. 2.

63. On Soviet policy toward religion, see Kolakowski, *Main Currents of Marxism*, 2:459–61, 3:53–56; Powell, *Anti-Religious Propaganda*, pp. 2–6; Robert Conquest, *Religion in the USSR* (New York: Frederick A. Praeger, 1968), passim.

64. See Powell, *Anti-Religious Propaganda*, pp. 22–30, 38, 40–45.

65. See ibid., pp. 24–28, 30.

66. See ibid., p. 24; Conquest, *Religion in the USSR*, pp. 15, 104–10. The statistics on Roman Catholic deaths are taken from *Catholic Almanac, 1988* (Huntington, Ind.: Our Sunday Visitor Publishing Division, 1987), p. 363, which cites a Congressional Report.

67. See Lenin, "On the Significance of Militant Materialism," in Lenin, *On Religion*, pp. 67–70; Powell, *Anti-Religious Propaganda*, pp. 35–39, 46–51.

68. See Powell, *Anti-Religious Propaganda*, pp. 66–84, 155–56.

69. See ibid., pp. 6, 34–44, 57–62, 86–89, 119–30.

70. See Kolakowski, *Main Currents of Marxism*, 2:460–61, 3:53–54.

71. See Powell, *Anti-Religious Propaganda*, pp. 3–9.

72. See ibid., pp. 15–16, 26, 29–30, 32–33; Conquest, *Religion in the USSR*, pp. 67–81; Janice A. Broun, "The Muslim Challenge Within the Soviet Union," *America*, 148 (February 12, 1983), 3–9.

73. For a brief survey of the situation, see Gerhard Simon, "The Catholic Church and the Communist State in the Soviet Union and Eastern Europe," in Bohdan R.. Bociurkiw and John W. Strong, eds., *Religion and Atheism in the U.S.S.R. and Eastern Europe* (Toronto: University of Toronto Press, 1975), pp. 190–221. In the same book are essays on Albania, Bulgaria, Czechoslovakia, East Germany, Hungary, Rumania, and Yugoslavia. Janice Broun, in *Conscience and Captivity: Religion in Eastern Europe* (Washington, D.C.: Ethics and Policy Center, 1988), presents similar surveys. On China, see Stuart R. Schram, *The Political Thought of Mao Tse-Tung*, rev. ed. (New York: Frederick A. Praeger, 1969), pp. 184–90, 258–59; "A Church in Crisis Weeps and Prays," *Time*, 124 (September 17, 1984), 73–76; "Debate on Religion in Nanking," *Ateismo e Dialogo*, 14 (September 1979), 130; Ren Gujiyu, "The Struggle to Develop a Marxist Science of Religion," ibid., 14 (December 1979), 165–71.

# 3

# Marxism's Influence in Africa: An Overview

ALTHOUGH MARXIST THEORY grew out of European experience, it came to have a considerable influence in Africa during the late decades of the twentieth century. The present chapter will look at how this happened. It will give a general picture of the social, economic, and political situation on the continent—the context in which Marxism exercised its influence.[1] It will describe the channels through which the influence made itself felt. And it will say something about the impact the theory had.

## COLONIZATION AND DECOLONIZATION

Sub-Saharan Africa was largely isolated from the rest of the world until about 1500. It was organized in scattered small communities. Conquests and alliances established a series of rising and falling "empires" among these.

Large-scale contact with Europe came in the late 1400s when Portuguese seamen began their exploration of the coastlands, and other nationalities followed. The Europeans traded with Africans along the coast, but they did not begin exploring the interior until the 1800s. Commerce followed exploration, and rival territorial claims among the Europeans led to a "scramble for Africa." To settle the claims peacefully, the Berlin Congress in 1885 parceled out the continent to the competing powers. The European countries then governed these territories as colonies or protectorates, often using force to subdue local resistance. The British, French, Belgians, and Portuguese ruled the largest blocs of population and territory; the Spanish ruled smaller areas; the German role ended in 1919 after World War I. The colonial powers gave shape to major elements of social organization that African countries brought with them when they became independent: government, administration, business, technology, education, and so forth.

The colonial era came to an end between 1956, when Great Britain granted independence to Sudan, and 1990, when Southwest Africa established its freedom as Namibia. A detailed account of the decolonization process is unnecessary. Nationalist movements gained momentum in the colonies especially after World War II. Their pressure and other considerations led the colonial regimes to transfer sovereignty to their colonies. The process in most areas was peaceful, although public demonstrations sometimes got out of hand and led to localized violence. The liberation movements in Portuguese territories, however, had to wage lengthy guerrilla wars against the colonial power; and in Rhodesia and Southwest Africa, they had to do likewise against territorial governments controlled by white settlers. Immediately after independence, moreover, rival nationalist factions in the Belgian Congo and Angola did battle with one another to control the new governments.

## THE AFRICAN CONTEXT: SOCIAL, ECONOMIC, POLITICAL

As the newly independent countries took charge of their own destinies, a number of common features appeared in their social situation.

The populations of these countries remained dominantly rural. Many of the people were nomadic pastoralists or peasant farmers. Age-old traditions powerfully influenced their ways of doing things. Great numbers of people had received little or no schooling. They worked hard but they had few comforts. They benefited marginally, at best, from independence. They were difficult to integrate into the modern economy. Nevertheless, many of the rural people began streaming into the cities. These were mostly young men looking for wage employment and for freedom from the toil and boredom of rural living. Because they had no marketable skills, they swelled the numbers of the unemployed. Their poverty led many of them into crime. Political agitators could use them, too, for public demonstrations which too easily became violent. Bettering the lot of the urban poor became an urgent challenge for the new African states.

The economies of these countries centered mostly on producing primary commodities for the developed world: rubber, cotton, palm oil, cocoa, diamonds, gold, copper, and petroleum. Economies of this kind were fragile and unstable. World prices for their products fluctuated widely, making it difficult to ensure a steady flow of money into the general economy and of revenue into the public treasury. Flood, drought, and other natural disasters damaged the productivity of farms and mines. In agriculture, the incentives for raising cash crops often led farmers to neglect production of food for local consumption, and this, in turn, compelled countries to spend on the importation of foodstuffs.

Many countries set up light industries to produce consumer goods for the local market and to expand employment. Even so, the industrial work force remained small. Manual workers who received regular wages were relatively privileged, so they hardly fit Marx's idea of a proletariat. And they were able through their trade unions to press governments for maintenance of their privileges, at the expense of their less fortunate countrymen.

Colonial governments had contributed to local development only to the extent needed for the effective functioning of their own enterprises. The new countries therefore began their lives with inadequate infrastructure and inadequate social services. They needed roads, communications, water supply, power, schools, and medical facilities. Nationalist leaders hastened to provide these and thus to meet their people's expectations. They often did so, however, through imprudent international borrowing and without making sure that they had the financial resources to maintain whatever they built or established. By the early 1980s, virtually all African countries were burdened with enormous foreign debts. In order to restore minimal economic health, they had to impose painful austerity programs and thus risk dangerous public discontent. The International Monetary Fund (IMF) financed most of these efforts at recovery and prescribed the medicine to be taken. Because its conditions were so demanding, African elites commonly criticized the agency and opposed acceptance of its prescriptions.

Among peoples' expectations, opportunity for education ranked especially high. Degrees, diplomas, and certificates were the passports to money, prestige, power, and comfort. The new states therefore vastly increased access to schooling at all levels. This policy, apart from placing pressure on public finance, introduced a volatile factor in political life. Young people brought together in schools could readily be roused to strikes and potentially violent demonstrations, not just about in-house issues such as academic regulations but also about political issues such as a country's policy toward South Africa.

Governmental systems at first followed the patterns of the respective colonizing countries: written constitutions, separation of powers, periodic elections, and pluralistic party systems. Generally speaking, however, the new arrangements soon lost momentum and underwent drastic change.

Charismatic presidents and prime ministers used their popularity and political skill to perpetuate themselves in office. Elections were rigged. Opposition parties were suppressed and one-party systems installed. Leaders of ruling parties concentrated control in their own hands. In many cases, military officers, complaining of corruption and ineffectiveness in government, ousted civilian leaders and took over their powers.

Typically, then, the emerging governments were authoritarian. This kind of government was actually the true legacy of colonialism. Although colonial powers had their constitutional regimes at home, their government of the colonies did not offer any model for democracy. Governors-general were virtual monarchs. Local legislatures, if they existed at all, had very limited powers. There was no place for political parties. Authorities censored the press and ignored procedural niceties in silencing vocal opposition.

Government administration similarly followed the systems used by the colonial powers. Unfortunately, the award of jobs in government service became a form of political patronage. This kind of patronage likewise reached into the many governmental corporations—the "parastatals"—which managed such enterprises as railways, electric power, and shipping. And because powerful patrons protected the tenure of clients for whom they had found jobs, administrators had great difficulty enforcing discipline. Bureaucracies, therefore, were often overstaffed, inefficient, expensive, and wasteful. When governments tried to reform and reduce them, their efforts again aroused dangerous discontent.

In many countries, too, financial corruption was common among politicians, administrative officials, and private entrepreneurs. Politicians demanded "kickbacks" for the award of lucrative government contracts. Entrepreneurs grossly overcharged government and supplied inferior goods and services. Officials accepted bribes for not enforcing regulations intended to protect the public interest. Government employees engaged in major business operations on their private account and used their "inside" contacts to ensure their profitability. Such people accumulated notable wealth and came to constitute a new upper class.

Another common feature of the African social situation was "tribalism." The numerous ethnic groups in each state competed with one another to ensure their "fair" share of the benefits brought by independence: strategic positions in government, higher education, contracts, and the siting of development projects. Political leaders built their constituencies from their own ethnic groups, and political parties often had ethnic identities. Each group was quick to complain about apparent discrimination in favor of others. Mutual mistrust spiraled upward and sometimes resulted in open violence and even civil war.

The colonial experience also left a legacy of interracial friction. During the colonial era, Europeans took it for granted that the black man's capacity for human progress and development was inherently inferior to their own. Whites, even of lower social status, enjoyed pay and perquisites far better than those available to blacks: housing, amenities, social services, and so forth. Where climate and other conditions were suitable for white settlers, law reserved the more fertile land for the white minority. Whites held all positions of significant responsibility. Schools offered blacks only enough schooling for jobs in lower echelons. Social segregation was maintained. Whites' treatment of blacks was commonly contemptuous and often cruel. When the African countries became independent, therefore, blacks objected to continued privilege for "Europeans." Government pressed for early "Africanization" of jobs at all levels. Land-hungry blacks wanted white "reserved areas" opened for their own resettlement. Owing to earlier educational policies, however, few Africans were skilled in technology, management, and modern agriculture. Because rapid departure of whites could therefore jeopardize the economy, the new governments had to make concessions in order to retain them.

Common features also appeared in the foreign policies of the newly independent countries. For one thing, they were determined to free the entire continent from colonial rule. They therefore gave abundant moral and material support to liberation movements in Angola, Guinea-Bissau, Mozambique, Zimbabwe, and Namibia. They likewise pressed to end apartheid in South Africa.

At the same time, however, they often disagreed violently on another issue—which also arose from the colonial experience. The boundaries drawn by the Congress of Berlin frequently cut through sizable ethnic groups, and some of the new countries were eager to reunite these divided peoples under their own sovereignty. Tensions over this issue offered non-African powers an opportunity to intervene in the affairs of the continent.

In world affairs generally, African countries remained "nonaligned" between East and West. Whereas the colonial governments had been cool toward Communist regimes, many new governments established diplomatic relations with members of the Eastern Bloc and with such countries as China, Cuba, North Korea, and Vietnam. They accepted economic and technical assistance from both sides. On occasion, some of them made defense agreements with one side or the other. They welcomed the arms, the military training, and the military advice that Communist countries provided for the liberation struggles. In international forums such as the United Nations, African countries co-operated among themselves in promoting their own agenda, frequently using the East–West rivalry to bargain for support in the organizations' debates and balloting.

## Growth of Marxist Influence

Such was the African context in which Marxism worked its influence. How did this influence insert itself? In this chapter we are looking at the overall picture; later we will examine particular cases. The overall view will begin with the development of Marxist influence in colonial times and during the transition to independence.

European Marxists made no attempt to introduce their theory to Africa until after the Bolshevik revolution in 1917.[2] The Soviet Union then became the primary force propagating Marxism, but its efforts in the colonial world initially focused on China, India, and the Middle East. It was in 1928 that the Sixth Comintern Congress began giving Communist parties directives on Africa.[3] Even then, the Soviet Union took no *direct* part in propagating Marxism there for several decades. Other forces were at work.[4] Western European Communists were befriending Africans who came to their countries for studies. In meetings and conversations, they reinforced the blacks' resentment of racism and colonial rule, and introduced them to Marxism. Through contacts of this kind, future African nationalists—men such as Kwame Nkrumah and Jomo Kenyatta— also came to know one another and to organize radical discussions among themselves. Communist trade unionists operated similarly with African workingmen in Europe. Members of the International Seamen and Harbor Workers Union carried the Marxist message to Africa's ports. The Communist-controlled Confédération Générale du Travail (CGT) in France affiliated unions in the colonies with itself—for example, the Confédération Générale Africaine du Travail (CGAT) in French Congo. European Communists who had jobs in the colonies were able to find local disciples and set up Communist cells among them.

These kinds of infiltration into the African countries did not result in any quick and widespread adoption of Marxism. They did lay a foundation for later development. Thus, though few leaders of the newly independent countries were full-blown Marxists, they often adopted particular Marxist ideas and they were open to cooperation with the Soviet Union. In addition, Communist organizational networks which had been established in the colonies were available to promote Marxist causes in later years.

Soviet involvement with Africa became more direct in the mid-1950s as the colonies approached and achieved their independence. Between 1956 and 1974, thirty-four sub-Saharan countries reached this goal. Their very independence made it easier for the Soviets, East Europeans, Chinese, and Cubans to operate. Soviet authorities strengthened agencies at home that were concerned with Africa. In an indication of heightened interest, they changed the names of two journals dealing with the colonial world: *Contemporary East* became *Asia and Africa Today*, and *Soviet Orientology* became *Peoples of Asia and Africa*. Initially the Soviets managed to set up strong positions in several countries. Thus, they established very cooperative relationships with Ghana, Guinea, and Lumumba's government in Congo-Leopoldville. But their own errors and other circumstances led to sudden, dramatic reversals. China also achieved a strong position in some places, for example in Congo-Brazzaville, but was similarly unable to hold it.[5]

By this time, of course, the cold war was under way. The United States and Western European countries were as active as the Communist countries in promoting their own objectives in Africa. They used many of the same methods, sometimes more successfully. But the focus here is on the efforts of the Marxists.

The reasons why the Communist powers sought to propagate Marxism in Africa related to their foreign policy and to their social theory. They could expect African countries leaning toward Marxism to be more cooperative in the rivalry between the Soviet Bloc and the "Western" powers. The Soviet Union in particular wanted access to strategic military positions and materials. Thus, it sought the use of seaports—such as Berbera, Maputo, Luanda, and Conakry—to facilitate naval surveillance of the Indian Ocean, the South Atlantic, and the passages through Suez and around the Cape of Good Hope. And when the Soviets could not establish naval bases, agreements on fishing could open the way for their trawlers to keep rival fleets under observation. Marxist-leaning African countries, moreover, were more likely to provide diplomatic support for the Communist countries in the United Nations and other international forums. The Chinese wanted help especially to break through the isolation which the United States imposed by keeping their country out of the United Nations. The Chinese were also competing for support and for favored positions in their bitter differences with the Soviet Union.[6]

The Communist powers' expectation of world revolution provided an ideological basis for their promotion of Marxism in Africa. Stalin himself extended this expectation from Europe to Africa and Asia. The colonial peoples, he argued, also had a right to national self-determination, and they could be enlisted in the struggle against the imperialist bourgeoisie. The proletariat everywhere should therefore support the liberation movement in the colonies. If a particular national movement conflicted with the development of the proletarian movement, however, such support was "out of the question."[7]

Promoting Marxism in Africa was not the work of Europeans alone. Africans labored to the same end. Their motives were various. Many of them accepted Marxist theory as the key to a better life for their people. Some saw that even after independence most of their fellow citizens remained poor, powerless, lacking opportunities and comforts, neglected and oppressed by those in power. They blamed the unfair distribution of benefits in their communities and in the world at large on the workings of the capitalist system. And they argued that organizing their countries along the lines of Marxian socialism would help their people lead more truly human lives. Other Africans, one suspects, espoused Marxism out of personal ambition. They were aware that Marxists elsewhere were adept with varied techniques for wringing concessions from governments and even for seizing political power. Africans who aspired to leadership saw possibilities of using such tactics to pressure colonial governments for independence or to oust and replace domestic rivals in the government of states that were already independent. Africans sometimes espoused Marxism, too, because they wanted military help from Communist powers in open warfare against competing forces at home, as in Angola, or against hostile neighbors, as in Ethiopia. One political analyst suggests that some African regimes chose the Marxist label because it gave them a distinctive identity. It raised their self-esteem by giving them a claim to "scientific" knowledge. It made it possible for them to maintain a bond with the Communist bloc at the same time that their commitment to "non-alignment" kept them at a safe distance.[8]

## CHANNELS

Advocates of Marxism-Leninism used many channels to make the theory known. Communist countries established embassies in Africa, attached economic and military missions to these, and set up offices for such agencies as their national press services. Personnel of these organizations were then well placed to disseminate Marxist ideas. In 1987 China had forty-four resident ambassadors in Africa, the Soviet Union thirty-nine, North Korea twenty-nine, and Cuba twenty-five; the six smaller East European powers had an average of fifteen. Offices of press services such as TASS, Novosti, and Xinhua were almost as numerous.[9] Some capitals had special importance because they offered contact with political activists from the entire continent; such was Dar es Salaam in the 1970s, the headquarters for the many groups involved in the liberation of Mozambique and Rhodesia. At times the disproportionate size of embassy staffs clearly indicated that personnel were engaged in other-than-routine diplomatic business; during the 1960s, for example, the Chinese mission in Brazzaville numbered one hundred.[10]

Countless "front" organizations were another channel for propagating Marxist perspectives. While their stated, praiseworthy objectives attracted the participation of outsiders, Marxists controlled their machinery and used it for their own purposes. Examples included the World Peace Council, the International Union of Democratic Jurists, and the World Federation of Democratic Youth.[11]

The media provided further channels for disseminating Marxist viewpoints. Communist countries transmitted shortwave radio broadcasts to Africa. They circulated periodicals, books, and other publications. Their press services offered news releases and feature stories to local newspapers. Marxist-leaning governments also used publicly owned radio and newspapers to advance Marxist perspectives.

The ones whom Marxists especially wanted to reach through these various channels were people who could sway others or who could seriously affect the course of public affairs. In countries still under colonial control, therefore, they directed their efforts at leaders of the struggle for independence. In already independent countries, they aimed mostly at government authorities; but sometimes, if these were not open to persuasion, they turned to people who might lead an alternative government. They sought also to influence civil servants, members of the security forces, leaders of trade unions, and organizations of women and youth. They likewise aimed at journalists, other writers, artists, and filmmakers, who could strongly affect public opinion. Finally, they wanted to influence students in schools and universities; these were leaders of the future who could also have a powerful impact on the present.

## TACTICS

Operating through these channels, Marxists used a multitude of tactics and techniques to win committed disciples. One device was the award of study grants in Marxist countries for education-hungry Africans. Grants were not just for university studies but also for many kinds of practical training. Lumumba University in Moscow was the best-known, but not the only, center for study in Russia. In other East European countries, students went especially to Budapest, Leipzig, Prague, and Sofia. China and Cuba also awarded grants to Africans. Sojourns in these countries allowed the hosts ample opportunity to instruct their guests in Marxist theory.[12]

Communist countries hosted Africans for short visits, too, as honored guests at meetings and conferences or for tours connected with their professional interests. Communist parties, for example, invited representatives of leftward-leaning but non-Marxist parties elsewhere to attend their party congresses. African delegates came to meetings of front organizations such as the Afro-Asian Writers' Association. Professional visitors toured model agricultural or industrial projects. Visits sometimes featured meetings with the head of state or other dignitaries. In some cases the host country bestowed a national honor, such as the Soviet Union's Lenin Prize, on prominent Africans. The front organizations often elected Africans to office or to board membership. It was expected that this generous VIP treatment would render its recipients more friendly to those who extended such hospitality and more open to their ideology.[13]

In 1980, radio stations in Communist countries were broadcasting to sub-Saharan Africa for several hundred hours a week.[14] They used both African and European languages. News broadcasts and commentaries extolled achievements in the home country, underlined the fraternal cooperation of progressive peoples against imperialism, exposed ongoing capitalist exploitation, and circulated disinformation about the Western countries. The printed word, too, was at work. Communist countries arranged wide distribution of books, free or at bargain prices, sometimes through specialist bookshops. The books were printed mostly in the locally used European language, especially English and French. They included the writings of Marx, Engels, Lenin, Stalin, Mao Tse-Tung, and Kim Il Sung; there were historical works focusing especially on the Bolshevik and Chinese Revolutions, Marxist analyses of world economic problems, textbooks in the social and natural sciences, and selected writings of African nationalist heroes. The books were attractively produced, and would appeal particularly to young people who had a taste for reading or who were engaged in private study of academic or practical subjects.[15]

Communist countries likewise circulated attractive periodicals for general readers. Their contributors interpreted the world in Marxist terms. Articles and pictures projected images of progress and happy living in Communist countries. Specialized journals of Marxist organizations dealt directly with Marxist theory and practice. *The World Marxist Review*, published in Canada, was the English version of *Problems of Peace and Socialism*, which was published in many other languages. It described itself as the theoretical and informational journal of Communist and Workers' Parties. In London the South African Communist Party published *The African Communist*. *The Journal of African Marxists* was published in Zambia. Some Marxist governments and parties in Africa put out their own periodicals and newspapers—*Tempo* in Mozambique, for example, and *Dipanda* in Congo.

Marxists in African countries sought to indoctrinate young people through the schools. Marxist governments put formal ideological instruction into the school syllabus. Marxists in non-Marxist countries tried to do likewise in their educational systems. African and expatriate university professors introduced students to Marxism and, one suspects, gave them tactical guidance on making Marxism a force in student government and other campus organizations. Two black writers, both from the Caribbean, had a notably powerful impact in radicalizing students at African universities. Walter Rodney's *How Europe Underdeveloped Africa*, published in 1972, was a critique of imperialist economics. It also argued that European-style education and the colonial cultural milieu had colonized African minds, imbuing them with individualist and capitalist values which blocked any vision of responsible socialist alternatives. A decade earlier, Frantz Fanon had stressed the psychological devastation that colonization had inflicted on the colonized. For independence to become real, he insisted, Africa had to break definitively with European cultural dominance.[16]

Ruling Marxist parties organized youth movements and incorporated ideological orientation in their programs. Marxists tried to parallel this tactic in non-Marxist countries. Marxist parties and governments also set up special institutes for ideological indoctrination and required party officials, civil servants, and members of other strategic groups to attend their courses.[17]

Communist governments outside Africa tried to extend Marxist influence by offering various kinds of material assistance to liberation movements and to the independent states. One such kind of aid was the training of military forces. Cubans, for example, instructed Mozambican guerrillas in Algeria, and organized the presidential guard in Guinea and Congo.[18] The assisting countries offered advanced training for officers as well. Communist countries also provided arms, financed by grants or loans. From 1975 to 1980, the Soviet Union delivered arms worth $633 million to Angola and $1.78 billion to Ethiopia.[19] Communist countries sent their own military personnel, too, to assist African troops engaged in armed conflict. In some cases, these were detachments of "military advisers," who helped with planning, logistics, and maintenance of equipment. In two cases, however, they were combat troops: In 1975 at least thirteen thousand Cubans, air-lifted by Russia, turned the tide for the MPLA against domestic rivals in Angola and set back a South African move to intervene in the struggle. Again, in 1977, Cuban troops in Ethiopia turned back a Somali invasion.[20]

Similarly, Communist countries offered technical and economic aid to African countries. They sent experts to help with particular functions or to give specialized training. They provided financial grants or loans for specific development projects. China, for example, constructed the Tazara railway, connecting Zambia's railway with the Tanzanian port of Dar es Salaam. Between 1973 and 1982, more than ten thousand Chinese technical assistants worked in the sub-Saharan region.[21] While economic and technical aid was intended to dispose the recipients favorably toward the donor countries, it also placed technical personnel in a position to disseminate Marxist ideology in local society and to engage in covert political activity if this seemed desirable.

By and large, too, Communist powers supported the positions of African countries in international diplomacy, particularly in the workings of the United Nations and similar organizations. In the UN's earliest years, Russia and the Communist bloc pressed for the immediate granting of independence to the colonies. Later, they turned their fire against the newly independent countries' continued economic dependence on the former colonial powers. Communist countries likewise supported African insistence that South Africa should end apartheid. This position contrasted sharply with the reluctance of the United States and other Western powers to exert real pressure on the South African regime.

Finally, Communist countries sought to extend Marxist influence by giving advice, financial help, and other assistance to local Marxists. These in turn could disseminate Marxist doctrine, and could even work to destabilize the home government and seize control. In the nature of the case it was hard to document undercover operations. But local Marxists certainly profited from the rioting at Brazzaville, which led to Fulbert Youlou's overthrow in 1963, and at Addis Ababa, which led to Haile Selassie's dethronement in 1974.

## REVERSES

Not all these tactics for spreading Marxist influence always worked as intended. In the early years of decolonization, some African leaders whom the Communists had cultivated chose to go their own way, and some lost their hold on power. African students in Communist countries did not always become converts. Some were disillusioned by the shortcomings they saw close up in Communist societies; some complained of racial discrimination at the hands of local people.[22] In African universities, the problem was different: Marxists among the students were never more than a small minority who made no long-term impact on the others; and after graduation the activists themselves found it easier to seek rewards within the existing system than to plot its overthrow.[23]

The tactic of granting military aid did not always work either. Some liberation movements were fragmented, and Communists sometimes backed the wrong faction. And when the Russians chose to help Ethiopia in its conflict with Somalia, they had to give up major privileges they had acquired in Somalia through seven years of patient diplomacy. This kind of intervention, moreover, made other African states uneasy; in a 1978 address to the Organization of African Unity, Nigeria's chief of state reminded "the Soviets and their friends . . . that having been invited to Africa in order to assist the liberation struggle, . . . they should not overstay their welcome."[24] On a number of occasions, too, when African governments had reason to believe that Communist governments were cooperating in the subversive activities of local Marxists, they reacted sharply; such situations led Burundi to close the Chinese embassy in Bujumbura in 1965, and in 1971 ended the previously cordial relations between Jaafar al-Nimeri in Sudan and the Soviet government.[25]

As for economic aid, the constricted economies of Communist states limited the amount of assistance they could offer to African countries. In 1983, for example, the Soviet Union had to turn down Ghana's request for help and advise the Rawlings government to approach the IMF.[26] Even when Communist governments did grant economic and technical assistance, moreover, this sometimes led to strained relations. The donor's inefficient management could cause friction with the recipient, or the recipient could become suspicious of the donor's opportunism. In some places, too, real or seemingly arrogant behavior on the part of foreign personnel could arouse antagonism among the local people.

### MORE AND LESS MARXISM

Even though Communist tactics for promoting Marxism sometimes failed, the ideology's influence in Africa nevertheless expanded after 1974. In assessing this expansion, however, a problem arises about the use of the term "Marxism." Some African countries called themselves "Marxist," but the older Marxist countries, such as the Soviet Union, would not apply this label to them; and in fact, they did not fully implement characteristically Marxist policies. Other African countries called themselves "socialist," and critics incorrectly took this to mean the same as "Marxist." To help clear up this confusion, we will note the typical lines that Marxist governments follow. Few of these are followed only by Marxist governments in Africa, and few "Marxist" governments follow them fully. Some of them are characteristic of governments that are merely "authoritarian," regardless of their ideological leanings, and many African governments were of this kind. The intent here, however, is not to set up a theoretical model of a Marxist regime; it is to indicate features that commonly appear in governments inclining toward Marxism. For practical purposes, we can say that the more such features a government does manifest, the more Marxist it is—provided it also has some degree of commitment to Marxist ideology.[27]

Marxist regimes explicitly declare their adoption of Marxism as the official ideology of the country. Commonly, too, they will assert their Marxist identity by giving the country a new name such as "Democratic Republic of . . ." or "People's Republic of. . . ."

Marxist governments are one-party regimes. They suppress opposition parties. They structure their party on Leninist lines, concentrating real power in a small political bureau. The party sets public policies, and the government merely executes them. Although Marxist parties in Africa commonly call themselves "vanguard" parties, most of them are, in fact, mass parties, not the disciplined elites that Lenin had in mind; they neverthless seek to bar all internal dissent. To mobilize women and youth, the regimes set up special party sections for these people and suppress any rival organizations. They may similarly bring other special constituencies into party-dominated organizations. They may, for example, set up a single federation of trade unions. At the same time, they may follow the practice of some older Marxist regimes by trying to arrange for workers to take at least a nominal part in managing enterprises.

Although Marxist regimes centralize the power to make important decisions at the top, they describe their system as "participatory democracy" or "democratic centralism." They may, in fact, arrange for a particular kind of popular participation in local government and party affairs—which is also a device for indoctrinating the people and mobilizing their support. The party organizes regular meetings of small groups in villages, urban neighborhoods, and work places. Party representatives explain ideology and decisions. They guide the groups in exercises of "self-criticism"—evaluation of their performance in pursuing the regime's objectives. This kind of face-to-face dialogue also becomes a form of mutual surveillance, pressuring potential dissenters to conform.

Marxist regimes likewise establish "people's courts" at the local level to administer justice. Commonly the judges have no legal training. Much of the courts' business is the trial of people accused of sharing the blame and the profits of the previous regime's evil deeds. The courts tend to brush aside procedural safeguards as needless formalities. Appeals of decisions that seem unwarranted are barred or severely restricted.

Marxist governments are acutely concerned with internal security. They tend to mistrust the regular army. So they assign political commissars to military units to ensure the ideological orthodoxy of the troops. They set up elite units, such as presidential guards, and give them intensive ideological training. They may also organize "people's militias" as counterweights to the regular armed forces. In addition, these governments may use secret police, investigation by "third degree," politically controlled judiciary, and harsh prisons and prison camps.

Marxist regimes control public information. They often assume exclusive ownership of the media. They may exercise formal censorship of press, radio, and television, or may merely harass indiscreet journalists and programmers into conformity.

Marxist governments customarily lay down comprehensive development plans. They nationalize economic enterprises on a large scale: banking, insurance, mining, manufacturing, shipping, transportation, and commerce. In addition, they reform land holding in various ways. They collectivize agriculture, setting up either state farms or large cooperatives; or, especially in countries where landlords exploit rural populations, they nationalize landed property and distribute it to landless people. They may also move toward expanding health care and education by nationalizing hospitals, clinics, and schools owned by voluntary agencies.

## THE IMPACT OF MARXIST INFLUENCE

We return here to the actual impact of Marxism in Africa. Most of the first countries to achieve independence adopted some kind of "socialist" ideology: either the democratic socialism of Western Europe or "African socialism," which linked public ownership of major enterprises with the traditional communalism of many African societies. But Ghana, Guinea, and Congo-Leopoldville (during the brief ascendancy of Lumumba) showed strong leanings toward Marxism. Beginning in 1964, a series of coups in Congo-Brazzaville brought to power several governments each more radical than the last; in 1969, Marien Ngouabi's regime adopted Marxism as its official ideology. In the same year, Nimeri in Sudan and Siad Barre in Somalia turned their countries in the same direction. Marxist influence, however, faded in Ghana, Mali, and Congo-Leopoldville when Nkrumah, Keita, and Lumumba, respectively, were overthrown— all before the end of the decade; Nimeri turned against Marxism in 1971. On balance, then, despite early successes, Marxism lost ground.

The 1970s were different. Matthieu Kerekou, who seized power in Dahomey (soon renamed Benin) in 1972, formally adopted Marxism-Leninism as the country's ideology three years later. In Ethiopia, Mengistu Haile Mariam seized leadership in the military government that succeeded Haile Selassie, and ultimately made Marxism the official ideology. By 1975 all the Portuguese colonies had won their independence. The governments of Angola and Mozambique were professedly Marxist; those of Cape Verde, Guinea-Bissau, and São Tomé and Principe had strong Marxist leanings. In 1975, Didier Ratsiraka turned Madagascar's domestic policies toward Marxism. After Zimbabwe achieved its independence under black majority rule in 1980, Robert Mugabe proposed to organize the country along the lines of "scientific socialism." Military coups in 1981 and 1983 brought Jerry Rawlings to power in Ghana and Thomas Sankara in Upper Volta (which he renamed Burkina Faso). The governments of both men leaned toward Marxism. And in the late 1970s, the government of Kenneth Kaunda in Zambia began to flirt with "scientific socialism."

Down to the mid-1980s, then, Marxism won acceptance as the ideology of an increasing number of African states. For the most part, however, governments were not very much concerned with doctrinal purity, and they paid little attention to Karl Marx's complete theory. Instead they followed selected practices of older Marxist-Leninist countries. The acceptance of Marxist ideology by governments did not imply, either, any widespread acceptance of Marxist theory by the people at large—at least not in the short run. Although a considerable number of intellectuals and academics regarded themselves as Marxists, few of them appeared to have a clear and accurate understanding of the doctrine or a concrete program for improving the social situation of their respective countries.

Even though the Marxism of African governments was selective and ambivalent in all but a few cases, then, the theory's increasing popularity raised a real possibility of serious problems for African peoples. Attempts to implement faithfully a Marxist-Leninist style of government and economy could give permanence to the common shortcomings of Communist societies elsewhere. It could slow down development instead of speeding it up. It could leave unchanged the oppressions the masses suffered or even make them worse. It could hamper the full growth of human persons. And serious Marxist indoctrination, sponsored by party and government, in ideological institutes, schools, and public media could lead people to the uncritical acceptance of defective principles of thought and action—and thus make it even more difficult to find remedies for their problems.

## NOTES

1. See the yearbook *Africa South of the Sahara* (London: Europa Publications) for up-to-date country-by-country surveys of African geography, history, politics, and economics.

2. Curiously, Samuel Moore, whom Engels personally recruited to translate Marx's *Das Kapital* into English, later became Chief Justice for Britain's Royal Niger Company and served for many years in present-day Nigeria. He made no effort, apparently, to propagate Marx's theories. See Henderson, *Life of Friedrich Engels*, pp. 281–82.

3. See Edward T. Wilson, "Russia's Historic Stake in Black Africa," in David E. Albright, ed., *Communism in Africa* (Bloomington: Indiana University Press, 1980), pp. 81–82.

4. Ibid., pp. 81–86, Here Wilson sketches the efforts that the Comintern inspired.

5. See Alexander Dallin, "The Soviet Union: Political Activity," in Zbigniew Brzezinski, ed., *Africa and the Communist World* (Stanford, Calif.: Stanford

University Press, 1963), pp. 7, 20–21, 32–35, 43; David Ottaway and Marina Ottaway, *Afro-Communism* (New York: Africana Publishing, 1981), pp. 4–5.

6. See David E. Albright, "Moscow's African Policy of the 1970s," in Albright, ed., *Communism in Africa*, pp. 50–58; George T. Yu, "Sino-Soviet Rivalry in Africa," in ibid., pp. 168–69; Dallin, "Soviet Union: Political Activity," pp. 12–13.

7. Stalin, *Foundations of Leninism*, pp. 76–80, 82–84.

8. See Kenneth Jowitt, "Scientific Socialist Regimes in Africa: Political Differentiation, Avoidance, and Unawareness," in Carl G. Rosberg and Thomas M. Callaghy, eds., *Socialism in Sub-Saharan Africa: A New Assessment* (Berkeley: University of California Press, 1979), pp. 136–44, 147–50, 165–67.

9. I derived these figures from the lists of diplomatic missions and foreign press agencies in *Africa South of the Sahara 1988* (London: Europa Publications, 1987).

10. See Vezeau, *L'Afrique face au communisme*, pp. 99–100; Fritz Schatten, *Communism in Africa* (New York: Frederick A. Praeger, 1966), pp. 215, 285.

11. See Schatten, *Communism in Africa*, pp. 229–39.

12. See ibid., pp. 302–308; Richard Lowenthal, "China," in Brzezinski, ed., *Africa and the Communist World*, pp. 159–60; "Angola," *West Africa*, August 15, 1982, p. 2133; "Students Leave for Cuba," ibid., September 5, 1983, p. 2087; "Tsikata in Cuba," ibid., September 26, 1983, p. 2259.

13. See Dallin, "Soviet Union: Political Activity," p. 22.

14. John L. Shirer, ed., *China Facts and Figures Annual*, vol. 6 (Gulf Breeze, Fla.: Academic International Press, 1983), p. 326.

15. There was a typical selection of such books at a Soviet-sponsored bookshop in Antananarivo, Madagascar, in May 1982. In Nigeria, in October 1982, the University of Ibadan's bookstore carried a considerable stock of Soviet publications. Likewise in Nigeria two commercial distributors advertised an entire line of Soviet books in widely circulated newspapers and invited orders by mail: Progressive and Socialist Book Depot, Ibadan, in *Daily Sketch* (Ibadan), September 9, 1983, p. 13; and John West Publications with MIR/Progress Publications, *National Concord* (Lagos), August 31, 1983, p. 20.

16. See Walter Rodney, *How Europe Underdeveloped Africa* (Washington, D.C.: Howard University Press, 1974), pp. 24–27 and passim; Frantz Fanon, *The Wretched of the Earth*, trans. Constance Farrington (New York: Grove Press, 1968), pp. 249–316; idem, *Black Skin, White Masks*, trans. Charles Lam Markham (New York: Grove Press, 1965), pp. 223–32 and passim.

17. Angola's MPLA had an *Escola de Quadros* at Leopoldville, and then in Congo-Brazzaville, from 1963. Ethiopia's Derg organized a school in 1976; see Ottaway and Ottaway, *Afro-Communism*, pp. 85, 103, 147. *Escolas do Partido* were established in Angola in 1977; see Kevin Brown, "Angolan Socialism," in Rosberg and Callaghy, eds., *Socialism in Sub-Saharan Africa*, p. 306.

18. See René Gauze, *The Politics of Congo-Brazzaville*, trans., ed., and suppl.

Virginia Thompson and Richard Adloff (Stanford: Hoover Institution, 1973), p. 225; Edward Gonzalez, "Cuba, the Soviet Union and Africa," in Albright, ed., *Communism in Africa*, pp. 148–49.

19. These figures were calculated from data in John E. Shirer, ed., *USSR Facts and Figures Annual*, vol. 8 (Gulf Breeze, Fla.: Academic International Press, 1984), p. 200.

20. Gonzalez, in "Cuba, the Soviet Union and Africa," 155, puts the number of Cuban troops in Angola at 15,000 and the number in Ethiopia at 16,000. Other writers give higher figures.

21. Shirer, *China Facts and Figures Annual*, 7:164.

22. See Schatten, *Communism in Africa*, pp. 303–307; Robert Bass and Elizabeth Bass, "Eastern Europe," in Brzezinski, ed., *Africa and the Communist World*, p. 102; Emmanuel John Hevi, *African Student in China* (New York: Frederick A. Praeger, 1962), pp. 76–84 and passim.

23. See Stanley Mulenga, "Ex-UNZA Militants Disown Socialist Ideals," *Times of Zambia* (Lusaka), September 28, 1985, p. 4.

24. Quoted in Colum Legum, "African Outlooks Toward the USSR," in Albright, ed., *Communism in Africa*, p. 28.

25. See Vezeau, *L'Afrique face au communisme*, pp. 91–95, 112–14; Schatten, *Communism in Africa*, pp. 141–42; Ottaway and Ottaway, *Afro-Communism*, p. 5.

26. See Onyema Ugochukwu, "The Lost Revolution," *West Africa*, February 25, 1985, pp. 346–47.

27. Neil Harding discusses the problem of classifying regimes as Marxist: "What Does It Mean to Call a Regime Marxist?" in Bogdan Szajkowski, ed., *Marxist Governments: A World Survey*, 3 vols. (London: Macmillan, 1981), 1:20–33. See similar discussions by Edmond J. Keller, "Afro-Marxist Regimes," in Edmond J. Keller and Donald Rothchild, eds., *Afro-Marxist Regimes: Ideology and Public Policy* (Boulder, Colo.: Lynne Rienner, 1987), pp. 7–11; and by Donald Rothchild and Michael Foley, "Ideology and Public Policy in Afro-Marxist Regimes: The Effort to Cope with Domestic and International Constraints," in Keller and Rothchild eds., *Afro-Marxist Regimes*, pp. 282–86.

# 4

# The Church in Africa
# and Its Encounter with Marxism:
# An Overview

THE OVERVIEW OF Marxist influence in Africa in the previous chapter
said nothing of the policies and practices of Marxist and Marxist-leaning
governments toward religion and the churches. But our central concern
is precisely with the meeting of Marxism and the Catholic Church. To
bring this topic into focus, this chapter will give a general picture of the
Church in sub-Saharan Africa and of the ways in which Marxist influences affected its mission.

### NATURE AND MISSION OF THE CHURCH

It will be useful at the outset to say something about the Church's understanding of its own nature, from which its mission flows. In recent decades, theology has deepened Catholic insight into the nature of the
Church. Official expression of this insight appeared particularly in the
documents coming from and following upon Vatican Council II. Especially in point were the Council's constitutions on the Church (*Lumen
Gentium*) and the Church in the Modern World (*Gaudium et Spes*), the
Decree on Missionary Activity (*Ad Gentes*), Pope Paul VI's Apostolic
Exhortation on Evangelization in the Modern World (*Evangelii Nuntiandi*), and the final document of the Synod of Bishops in 1971.[1]

Viewed theologically, the Church is a multifaceted entity. A complete
picture must include all its facets together, but it is helpful to begin by
looking at them separately.[2] The Church is, most obviously, an "institution,"[3] a visible society of men and women organized for cooperative
work toward a common good. Only by being an institution can the

Church act in a human way in a world of humans. It can coordinate the efforts of its members by providing centers for planning, deciding, initiating, and controlling action, and it can maintain continuity in pursuing its mission. Its organization, moreover, is international. The Church has members in virtually every nation of the world. Because the bishop of Rome, as successor to Saint Peter, heads it, its administrative center is in that city.

But the relationship among people in the Church is not the quasi-contractual relationship characteristic of ordinary organizations. In faith, members see the Church as a "communion"[4] or "fellowship" bound together by mutual love and service among themselves and by the divine grace that brings them into communion also with Christ. Members also see the Church as a "sign"[5]—a visible sign of the inner reality of divine grace. It not merely signifies this reality; it also carries on God's grace-giving action in the world. One particular way it does this is by its "sacraments," the external rituals which God has made channels of interior grace. The Church, further, is a "herald."[6] God commissioned it to proclaim his message, to teach what he has revealed through Christ and the Bible. The Church also holds God's commission to be the authentic interpreter of the message.

In addition, the Church is "servant."[7] It must serve the world in its temporal as well as its spiritual needs. Jesus blessed those who fed the hungry, clothed the naked, and visited the imprisoned. From its beginnings, the Church engaged in such works of mercy as care of the sick. From early centuries, too, popes, bishops, and theologians spoke out on the effective organization of secular society. Vatican II, however, stressed a sometimes neglected understanding of being "servant." It recalled that men and women grow in their personalities by dealing with the world and helping to establish a well-ordered society. The Church, therefore, is to work for human dignity, social justice, and peace. The secular aspects of life have value in themselves. By promoting this value, the Church labors to fulfill God's intentions for humankind. But it should not lose sight of the fuller, more sublime, otherworldly destiny which the word of God proclaimed, or of people's need for the interior grace which the Church can make available to them.[8]

With this understanding of the Church's nature in mind, we can look more closely at its mission—at its purposes and the functions through which it pursues these. Its fundamental purpose is to continue the saving work of Christ throughout history, to bring men and women everywhere into contact with this work. Jesus's life on earth was limited in time and place, but he intended his work for everyone who would ever live. So he established the Church to teach, sanctify, and serve all humankind on his behalf in all the ages that were to follow.

In order to fulfill its purpose, the Church must proclaim the gospel, teach, and offer guidance. It must not merely pass knowledge along but also move people's hearts to respond. It must continue to evangelize people who are already in the Church, striving to deepen their faith and their love of God and neighbor and to strengthen the bonds of unity among them. It must also make God's message known to people outside the Church, leading them to belief in Christ and conversion of heart.

The need to teach implies an obligation to educate the young. The Church must help Christian families provide religious formation, intellectual and otherwise, for their children. This normally entails involvement with schools. The objective is not just to hand on a body of doctrine. The Church school should help its students to integrate religion into their lives, to deepen their conviction and commitment. In circumstances where the Church cannot reach young people through the schools, it should organize other ways of giving them whatever religious training it can. In order to teach, the Church must also use other channels of communication: private conversations and private associations, public forums, books, newspapers, periodicals, pamphlets, cassette recordings, radio, films, and television.

The Church must make available to the faithful the sacraments, the external rites aimed at deepening their inward holiness and strengthening their union with God and one another. Among these, the Church's central act of worship and praise for God is supremely important: the Mass, the Eucharistic sacrifice.

The Church must promote human development in the secular sphere. It must foster the full growth of persons, following the lines of Christian humanism, and must advance the development of civil society as an extension of human growth and a support for it. This work touches culture, economics, society, and politics. But here the Church should bring a distinctive "gospel" perspective to development; it should make clear the dignity of the human person and the linkage of human growth with divine purpose. In pursuing this part of its mission, the Church frequently offers moral guidance on social matters. Especially since the time of Leo XIII, popes have presented more or less systematic teaching on the family, legal and constitutional institutions, economic organization, international peace, and so forth. Similar pronouncements were found in patristic times. They are found today also in the pastoral letters of ordinary bishops. Church authorities in recent times have tried in this way to combat such injustices as racism, economic abuses that keep people permanently destitute, and political controls that reduce whole populations to powerlessness, fear, and servility. The Church, then, must be social advocate, mobilizing its members to exert political pressure for or against specific measures of public policy.

The Church's mission requires it, in principle, to reach all human beings in all times and all places. It will not, in fact, accomplish this, but this duty of the Church does bar any interference in its communication with any human person.

Finally, to pursue all these tasks the Church must organize itself and its activities. It can work until "the close of the age" only if it establishes, maintains, and operates its institutional structures. It must possess and manage physical facilities; recruit, train, and direct its personnel; arrange for ongoing cooperation of the faithful at many levels; lay out lines of responsibility; and use standard channels of internal communication.

It is true that the Church in its actuality always falls short of the ideal here described, partly because its members take a one-sided view of what it is and does. Church officials are sometimes excessively conscious of their authority and overbearing in their dealings with the faithful. Their concern for the smooth functioning of the institution sometimes distracts them from the weightier issues of justice and Christian charity. Some layfolk regard the Church's mission as the responsibility of the clergy alone and remain merely passive recipients of its services. Other layfolk are more active but nevertheless see religion as a matter only of personal piety, unrelated to the everyday life of workshop and marketplace. Still other Catholics do give themselves to the promotion of justice, development, and peace, but find themselves aiming at merely temporal objectives, unmindful of people's need for God's saving grace. Some of these shortcomings were perhaps more widespread in history than they are today because the comprehensive understanding of the Church outlined here has gained prominence only in the past twenty-five years. Sometimes the Church's current conflicts with Marxism in Africa are rooted in the shortcomings of earlier days.

## THE CHURCH'S HISTORICAL DEVELOPMENT IN AFRICA

We turn here to the actual development of the Church in Africa. Its responses to Marxist influence are better understood in the context of its history and its total pastoral effort. Even though the pace and style of the Church's development differed in the differing environments of the various countries, there is room here for valid generalization.

The work of the Portuguese missionaries in the fifteenth and sixteenth centuries did not take permanent root. A new thrust in the nineteenth century had more lasting effect, and largely shaped the Church as it was at the time of independence. This effort began in the heyday of colonization, when the European powers were penetrating inland and setting up their own administrations. The missionaries came mostly from Western Europe. The Church tended to be more visible in the colonies of countries that were at least nominally Catholic: Belgium, France, Portugal, and Spain. But it also functioned in the British and German colonies, where there was also a marked Protestant presence.

During the colonial era, the Church established its basic structures and methods of operation: vicariates and prefectures (in lieu of dioceses), parishes and mission stations, primary evangelization and catechumenate. Lay catechists had a key role in carrying on the Church's work, partly because the missionaries were so few and were handicapped by the multiplicity of local languages. The Catholic Church was slow in recruiting indigenous clergy and religious, partly because of the high educational qualifications needed for priestly training and the resistance of African cultures to the requirement of clerical celibacy. In many places the Church built up an extensive school system. Missionaries supervised primary and secondary schools and taught in the latter. They thus gave a basic Catholic formation to students who were Catholic and evangelized those who were not; they also won the good will of elders who wanted education for their offspring. The Church established medical clinics and small hospitals, too, mostly emphasizing maternal and child care and usually conducted by professionally qualified women religious.

As people of their own day, missionary personnel largely took for granted the legitimacy of foreign rule, at least for a period of time. When the nationalist movement gained momentum, their opinions on the desirability of independence divided. Some missionaries believed that a longer period of tutelage was needed, lest premature liberation lead to political and economic chaos. The socialist rhetoric of nationalist leaders also aroused their fears that the new governments would be Marxist and hostile to the Church. In the view of others, justice demanded the early concession of independence.

When the African countries in fact came close to achieving their freedom, the Holy See raised the status of their Catholic vicariates and prefectures into dioceses, and gathered these into national hierarchies. As

missionary bishops retired or died, it began to replace them with indigenous bishops. It accelerated this process in the 1970s.

The Church was an impressive presence in a number of countries.
Although it is hard to get accurate statistics, the figures in Table 1 give a
reasonable approximation of its size. In 1985, there were 69 million Catholics in sub-Saharan Africa. These constituted about 16 percent of the
total population. Their proportion was generally smaller, however, in
the countries of the Sahel (where Muslims were dominant) than in the
countries further south. Bishops numbered 356, priests 16,200, religious
brothers 4,700, and sisters 31,300. No figures were available on the proportions of foreign and African personnel; an impressionistic judgment
would be that 80 percent of the bishops and 50 percent of other categories
were indigenous. Catholics numbered more than 500,000 and constituted
more than 10 percent of the population in 19 countries.

The Church's basic organization at its highest level in each country
was by dioceses. The hierarchies organized themselves into national
"bishops' conferences," which commonly developed joint pastoral initiatives and coordinated the bishops' approaches to public issues. Further,
the hierarchies established international bishops' conferences (or, more
precisely, associations of national conferences). Some of these were regional: AMECEA for East Africa, AECAWA and CERAO for West
Africa, and IMBISA for southern Africa; and one was continent-wide:
SECAM.[9] These fostered cooperative initiatives in both the sacral and
the secular realm. The Holy See conducted its business with the African
churches through the Sacred Congregation for the Evangelization of
Peoples (SCEP) in Rome, and through Apostolic Nuncios or Delegates
who represented the Holy See in each nation's capital.[10] These sometimes
played a prominent part in the relations of the Church with government.

After independence, the operational center of the Church's pastoral
work continued to be the parish, served by a resident priest. Because the
parish was often extensive in area and priests were few, it was commonly
divided into out-stations which the priest visited periodically to instruct,
offer the Eucharist, and administer the other sacraments. Between his
visits, full-time lay catechists provided instruction and whatever religious
services a nonordained person could provide. An elected committee of
church members supervised the business of parish or out-station, especially its material concerns, in consultation with the priest.

Church schools continued to play an important part in the religious
formation of Catholic children and the evangelization of non-Catholic
ones. Health services remained a high priority, especially in remote areas.

TABLE I: POPULATION, CATHOLIC POPULATION, AND CHURCH PERSONNEL
IN THE COUNTRIES OF SUB-SAHARAN AFRICA.*

| | Total Population | Catholic Population | % Catholic | Priests | Brothers | Sisters |
|---|---|---|---|---|---|---|
| Angola | 8,750,000 | 4,663,000 | 53.2 | 299 | 46 | 852 |
| Benin | 3,930,000 | 671,000 | 17.0 | 192 | 18 | 358 |
| Botswana | 1,080,000 | 42,000 | 3.8 | 34 | 5 | 60 |
| Burkina Faso | 6,640,000 | 629,000 | 9.4 | 390 | 132 | 635 |
| Burundi | 4,720,000 | 2,688,000 | 56.9 | 270 | 147 | 646 |
| Cameroon | 10,110,000 | 2,741,000 | 27.1 | 830 | 213 | 1,291 |
| Cape Verde | 330,000 | 303,000 | 91.8 | 32 | 6 | 70 |
| Central African Republic | 2,610,000 | 429,000 | 16.4 | 216 | 57 | 276 |
| Chad | 5,020,000 | 311,000 | 6.1 | 141 | 41 | 227 |
| Comoros | 440,000 | 2,000 | 0.4 | 2 | 0 | 8 |
| Congo | 1,740,000 | 817,000 | 46.9 | 159 | 44 | 228 |
| Côte d'Ivoire | 9,810,000 | 1,015,000 | 10.3 | 406 | 86 | 546 |
| Djibouti | 430,000 | 10,000 | 0.2 | 9 | 8 | 26 |
| Equatorial Guinea | 390,000 | 320,000 | 82.0 | 72 | 17 | 147 |
| Ethiopia | 43,350,000 | 271,000 | 0.6 | 486 | 76 | 796 |
| Gabon | 1,150,000 | 621,000 | 54.0 | 101 | 29 | 157 |
| Gambia | 640,000 | 14,000 | 2.0 | 20 | 3 | 34 |
| Ghana | 13,590,000 | 1,621,000 | 11.9 | 531 | 135 | 557 |
| Guinea | 6,070,000 | 54,000 | 0.9 | 21 | 2 | 22 |
| Guinea-Bissau | 890,000 | 50,000 | 5.6 | 52 | 11 | 56 |
| Kenya | 20,330,000 | 4,212,000 | 20.7 | 1,032 | 239 | 2,390 |
| Lesotho | 1,530,000 | 647,000 | 42.0 | 134 | 47 | 662 |
| Liberia | 2,190,000 | 54,000 | 2.4 | 53 | 32 | 110 |
| Madagascar | 9,980,000 | 2,281,000 | 22.8 | 689 | 385 | 1,897 |
| Malawi | 7,060,000 | 1,490,000 | 21.2 | 377 | 148 | 607 |
| Mali | 8,210,000 | 70,000 | 0.9 | 135 | 25 | 169 |
| Mauritania | 1,890,000 | 6,000 | 0.3 | 11 | 2 | 32 |
| Mauritius | 990,000 | 330,000 | 33.0 | 86 | 35 | 287 |
| Mozambique | 13,960,000 | 1,854,000 | 13.2 | 270 | 71 | 512 |
| Niger | 6,100,000 | 15,000 | 0.2 | 36 | 10 | 82 |
| Nigeria | 95,200,000 | 7,207,000 | 7.5 | 1,588 | 281 | 1,521 |

| | Total Population | Catholic Population | % Catholic | Priests | Brothers | Sisters |
|---|---|---|---|---|---|---|
| Rwanda | 6,070,000 | 2,621,000 | 43.0 | 508 | 241 | 933 |
| São Tomé | 110,000 | 90,000 | 81.0 | 10 | 3 | 15 |
| Senegal | 6,440,000 | 299,000 | 4.6 | 236 | 137 | 553 |
| Seychelles | 66,000 | 60,000 | 90.0 | 16 | 9 | 58 |
| Sierra Leone | 3,600,000 | 47,000 | 1.3 | 121 | 13 | 109 |
| Somalia | 4,650,000 | 2,000 | 0.0 | 5 | 1 | 59 |
| Sudan | 21,550,000 | 1,521,000 | 7.0 | 270 | 73 | 263 |
| Swaziland | 650,000 | 37,000 | 6.0 | 37 | 8 | 115 |
| Tanzania | 21,730,000 | 4,539,000 | 20.8 | 1,503 | 368 | 4,675 |
| Togo | 2,960,000 | 646,000 | 21.8 | 218 | 78 | 319 |
| Uganda | 15,480,000 | 6,406,000 | 41.3 | 1,037 | 307 | 2,247 |
| Zaïre | 30,360,000 | 14,774,000 | 48.6 | 2,689 | 842 | 4,897 |
| Zambia | 6,670,000 | 1,914,000 | 28.6 | 543 | 161 | 798 |
| Zimbabwe | 8,300,000 | 718,000 | 8.6 | 318 | 124 | 1,021 |
| Total | 417,756,000 | 69,154,000 | 16.5 † | 16,185 | 4716 | 31,323 |

*Source: Catholic Almanac, 1988.* Huntington, Indiana: Our Sunday Visitor Publishing Division, 1987, pp. 332–366. Namibia and the Republic of South Africa have been omitted.

†Percent of Catholics among entire African population.

Responding to Vatican II's teaching that Christians must labor for the secular as well as the religious welfare of mankind, the Church expanded its social commitment, engaging in a wider variety of activities than it had earlier. The Church labored, too, to enlist young men and women into the clergy and religious congregations. To this end it still conducted seminaries and novitiates. The factors that slowed vocational recruitment in the missionary era, however, persisted in many countries; this remained a matter of special concern, because the number of missionary vocations abroad was declining and the new governments sometimes restricted the entry of foreign priests and religious. The Church also continued to promote organizations of the laity at both the local and the national level, particularly such groups as the Catholic Women, the Catholic Family Movement, Catholic Workers, and Catholic Youth. Bishops and religious congregations often sponsored modest publishing enterprises. These turned out devotional books, catechisms, and popular pamphlets as well as newspapers (weekly) and magazines for a Catholic readership. In Angola the Church controlled its own radio station.

Church finance followed the pattern established by the missionaries. Local communities often donated land and labor for building churches and other facilities. Church members paid a fixed annual contribution to their parish and made additional free-will offerings each week— sometimes in kind rather than in cash. They also paid "stole fees" to the priest on the occasion of receiving particular personal services. In some countries, government paid salaries of teachers and health workers in church-run schools, clinics, and hospitals. Church personnel working in these places continued the missionaries' practice of contributing part of their salaries to their respective institutions. The Holy See partially subsidized the maintenance of priests, seminarians, religious novices, and catechists. Catholic funding agencies abroad gave grants for capital projects. Critics sometimes complained that the insistence on annual contributions, stole fees, school fees, and fees for medical services exploited the poor. Yet it was appropriate that members take responsibility for their own church. Although shameful abuses did occur, most church personnel were sympathetic with the problems of their people and thus flexible in their expectations of payment.

For the most part, the faithful took their Catholic commitment seriously. They attended Church services regularly, were earnest in their devotional life, and were generous in their material support. Still, some shortcomings gave rise to problems that could acquire special urgency in a Marxist environment. Although the basic religious knowledge of at least older Catholics was solid, it remained quite elementary. In different ways, inadequate formation led to some "leakage" of members. Catholics among the elite often drifted away because their merely elementary religious training did not prepare them for the secularizing atmosphere of university education. Catholic young people flooding into the cities drifted because the Church had trouble keeping contact in the unsettled conditions of the burgeoning slums. In some countries, too, the Church could no longer rely on the schools to give religious instruction to young people, because governments took over schools that belonged to voluntary agencies.

## CRITICISMS, PROBLEMS, AND CORRECTIVES

In some places the Church had a problem of "public image." People criticized it for tendencies that had marked it in colonial times. Some missionaries were racist in their attitude toward Africans. To a considerable degree missionaries imposed their European cultural perspectives on African expressions of faith, prohibiting local customs that were, in fact, compatible with Christian belief. The Roman liturgy was used universally in that era; it was only after Vatican II that the Church began to encourage rituals expressive of indigenous cultures. Some Africans, too, tended to identify Christian missionaries with the colonizers. They charged that the Church consciously conspired with the colonial powers to subjugate the continent politically and that it had been hostile to independence. But they overlooked contrary considerations. Colonial governments sometimes barred missionaries from certain areas for fear of provoking public disturbances. Anticlerical European governments extended restrictions on the Church from the metropole to the colonies. In some territories, missionaries pressed colonial governments to remedy oppressive and unjust ways of dealing with indigenous populations. And missionaries did not uniformly oppose independence; many of them favored it; some Church publications supported the nationalist cause.

Two other problems of African churches were matters of substance rather than image. One was that the churches remained strongly "clerical." They relied almost exclusively on priests not only for sacral ministries but also for all forms of initiative, direction, and leadership. Catechists and parish committees performed essential functions, but their scope was limited. The laity, then, were not yet assuming the role that Vatican II accorded them, especially their role in the Church's task of evangelization.

The second problem was that many Catholics saw their religion in a way that was too sacral and too focused on individual piety and morality. They were faithful about their devotions but careless about applying their moral principles in the ordinary work of every day: in industry, commerce, and government. With exceptions to which we will return in later chapters, the missionary Church did not teach much about the social aspects of Catholicism, perhaps because the Church's social doctrine seemed largely directed to situations in the developed world. As a result, even political leaders who were Catholic in the newly independent states had little knowledge of the Church's teachings on social justice and little understanding of its critical attitude toward Marxism.

The young African churches' efforts to deal with these problems were an important part of their coming to maturity. Some of their initiatives manifested an awakened concern for justice, peace, and related issues in the structure and functioning of social institutions. They thus related, directly or indirectly, to the rise of Marxist influence and the central concern of the present study.

One initiative was the sponsorship of "small Christian communities." These were face-to-face groups of committed Christians in villages and urban neighborhoods. Their commitment came from their reflection together on God's revelation and on their practical application of this to their living together. The communities carried on both religious and secular functions: prayer services, assistance to the sick, mutual help, and modest development projects. While they fit organically into the more formal organization of out-station and parish, their main purpose was not to improve organization but to make Christian faith a more powerful reality in the lives of the members. The communities fostered active involvement of the laity in both the religious and the social elements of the Church's mission. In 1976 the AMECEA bishops declared them a "pastoral priority" in the countries the bishops represented. The communities in Africa did not take on a political orientation as the similar "basic Christian communities" in Latin America did.

The postcolonial Church also gave more explicit attention to its role as "servant." Taking a fresh view of the social services it had offered for so long, it saw these not just as leading people to faith but also as an integral part of Christian spirituality. By laboring to improve the circumstances in which they lived, people were also helping one another to become more human and humane and thus to become the more complete persons God wanted them to be. The Church accordingly fostered adult literacy and vocational training. It encouraged and helped its members to improve such amenities as local roads and water supply, to use "appropriate technology" and more productive methods of farming and stock raising, and to participate in cooperatives and credit unions. It promoted efforts to raise social consciousness through such organizations as the Young Christian Workers and Young Christian Farmers.

The Church also moved to teach its social doctrine to its members. The Gaba religious education syllabus for secondary schools, which was used in many English-speaking countries, included a section on social responsibility.[11] Bishops touched on Christian social principles in the pastoral letters they published at independence, but did not immediately go further. When particular crises arose in particular countries, however, their respective bishops took steps to instruct the faithful on relevant moral considerations. This happened especially in the four countries we will deal with later: Mozambique, Madagascar, Zimbabwe, and Zambia.

Apart from the activities of national hierarchies, meetings of SECAM in 1977, 1978, and 1983 dealt with issues of social justice. In 1978 a statement by the organization strongly criticized unjust situations that were common in Africa. In 1983 SECAM decided to convene a Pan-African Conference on Justice and Peace. In 1987 the planners prepared points to guide discussions among Catholics in parishes and other communities of the member countries; a committee was then to synthesize national and regional reports on responses for presentation to the conference itself. This preparatory process was intended to enlist the laity's participation in pastoral planning and to stimulate ongoing reflection and involvement with issues of justice and peace. At the same time, the SECAM bishops addressed "to all apostolic workers" a remarkably good exhortation, incorporating sound theology and common sense, entitled "Justice and Evangelization in Africa." This stressed the need for Catholics to work actively for justice if the Church was to be credible, but it also recognized that some political situations could prevent local churches from speaking and acting effectively.[12]

## IMPACT OF MARXISM ON THE CHURCH

Such, then, were the general features of the Church in Africa most relevant to the present study. We turn now to the ways in which the rise of Marxist influence affected its life and work.

The Church in Africa saw some aspects of Marxist thought as threatening in themselves because they were directly opposed to the most basic Catholic beliefs. Karl Marx, as a materialist and an atheist, strongly attacked all religion. He denied, in effect, any objective way of determining what was morally good and bad. Lenin went further than Marx. He urged positive action to eradicate religious thinking and to end the churches' influence, and introduced in the Soviet Union the antireligious program which became standard for other Marxist-Leninist regimes. His concept of revolution, moreover, gave rise to a morality in which actions were regarded as good or bad only insofar as they helped or hindered the revolution. And in his theory, the party's leaders were the sole judges of whether people had particular rights—their judgment depending on whether the recognition of such rights was or was not for the party's good. As herald of the gospel, the Church was concerned about the spread of atheistic views and of false moral principles among its members. As promoter of social justice and Christian humanist ideals, it was concerned about ensuring citizens' rights. As institution, it was concerned about government measures that threatened its own existence and operations.

Authoritarian non-Marxist governments, it is true, likewise hampered the Church. In Zaïre, for example, Mobutu Sese Seko at one time abolished civil recognition of such religious holidays as Christmas. Jean Baptiste Bagaza in Burundi forbade people to attend Mass on weekdays.[13] Under Marxist regimes, however, such measures were more deeply rooted in ideology and evoked the unrelenting persecutions the older Marxist states had carried on.

Marxist governments commonly took over the ownership of the Church's primary and secondary schools and teacher-training colleges. Government then controlled the appointment of staff; it set a curriculum that prescribed the teaching of Marxism-Leninism and forbade religious instruction. It also prohibited assemblies for worship, prayer, discussion of religion, and other religious activities. It sometimes retained priests and religious as teachers because their skills were in short supply, but it kept them under surveillance to prevent their exercising any religious ministry for the students.

Marxist governments obstructed the Church's access to young people in other ways as well. Some governments forbade giving religious instruction to people younger than eighteen years of age. Ruling Marxist parties organized youth movements that young people had to join. Such groups' programs included Marxist-Leninist indoctrination; their activities took so much time that members had difficulty keeping in touch with the Church in any way. The ruling parties established similar organizations for other categories of people—women, for example—and forbade Church-sponsored organizations of this kind. The Marxist-leaning government of Alphonse Massamba-Débat in Congo forced three trade-union groupings to merge into a single federation under party control. When the (Christian) Confédération Africaine des Travailleurs Croyants (CATC) refused to join, the government dissolved it, and arrested some of its officers and harassed others.[14]

Marxist governments took complete control of the Church's hospitals and medical clinics. If medically skilled Church personnel continued to work in these, government restricted the religious ministries they could exercise for patients.

Marxist governments censored Church newspapers, periodicals, and other publications, or even suppressed them. Government penalized editors for indiscreet articles by suspending their authorization to publish. It prosecuted people who put out unauthorized publications. It obstructed publication of liturgical, devotional, and instructional books by curtailing the supply of printing materials. Massamba-Débat's government jailed the priest-editor of the Catholic paper *La Semaine Africaine*.[15] Other media experienced similar treatment. Angola took over the Catholic Church's Radio Ecclesia, and Ethiopia took over the Lutheran station, Radio Voice of the Gospel.[16]

Marxist governments used various tactics to reduce the number of Church personnel. They expelled some missionaries, refused to renew the residence permits of others, and stopped granting visas to new ones. As for indigenous priests and religious, some governments closed seminaries and so manipulated the requirements of national service as to impede young peoples' entering seminaries and novitiates.

Some Marxist governments deprived the Church of material resources for its functioning. They took over buildings that belonged to the Church and used them for other purposes. They forbade the Church to solicit donations from the local faithful and used their currency controls to cut off the flow of financial subsidies from overseas.

Marxist governments tended to keep all social development work in their own hands and thus prevented the Church as such from organizing the kinds of projects it customarily sponsored. If government did permit the Church to participate corporately in development, it kept this work under its own control.

Marxist governments—and individual advocates of Marxism—also used hostile propaganda to discredit the Church in the eyes of local people. As early as 1961, the *World Marxist Review* published an article by Laurice Galico entitled "The Catholic Church in Africa."[17] This provided propagandists with materials and lines of argument to shake people's confidence in the Church. According to Galico, the Church was hoping for a rapid and enormous expansion of its numbers in Africa, but contemporary developments were frustrating this hope. The basic reason was that the Church had always backed imperialist policies in the past, was now accepting African independence only reluctantly, and was still maneuvering to support neocolonial interests; Africans were turning away from the Church because they knew this. Galico argued his case mostly by innuendo. He connected the Church with the Nazis, the Fascists, and multinational financiers. He gave distorted interpretations of pastoral developments in the Church, ignoring its supernatural objectives and attributing all its activities to politics. He offered little documentation of his statements and when he did, it often consisted of citations taken out of context. Although he was able to adduce some painfully shortsighted judgments on the part of ecclesiastics and some real wrongs done by churchmen, many of his alleged facts were simply false, and his logic was fallacious. Even so, his arguments could appear authoritative to poorly informed readers or hearers. His conclusion was that "resolute and conscious action by the working people . . . including Catholics . . . is essential . . . if the march of events is to make a still greater breach in the crumbling walls of the Vatican."[18]

Marxist efforts to recruit followers among Catholics in Africa extended also to clergy and religious. They seem to have succeeded in only a few cases. In Mozambique, Fr. Mateus Gwenjere was active in FRELIMO, and in Angola, Fr. Joaquim Andrade was active in the MPLA, but both men fell from the good graces of the respective parties.[19] During the struggle against Ian Smith's government in Rhodesia, some Marxist guerrillas attempted to indoctrinate indigenous priests and religious. These people did support the fight for liberation and sometimes worked in it (as noncombatants), but they did not accept Marxist ideology.

An incidental but relevant point in this context was the effort Catholic theologians were making to work out an "African theology"—a theology that took into account the concrete and special experience of Africans. This experience was similar in some ways to the Latin American experience which had given rise to "liberation theology." But while some people tended to see the latter as a model for theologies everywhere in the Third World, Catholic theologians in Africa viewed it more judiciously. They agreed that the experience of oppression was a starting point for their theological reflection and that Christian living entailed an effort to overcome oppression, establish justice, and improve people's material circumstances. But they insisted that, in the final determination, temporal values were secondary to eternal values. They did not use Marxist concepts as tools for social analysis, and they did not endorse class warfare as a method of establishing justice. They would approve violence only to end the violent repression of regimes like those of the Portuguese colonies, Ian Smith's Rhodesia, and South Africa in Namibia. In their view, then, African theology had to be liberating, but this did not mean that it had to be liberation theology.[20]

Such, then, was the Catholic Church viewed globally in sub-Saharan Africa. Such were the problems it faced from Marxism. In the next four chapters we will look more closely at the Church in particular countries, at the development of Marxism in them, and at how the Church matured as it responded to the challenges this development presented.

## Notes

1. English translations of the Council's documents are published in Walter Abbot, ed., *The Documents of Vatican II* (New York: America Press, 1966). See also Pope Paul VI, *On Evangelization in the Modern World* [Apostolic Exhortation "Evangelii Nuntiandi," December 8, 1975] (Boston: Daughters of St. Paul Editions, n.d.). Synod of Bishops, *The Synodal Documents on Justice in the World, November 1971* (Boston: St. Paul Editions, n.d.).

2. I have adopted and adapted the approach of Avery Dulles, *Models of the Church* (Garden City, N.Y.: Doubleday, 1974).

3. See ibid., chap. 2.

4. See ibid., chap. 3.

5. See ibid., chap. 4.

6. See ibid., chap. 5.

7. See ibid., chap. 6.

8. See especially *Gaudium et Spes*, in Abbot, ed., *Documents of Vatican II*, paragraphs 17, 26, 27, 29–31, 34–37, 39, 65–66, 73, 77.

9. The acronymns mean: AMECEA, Association of Members of Episcopal Conferences of East Africa. AECAWA, Association of the Episcopal Conferences of Anglophone West Africa. CERAO, Conférence Épiscopale Régionale de l'Afrique de l'Ouest Francophone. IMBISA, Inter-Regional Meetings of Bishops of Southern Africa. SECAM, Symposium of Episcopal Conferences of Africa and Madagascar.

10. An Apostolic Nuncio is an accredited diplomatic representative of the Holy See to a country's civil government. An Apostolic Delegate is a purely ecclesiastical representative of the Holy See to the Catholic Church of a particular country; he does not have diplomatic status but sometimes engages in informal diplomacy.

11. The Gaba series is entitled *Christian Living Today: Christian Education for Secondary Schools. A Study of Life Themes*, 2 vols. (London: Geoffrey Chapman, 1974). See also *Christian Living Today. Teacher's Handbook* (London: Geoffrey Chapman, 1981). The series is intended for the 4th and 5th forms of secondary school.

12. See *Seeking Gospel Justice in Africa*, Spearhead Series No. 69 (Eldoret, Kenya: Gaba Publications, 1981), pp. 1–2, 29–30, and passim; "Spearhead" is a series of occasional monographs on topics of concern to the Church in Africa, published by AMECEA Gaba Publications at Eldoret. SECAM's project is described in "Pan-African Conference on Justice and Peace, 1983–1987," a circular of 4 mimeographed pages prepared by the Secretariat of SECAM, undated. The bishops' exhortation appears in *Justice and Evangelization in Africa* (Lusaka: Catholic Secretariat, [1983]); see especially pp. 6, 8–9, 11–12, 16–17, 22, 25–26. SECAM held the planned meeting at Roma, Lesotho, in May–June 1988; see

Jaime Gonçalves and P. Obinna Aguh, "Pan-African Justice and Peace Seminar, Held at Roma, Lesotho, 29 May–2 June 1988, Communiqué Issued on 3 June 1988," *AFER*, 30 (August 1988), 218–25, and *Rapport de la rencontre pan-africaine sur la justice et paix, Roma, Lesotho, du 29 mai au 3 juin 1988*, bound, mimeographed volume, obtained from SECAM's Secretariat, Accra, Ghana. The "Resolutions" of the seminar are printed separately on 7 mimeographed pages.

13. See "Burundi: Weekday Churchgoing Banned by Decree," *Tablet* [London], 238 (October 1984), 972.

14. See Gauze, *Politics of Congo-Brazzaville*, pp. 160–213.

15. See ibid., pp. 219–20.

16. See "Angola: 'Radio Ecclesia' Nationalized," *International Fides Press Service*, February 15, 1978, pp. NE 82–84; "Ethiopia: A Tale of Two Revolutions," *Pro Mundi Vita Dossiers*, Africa Dossier 5 (January–February 1978), 33.

17. See Laurice Galico, "The Catholic Church and Africa," *World Marxist Review*, 4 (April 1961), 34–40.

18. See ibid., 40.

19. See Kevin Brown, "Angolan Socialism," in Rosberg and Callaghy, eds., *Socialism in Sub-Saharan Africa*, p. 312; Barry Munslow, *Mozambique: The Revolution and Its Origins* (New York: Longman, 1983), pp. 98, 107, 111, 128, 135.

20. See, for example, the reserved viewpoint of Laurenti Magesa, *The Church and Liberation in Africa*, Spearhead Series No. 44 (Eldoret, Kenya: Gaba Publications, 1976), chaps. 3–4; idem, "Instruction on the 'Theology of Liberation': A Comment," *AFER*, 27 (February 1985), 2–8.

# 5

# Marxism and the Church in Mozambique

CLOSER STUDY OF THE INTERACTION of Marxism and the Church in Africa will begin with Mozambique. The situation here reflected especially the circumstances in the former Portuguese colonies, the others being Angola, Guinea-Bissau, Cape Verde, and São Tomé.

## GEOGRAPHICAL AND HISTORICAL BACKGROUND

Mozambique is on the continent's southeastern coast. Its neighbors are Tanzania and Malawi on the north, Zambia and Zimbabwe on the west, and South Africa and Swaziland on the south. Its area is 309,000 square miles. Its population is about ten million. Most of its people are black; a considerable number are *mestiços*; before independence there were several hundred thousand whites, but these are now far fewer. Agricultural capability is promising, but drought often seriously reduces productivity. Mineral resources are largely unexplored and unexploited. Seaports are good, notably Maputo and Beira, which connect by rail with Zimbabwe and South Africa. The Zambesi and other rivers cross the country from west to east and offer potentially abundant water power.

Portugal, the colonial ruler, established settlements along the coast in the fifteenth century but did not expand very much into the interior until the nineteenth. It established complete control only in the 1920s, in the face of vigorous local resistance. In this decade the government of Antonio Oliveira Salazar began efforts to strengthen the home country's weak economy by meshing Mozambique's economy with it. His government systematically used the existing practice of sending Mozambican workers to South Africa for work in the mines. It used forced labor on agricultural plantations, and imposed the raising of cash crops on peasant farmers. It took only modest steps to develop the colony's infrastructure and industry.[1]

Claiming that their policy toward the indigenous population was non-racial, the Portuguese granted full citizenship to blacks who were "assimilated." But the education that was prerequisite to assimilation was within the reach of only a minuscule minority; its thrust, moreover, was to transform the *assimilados* into "black Portuguese." In addition, from the 1950s Salazar encouraged Portuguese whites to settle in Mozambique. Although many of them were poorly educated peasants, migration brought them membership in a privileged class. Colonial Mozambique, then, was a racist society whose coercive political and economic system exploited and oppressed its black population.[2]

Blacks looked for escape. Thousands of Mozambicans worked as miners or farm laborers in South Africa, Rhodesia, and other neighboring countries. In some of these host countries the migrants experienced the era's continent-wide stirrings of nationalism and thrust toward independence. Mozambican liberation movements took shape in Rhodesia, Malawi, and Kenya. Other nationalists organized themselves overseas. Even though circumstances in their own land delayed the formation of any movement there, these externally based groups came together in 1962 to form the Frente de Liberação de Moçambique, FRELIMO. Its First Congress met at Dar es Salaam in September. This elected as the movement's president Eduardo Mondlane, who had been a university professor in the United States and was then a civil servant in the United Nations Secretariat.[3]

The Salazar government adamantly opposed granting independence to the Portuguese colonies. FRELIMO therefore began guerrilla operations against the regime in 1964, infiltrating into the north from Tanzania and ultimately advancing into the center but not the south. In the areas it controlled, FRELIMO sought the support of local populations. It organized production, provided educational and medical services, and maintained tight discipline over its officials and troops in order to curb corruption and highhanded conduct, which would alienate the locals. In areas where its forces were not yet active, it secretly disseminated propaganda and organized underground discussions in order to win over the local people to its side.[4]

The war dragged on for ten years. As it continued, the Portuguese armed forces, mostly conscripts, became severely demoralized. They gradually abandoned large blocks of territory to FRELIMO, which then governed these areas as "liberated zones." One Portuguese tactic must be mentioned here because it came to affect social organization after independence. This was the establishment of "safe villages." The people traditionally lived in isolated homesteads. To keep guerrillas from hiding among them, the Portuguese brought them into new settlements and limited their freedom to move about.[5] Meanwhile, guerrilla wars in Angola and Guinea-Bissau multiplied the pressures on Portugal, placing heavy strain on the national economy. Salazar died in 1968. Radical army officers overthrew his successor in April 1974. And in June the new government promised to grant Mozambique's independence in one year's time. FRELIMO, the only organization resembling a political party in the colony, took over the government of the independent country in June 1975. Mondlane had been assassinated in 1969. Samora Machel, who had succeeded him as head of FRELIMO, became Mozambique's president.

## FRELIMO's Marxist Leanings

FRELIMO was not originally a Marxist organization, but it leaned increasingly toward Marxism during the struggle for independence. A curious feature of the background was Salazar's vigorous anti-Communist stance. PIDE, his powerful secret police force, tried hard to uproot Communist influence in Portugal and the colonies. Yet Communists managed to continue their clandestine operations. Seamen brought their message to stevedores in Mozambique's ports. *Mestiços* and *assimilados* learned Marxism in university circles at Lisbon and Coimbra. Some white settlers were Communists. Communists were a force even in the Portuguese armed services. Not surprisingly, then, some organizers of the independence movement were Marxists at its very beginning.[6]

But people of other persuasions were also members of the movement, and differences among factions gave rise to serious tensions. One faction, for example, wanted to end the power of traditional chiefs in territory under FRELIMO's control. It wanted to set up new structures that would draw local people into participation. It wanted to collectivize agriculture. It urged clemency toward captured Portuguese soldiers as a way to undermine the army's morale. Another faction charged that this group was counterrevolutionary, not interested in true liberation, and aiming only to drive out the Portuguese bourgeoisie and set themselves up in its place. Mondlane summoned the second FRELIMO Congress in July 1968 to deal with these tensions. The radical faction here became dominant.[7]

Samora Machel was among this group's leaders. Machel was born in 1933. He was raised a Protestant, but after finishing primary school, he became a Catholic in order to gain access to higher education, and spent several years living and working in mission compounds. He later trained as a nurse. In 1962 he joined FRELIMO's Popular Forces for the Liberation of Mozambique (FPLM) and went to Algeria for military training. In time, he moved into the Front's leadership circles and into the presidency of party and country.[8]

Under Machel FRELIMO did not explicitly adopt Marxist ideology right away. From its early days Marxist catchwords had appeared in its pronouncements. Documents of 1969 and 1970 showed the outlines of Marxist thought more clearly. Leaders also (so they said) were consciously using Marxist analysis to find the "correct" revolutionary line. But they did not call their movement Marxist-Leninist, because ordinary people would not have understood this. In their view, people supported the movement because of its content and its style of implementing this, and were not interested in labels.

In the early 1970s, however, Machel was moving to change the Front into a Marxist-Leninist party. The Front began to form party committees inside the FPLM in 1973. It established a party school in 1974 to give cadres a solid theoretical basis for their work. Both Machel and FRELIMO's vice president, Marcelino dos Santos, gave lectures in the school. Marxism came to full flower in 1975, both in the government's public policies and in the party's restructuring. FRELIMO'S Third Congress, in January 1977, officially transformed the movement into a Marxist-Leninist vanguard party which would lead the workers and peasants into the new society.

Several elements in the background apparently led Machel to his adoption of Marxist theory. His military training in Algeria included indoctrination by Cubans. Chinese Communists, assisting in the guerrilla war, customarily taught ideology to the military and to civilians in guerrilla-controlled areas, and FRELIMO's tactics, early on, reflected Mao's ideas. The movement enlisted the peasants to support guerrilla operations. It undermined traditional chiefs government. It involved the peasants in talking together about their situation. It insisted on frequent use of "self-criticism." Meanwhile, the party school familiarized cadres with more classical Marxist-Leninist concepts. Machel and his close associates particularly emphasized the need for class analysis, class conflict, and the structuring of a vanguard party.[9]

## FRELIMO's Policies and Programs

The FRELIMO government, then, took Marxism-Leninism as its guide for determining policies and programs. As it set about its work, however, several circumstances caused it to be confronted with major difficulties. The first of these touched classic Marxist theory. According to Marx, socialists would take over a country only after capitalists had developed it. But the Portuguese were not very effective capitalists and did not bequeath FRELIMO a very thriving economy; the war of liberation had damaged even what they did bequeath. Natural calamities aggravated the country's economic plight. Drought overtook the north in 1976. Floods struck the south in 1977. More drought in 1982–1983 affected eight of the ten provinces. Animal diseases devastated livestock.

The liberation struggle in Rhodesia also had repercussions in Mozambique. The Rhodesian army wrought havoc in its pursuit of freedom fighters who took advantage of the sanctuary offered by Mozambique. The FRELIMO regime, moreover, voluntarily sacrificed substantial income when it imposed sanctions on Ian Smith's government, closing the border and denying Rhodesia the use of Mozambican railways and ports. To complicate matters further, from 1975 to 1979 Ian Smith tried to weaken FRELIMO's support of his opponents by sponsoring a Movimento Nacional da Resistencia de Moçambique (MNR or Renamo). When Zimbabwe became independent in 1980, South Africa took over this sponsorship in order to destabilize Machel's regime. The movement damaged the economy by sabotaging pipelines and rail lines, ambushing convoys that carried people and goods on the highways, and harassing peasants into abandonment of their farms.[10]

Further, Portuguese and other foreigners were anxious about their safety, and early steps to nationalize enterprises confirmed fears about their investments. Some 150,000 of these people departed and only 20,000 remained. Their going deprived the country of almost all managerial and technical skills in agriculture, industry, transport, commerce, and public service. Roads and other infrastructure deteriorated from lack of maintenance. Some emigrants took vehicles and other machines with them or sabotaged the equipment they left behind. The rural population lost the middlemen who had bought their produce and sold them kerosene, soap, farm tools, and other commodities.[11]

The FRELIMO government itself was notably inexperienced. Although the party had governed the liberated zone in the north, this zone was only a small and sparsely populated part of the country; the party had not established a solid base in the south. Now it faced the complications of the cities; of industry, national defense, international trade, and foreign affairs; and of raising revenue and meeting demands for expenditure. Because the Portuguese had excluded virtually all blacks from positions of responsibility, the new government had only a handful of highly trained cadres, with only a modest pool of "middle managers" to back them up. Wartime governance of the liberated zones did not prepare FRELIMO very well to rule the whole country.[12]

FRELIMO's major aims were to end exploitation in Mozambique, to expand the country's material riches, and to raise the people's living standards through equitable distribution of wealth and social services. The government's early policies followed classic Marxist-Leninist lines. It nationalized land, transport, shipping, insurance, export–import trade, medical facilities, most banks, many plantations, and half the industries. It pressed collectivization of agriculture. For this it used different formulas: it set up state farms on which peasants were employed; it encouraged other peasants to form producers' cooperatives. It also set up a system of *aldeis communais* (communal villages). For many of these villages, ironically, it used the facilities the Portuguese had laid out for their "strategic hamlets." FRELIMO intended the villages to be "centers of production" but also communities enjoying ready access to such amenities as education and improved water supply. They were also to feature ideological training. There were about a thousand villages in 1979, with a total population of about 1.6 million.[13]

The government received some foreign aid, mostly from international organizations and Western countries. Foreign personnel helped fill the dearth of technical and managerial skills; at first, these came chiefly from Eastern Europe and Cuba. Reluctantly, Mozambique subscribed to the Lomé Convention so as to benefit from trade concessions and grants offered by the European Economic Community. Sheer necessity compelled FRELIMO to continue economic and diplomatic connections with South Africa. In Portuguese days, South Africa had hired more than 100,000 migrant Mozambican mine workers annually, and had remitted 60 percent of their wages, in gold, to the colonial government. South Africa now carried on this arrangement until 1978, although in 1977 it cut the number of migrants. South Africa sent personnel to maintain and operate the ports and railways, which were important for its own foreign trade. South Africa bought 98 percent of the Cabora Dam's output of electricity. The miners' remittances brought Mozambique $37 million a year, the ports and railways $93 million, and the Dam $50 million.[14]

FRELIMO first approved a comprehensive development plan only in 1981. This made agriculture the country's principal activity. It would take up 80 percent of the labor force, and 90 percent of these workers would be in cooperatives. Heavy industry would have second priority. But the party quickly recognized that the plans were too ambitious, and scaled them down.[15]

The party's economic policies did not work very well. Both agricultural and industrial productivity dropped drastically in the first year of independence. Machel put the figure at 75 percent. The figures moved generally upward in later years, but with notable setbacks. The attitudes of the peasants and the disorganization of the rural economic structure contributed significantly to the low agricultural productivity. Although peasants were willing to work the land for themselves, they resisted collectivized cultivation. The government was using heavy pressure to move them into the communal villages. And the government found no effective organizational substitute for the bush traders who had collected produce and transported it to the cities.[16]

The international balance of payments was in the same shaky condition as that of most African countries. The debt to Western countries in 1984 was $1.4 billion. Interest alone constituted an oppressive burden. In that year, the government asked its Western creditors for a moratorium on payments.[17]

Machel and FRELIMO acknowledged the weakness of the country's economic performance and took some steps to correct it. In 1977 Machel moved to control the operations of worker-councils in various enterprises so that management could function more efficiently. In 1979 he tried to attract foreign investment. In 1980 he campaigned against corruption, parasitism, indiscipline, and incompetent leadership. He handed "people's shops" over to private entrepreneurs or to cooperatives. He reintroduced wage incentives for some industries and plantations. The Fourth Party Congress in 1983 decided to emphasize family agriculture and to decentralize economic administration. But it did not notably change the main lines of the party's policies.[18]

One of FRELIMO's social objectives was to make education more widely available. At independence only 15 percent of the population was literate. The government began literacy classes at night in barracks, workplaces, and agricultural production centers. In 1975, it temporarily suspended university programs and sent the students to teach in adult literacy classes and schools. It expanded opportunities for primary and secondary schooling. This entailed nationalization of all existing schools, most of which were run by the Catholic Church. Many observers regarded the party's educational achievement as creditable. Enrollments rose from 690,000 in 1974 to 1,495,000 in 1979. University students numbered 836 in 1982. Graduates had to do national service for as many years as they had spent in studies.[19]

To make medical care more available, government nationalized all medical facilities and practices. It took over hospitals, clinics, and maternity centers, including those run by the Church. It was not clear, however, that government was providing adequate medical supplies and supporting services for these institutions or that it was increasing the capacity of the facilities as the demand for health care increased.[20]

To provide more and better housing, at least in urban areas, government nationalized homes abandoned by people who had left the country, homes whose owners were renting them out, and many residences belonging to the Church. It forbade people to own more than one house in a single locality, and it confiscated houses which thus became "surplus." In this way it obtained about 50,000 substantial dwellings with which it could help some people escape from marginal housing near the towns.[21]

As part of its social policy, FRELIMO tried to weaken the authority of traditional chiefs and to change the attitudes that decidedly subordinated women. Correspondingly, in classic Marxist-Leninist fashion it sought to develop "the new man," the man who was liberated from custom and superstition and who ruled his life by "science." It was not clear that these efforts had much impact. FRELIMO also insisted on an almost puritanical moral rectitude; the government campaigned against prostitution, drug dealing, long hair, beards, and the deviant styles of dress popularized by Western films.[22]

The party fought, too, against the bourgeois mentality. Presumably this mentality entailed a disposition to individualism, lack of concern for other people's welfare, and subordination of others to one's own material well-being. Even though the departure of Portuguese settlers left few classic bourgeoisie in Mozambique, FRELIMO wanted to keep the people who took their positions from assuming their attitudes. The party's success was doubtful. It persistently complained that its own cadres were becoming distant from the masses. As early as 1975, by raising civil servants' but not soldiers' salaries, the party provoked a brief mutiny by the troops around Maputo.[23]

FRELIMO's politics followed the lines of Marxism-Leninism in Eastern Europe and China. During and after the independence struggle, it organized small "dynamizing groups" in villages, neighborhoods, workplaces, and institutions. These engaged in self-criticism and in discussion of local needs. They also served as channels through which its cadres made the party's ideas known and accepted. But FRELIMO'S decision in 1977 to become a vanguard party meant substituting a highly trained and dedicated revolutionary elite for the earlier mass membership. The dynamizing groups did not fit the new structure very well; so the party then tended to neglect them. FRELIMO's new vanguard role also gave rise to potentially embarrassing questions. How could a group of "intellectuals" represent a proletariat that had no commitment to ideology? How could the proletariat itself be the leading force in a social revolution when there really was no proletariat but only a massive peasantry? Would the leadership only use the peasants, as Lenin had done, to achieve the objectives of other people?[24]

Professing to lead the new society in its "class warfare," the party urged citizens to vigilance against the "enemy." The law encouraged citizens to inform on one another, thus fostering general mistrust. The party used the dynamizing groups' self-criticism sessions to press dissidents into conformity. In 1975 the government set up a political police force, the Servição Nacional de Segurança Popular (SNASP) to repress hostile activity. Like Portugal's oppressive PIDE, this organization had almost unlimited powers of search, seizure, arrest, and detention. It used its powers not just against the armed rebels of the MNR but also against people who merely criticized the regime. The government also set up "reeducation camps" for ideological dissidents, prostitutes, drug dealers, and corrupt officials.[25]

FRELIMO'S structures and its relationship to government were like those of Eastern Europe. A general party congress met periodically but infrequently. The Central Committee looked after ongoing management. A small Politburo held the real power. And Machel, by force of personality, dominated the Politburo. The party gave directives to government and government implemented them.

The national constitution established a legislature, the People's Assembly; its members were elected indirectly by regional bodies. The constitution also granted enormous power to the national president, who was, in fact, the party's president as well. FRELIMO professed "democratic centralism," governance that was supposed to enlist wide popular participation but did not. According to the constitution, power belonged to the workers and peasants united and led by FRELIMO, and was exercised by the organs of "people's power" (*poder popular*). In reality, it was Machel and his close associates who controlled the system from the top down.

The constitution guaranteed human rights and set up an "independent judiciary." In practice, however, citizens' rights were often at risk, not least from the operations of SNASP. Lower courts could include judges who had no legal training. And in any case it was doubtful that the courts were truly independent.[26]

FRELIMO acknowledged weaknesses in its structures and functioning, but saw these as failures of implementation rather than of policy. In 1981 the party's section for ideological work identified some of the flaws. Party workers were staying in their offices and not getting out with the people. The public addresses they gave were set speeches having no relation to their audience's problems. They were not listening to the questions people asked. They were not encouraging people to analyze their own situations. There was need to plan better, define tasks more clearly, and set deadlines more carefully. The Fourth Party Congress decentralized operations somewhat, calling for more responsibility by regional and local officials. It also adjusted the economic program, favoring family farming, offering more incentives to peasants, and giving more opportunity to private entrepreneurs. It was thus reminiscent of Lenin's NEP.[27]

Mozambique's links with the Communist bloc were like those of other professedly Marxist countries. FRELIMO had ties with Communist parties in the Soviet Union and elsewhere; representatives of twenty-three such parties attended its Third Congress. The parties exchanged visits and formally agreed to cooperate. Units of FRELIMO sent delegates to the meetings of Communist front organizations. Delegates from the Organization of Mozambican Women went to East Germany in 1981 for a meeting of women leaders from socialist countries, and to Czechoslovakia for the World Congress of the International Federation of Democratic Women. The same year, the International Organization of Journalists in Moscow elected Mozambique's National Organization of Journalists to its presidium. Mozambique was chosen to be vice president of the second radio festival of non-aligned countries, meeting in Cuba. The Mozambican Friendship Organization sent delegations to Russia, China, and North Korea. Government delegates attended a COMECON meeting in Bulgaria and a Conference of Ministers of Education from socialist countries in East Berlin.[28]

In addition, Communist countries sent material aid to Mozambique. East European countries supplied arms. Cuba was educating two thousand Mozambican children on the Isle of Youth. Cuban technicians helped with sugar plantations, East Germans with coal mines, Russians and others with armed forces. China provided equipment and advisers during the war of liberation, but lost influence when its policies in Angola diverged from Mozambique's. It must be said, nevertheless, that Mozambique did not surrender control of its foreign or domestic policy to any of its Communist benefactors. Strikingly, it did not allow the Russians to establish a naval base on Bazanuto Island, fifteen miles off its coast.[29]

FRELIMO faced an especially complicated problem in dealing with South Africa. Although it strongly opposed apartheid and the subjugation of Namibia, it recognized its neighbor's importance for its own security as well as its economy. South Africa's military power directly threatened Mozambican territory, and the surrogate forces of the MNR were undermining the country's public order and economic well-being. In addition, Mozambique needed the money it earned from South Africa. For its part, however, South Africa needed the economic services Mozambique was providing, and also wanted to keep its own exiled anti-apartheid movements from using Mozambique as a base for their operations. These considerations offered a basis for negotiation between the two governments and resulted in the Nkomati Accord of 1984, which Machel reluctantly accepted: Mozambique would exclude from its territory virtually all members of South African liberation groups; South Africa would stop supporting the MNR. A year later, South Africa was clearly violating its undertaking, but Mozambique had no feasible way to enforce it. Mozambique did join eight nearby countries in the Southern African Development Coordination Conference (SADCC); its members aimed, among other things, to build a regional infrastructure that would end their critical economic dependence on their oppressive neighbor.[30]

## History and Development of the Church in Mozambique

FRELIMO's policies also touched religion. Before explaining these, however, we will say something about the history and structure of the Catholic Church in Mozambique.

The missionaries who arrived in the fifteenth century mostly looked after the religious needs of the Portuguese merchants and soldiers, and they had little success in evangelizing the local peoples. Critics charge that they actively joined in conquest—an alliance of "cross and sword." Some of them certainly engaged in trading, even in slave trading—

conduct which became painfully embarrassing to the Church. After 1750, tension between the government and the Church hampered more active evangelization; Portuguese governments from then until the mid-1920s were anticlerical, and their policies were often hostile to the Church.[31]

This stance changed with the Salazar regime. Portugal and the Holy See negotiated a Concordat in 1940 aimed at easing the troubled relations between Church and State. At the same time, the two parties entered into a "Missionary Agreement" intended to regulate the Church's work in the colonies, and the government passed a "Missionary Statute" to implement the agreement. These documents gave the Church a near monopoly of access to the colonies by severely restricting the entry of Protestant missionaries. They gave Catholic schools a favored position over those of other religious denominations. They provided government subsidies for maintaining missionaries and their works. But they also gave the government important controls over Church personnel. Missionaries had to be Portuguese unless Church authorities could demonstrate a need for others. The Church could not appoint non-Portuguese bishops without government approval. The Apostolic Nuncio in Lisbon needed government authorization to visit the colonies. The government's concessions, in effect, made churchmen cautious about challenging its wishes.[32]

The Church's pastoral activities followed the pattern used elsewhere in Africa. It organized parishes and out-stations. Cathechists supplemented the work of priests, giving instruction and leading paraliturgical worship. The Church provided most primary and all secondary education. It administered many medical facilities. In the early 1960s there were eight dioceses, and the bishops had organized a Conferencia Episcopale de Moçambique (CEM). All the bishops were Portuguese. Most priests belonged to religious congregations. Many congregations, both of men and of women, worked in the colony. Some of their members were not Portuguese. In 1974, when independence was near, the estimated numbers of personnel were 513 priests, 187 brothers, and 1,122 sisters. The development of indigenous vocations had been slow. Mozambican priests numbered only about 35; brothers and sisters were similarly few. Parish centers totaled 715. The number and quality of medical establishments and schools were hard to determine. FRELIMO later charged that, in 1963, only 20 percent of the students in primary schools and 5 percent in secondary schools were black, that black children were made to work on mission-farms, and that their primary education was inferior. Literacy among blacks in 1958 was estimated at only 2.2 percent.[33]

The war of liberation sharply divided opinion among Church personnel. Most bishops supported government. Many priests and religious,
especially non-Portuguese, favored independence. They deprecated the
colonial structure's systematic injustices: neglect of basic amenities and
services for blacks, exploitation of their labor, discrimination in employment and remuneration, and brutal police action in the name of public
order. They decried especially the cruelties of the war itself: interrogation
of people who might have military information, collective punishment
of villages that might be collaborating with guerrillas, and the massacre
of civilians.[34] In the missionaries' view, fidelity to the gospel required
them to support justice and protest its violation. They wanted the bishops
to reject Portugal's clinging to the status quo. They wanted them to take
a public stand against appalling cases of injustice. They wanted them to
give moral support to Church personnel whom government detained or
deported. For their part, the bishops did not publicly protest to government about anything, and did not exercise much pressure to help their
personnel who were in trouble with the police. They did sometimes
criticize serious abuses that arose in the fighting—"whichever side might
be responsible for them." And they did protest privately to government
over the massacre of civilians at Wiryamu in December 1972.[35]

The missionaries' attitudes led to several dramatic incidents. In 1965
the Portuguese authorities compelled thirteen Montfort Fathers to leave
posts in the guerrilla areas because they did not trust them. In 1971 all
the White Fathers, thirty-seven of them, left the colony as a gesture of
protest. In 1973 government expelled ten Burgos Fathers for publicizing
the Wiryamu massacre. In 1974 the authorities deported six Verona Fathers for supporting a black protest against a particular government action, and five Picpus Fathers followed them out.[36]

Tension inside the Church became especially acute in 1974. In February the Combonian missionaries of the Nampula diocese wrote a confidential letter to the bishops' conference stating their position on several
sensitive issues and making several requests. The letter somehow became
public. Portuguese authorities rounded up several of its signatories for
questioning. The missionaries and the bishops' conference then engaged
in an angry exchange about which party had leaked the letter. The
bishop of Nampula, Manuel Vieira Pinto, saw the situation differently
from his fellow-bishops. He was sympathetic with the Mozambicans'
quest for liberation and their critique of colonial oppression, and shared
with his priests in drafting the letter. Whites mounted a demonstration
against him at his cathedral, threatening his personal safety. In early

April, security officers forced him and eleven of his clergy to leave the colony.[37]

In August 1974 an organization of indigenous clergy met—União de Sacerdotes e Religiosos de Moçambique (USAREMO). At the meeting, Fr. Brazão Mazula delivered a passionate critique of the Church: the colonialist, bourgeois, imperialist Church was false; it was centered on institutions, organizations, religious institutes, schools, seminaries, and hospitals. These were run for the benefit of their founders. They were nothing more than centers of tourism. We reject this Church. We cannot africanize a Church that is old and false.[38]

The controversy in the Church also involved the laity. A group of these, likewise in 1974, presented a memorandum to the bishops' conference, posing some challenging questions:

> What is the Church doing to reconcile the opposing sides in the colonial war? . . . Has not the people of Mozambique the right to self-determination? Has the Church nothing to say about the right of people to work out their own history? Has the Church nothing to say about the fact that the greater part of the cultivable land and the economy are in the hands of a few? What has the Church to say about the denunciation, arrests, . . . torture, confiscation of property, people disappearing, retaliation, intimidation? . . . Does making people Christians mean making them into Portuguese? Is there not good reason to denounce the Concordat, the Missionary Agreement, and the Missionary Statute?[39]

The rumblings within the Church in Mozambique were felt in Rome. Missionaries were telling their superiors-general about their uneasiness with the bishops' position. They spoke of their personal problems, in conscience, about remaining silent. From late 1973 the superiors, through the Union of Superiors General (USG), were discussing the matter with the Vatican Secretariat of State. The Holy See sent the Apostolic Nuncio in Lisbon to work out some solution on the spot, but he did not succeed. The Holy See did protest confidentially to Portugal about some incidents during the war. But it apparently decided not to make any public pronouncement favoring either independence or continued colonial rule. It was clearly anxious for missionaries to remain in the colony to serve the people's religious needs. It feared, perhaps, that a hostile gesture against Portugal would risk large-scale expulsion.[40]

Despite the wide differences of view and the intense emotions of the debate within the Church, in the present context a curious fact seems noteworthy: in the public record of the controversy about liberation there was almost no mention of the possibility that FRELIMO's coming to power would give entry to Marxism or Communism in Mozambique.[41]

## FRELIMO's POLICIES TOWARD THE CHURCH

We turn now to FRELIMO's policies with respect to religion. In 1976, the year after FRELIMO's accession to power, the total number of Catholics was about 1.6 million, or 17 percent of the population. Protestants were about 0.5 million, 5 percent. Muslims were about 1.1 million, 12 percent. The remaining 66 percent followed traditional religions.[42]

Machel's thinking about religion followed classic Marxist lines. Religion was unscientific. It made people submissive and passive in dealing with challenges of nature and of social organization. It kept them from rational analysis of their problems and tied them to traditional ways of doing things. Religious sectarianism divided societies that needed unity. The Catholic Church in particular had allied itself with the Portuguese colonialists to hold the Mozambican peoples in subjection and was still allied with neocolonialists to restore that subjugation.[43] Machel accordingly sought to eliminate the influence of this mentality which impeded the emergence of the new liberated man and the new socialist society. His government therefore harassed the Catholic Church and other religious bodies, but avoided making martyrs. Its concrete measures varied from place to place and time to time, but followed lines used in other Communist countries.

In the first month of independence, the government nationalized all schools. The takeover of the schools often entailed the takeover of whole mission-compounds that had also served other purposes besides schooling. The government made these into "educational centers" and banned their use for all religious activities, including the teaching of catechism after school hours. The government likewise nationalized all medical facilities.[44]

The government took over church residences as part of its move to nationalize housing. Although priests and religious might remain as tenants, other people then moved in with them to take up "surplus" space. Government seized most of the cars owned by the Church. It blocked Church bank accounts, arguing that the Portuguese subsidies to the Church really belonged to the exploited Mozambican people. For a period of time, it proscribed other foreign donations to the Church, claiming that these were intended for subversive activities.[45]

The government imposed severe limitations on almost all the

Church's traditional ministries. It ordered missionaries to leave their rural stations and collected them in the larger urban centers. They then had to obtain passes from local authorities in order to travel. This regulation, so government said, was intended to protect missionaries from MNR guerrillas; it did not wish to be blamed for any harm these might inflict. But local authorities did not readily issue passes; so priests found it almost impossible to offer Mass or hear confessions in the bush. Even when the clergy were allowed to move, the dearth of motor vehicles drastically reduced their mobility.

Regulations forbade religious services and instructions anywhere except in church compounds. But they also forbade the use even of churches and other buildings in "educational centers" for any religious purposes. They forbade, too, such use of existing church buildings in the "communal villages" and the erection there of new buildings. In fact, they prohibited religious activities of any kind inside the villages. Government aggravated the shortage of facilities by closing some churches in the towns or taking them over for other purposes.

The clergy, moreover, had to get government permission to build new churches, even makeshift chapels—a permission not readily granted. Government claimed that it had to set priorities in the use of construction materials because these were so scarce. To top off all this, government described even the edifices that were still functioning as part of the "national patrimony," and set aside some churches as "national monuments"; it then made Catholic authorities responsible for maintaining them.

Regulations also forbade anyone to give religious instruction or baptism to persons less than eighteen years old—though some local officials did not press this restriction. This rule hampered the ministry to youth. In addition the programs of the national youth organization kept young people too busy to engage in religious activities. Further, youth who showed interest in religion risked being excluded from educational and other opportunities, a factor which discouraged even visits to clergy.[46]

FRELIMO's policies impeded efforts to attract new Church personnel among young Mozambicans. Government closed the minor seminaries. It forbade admitting candidates to a seminary or novitiate before they reached the age of eighteen. It required young men and women of this age to do two years of national service. And party and government tried to entice talented young people from seminaries and convents into public employment.[47]

FRELIMO insisted that only organizations it sponsored could exist. It claimed that societies founded on other bases, particularly religious, would be divisive. So it forbade the functioning of standard parish societies such as societies for Christian family life.[48]

Government severely restricted the Catholic press. The Church had to arrange for the publication and distribution of printed and mimeographed materials through the National Institute of Books and Records (INLD). Government's justification was its need to control the allocation of scarce resources: paper, ink, use of presses, and foreign exchange for overseas purchases. School textbooks, it argued, were more important than religious literature. Actually, authorities used these controls for censorship. They made clear their displeasure that both local and imported Catholic publications were criticizing Marxism and Communist states.[49]

In 1979 the government set up the Serviços para as Actividades Associativas e Religiosas (SPAAR) to manage its relations with the churches. This institution looked like the Ministries of Religion in Eastern Europe. Together with other agencies it exercised wide discretion in administering the many regulations concerning the churches.[50]

The policies that hampered religion applied to Islam and the Protestant churches as well as to the Catholic Church. But after initial frictions, the Protestants seemed to get along more easily than the Catholics, probably because they had been more distant from the colonial government.[51]

In point of fact, the FRELIMO regime directed a propaganda campaign specifically against the Catholic Church. At a meeting with the bishops in December 1978 a government spokesman bitterly attacked the Church for its past and present failings in Mozambique. A few months later, the government's weekly magazine, *Tempo*, ran a series of articles that went over the same ground as the meeting. The editors illustrated the articles with pre-independence photos that linked prominent churchmen with Portuguese authorities and with the Portuguese armed forces. Articles in the government daily, *Noticias*, presented something very like the minutes of the December meeting itself. It drew these from a publication put out by a Spanish organization that had somehow obtained them: the Instituto de Estudios Politicos para America Latina y Africa (IEPALA). *Tempo* had earlier published a piece entitled "Religion and the Submission of Man." Its leading illustration suggested its main point; it was a photo of black candidates for the priesthood, prostrating themselves at the litanies during an ordination ceremony.[52]

## THE CHURCH'S RESPONSE TO ITS NEW SITUATION

We look now at how the Church responded to the situation in Mozambique after independence and to FRELIMO's religious policies.

During the transition from Portuguese to Mozambican rule, in December 1974, the Holy See was able to set up an Apostolic Delegation in Mozambique. Pope Paul VI's personal representative, Cardinal Umberto Mozzoni, was able to visit the country several times during this period. The first two indigenous bishops were consecrated in March 1975, for Lourenço Marques (later Maputo) and Pemba. Four others joined them by October 1976. Two Portuguese bishops remained: Vieira Pinto at Nampula and Ferreira da Silva at Lichinga (formerly Vila Cabral). The Apostolic Delegate provided communication with the FRELIMO government. But the belated appointment of Mozambican bishops did not impress FRELIMO, which considered them "mentally colonized" and their appointment cosmetic—changing only the Church's "identity card."[53]

Some indigenous church personnel had organized USAREMO in 1974. Representatives of this group visited FRELIMO's camps in Tanzania. The organization invited Machel to send a message to its first meeting. As previously mentioned, Fr. Mazula spoke of the Church as colonialist, bourgeois, and capitalist. It promoted repression, profited from its institutions, alienated Mozambican priests and religious from their culture and their people, and taught them to seek wealth without working for it and to seek prestige instead of service. Yet the Church also brought faith in Christ. Those attending the meeting needed self-criticism and conversion in order to become authentic missionaries who were sharing the revolution. Several formulas for society were not suitable for Mozambique: American capitalism, Russian Communism, and Chinese Marxism. Father Mazula's description of the colonial church as "capitalist" and his apparent belief that FRELIMO's policies were not Marxist are noteworthy. USAREMO met a year later. Its final statement did not repeat explicit agreement with FRELIMO's philosophy. The group reaffirmed its commitment to Christ, and urged work for development along the lines of *Gaudium et Spes*.[54]

Initially, some missionaries supported the revolution enthusiastically. In November 1975 a group of Burgos Fathers, without consulting or informing the bishops or the other religious congregations or USAREMO, issued an extraordinary statement:

Following a scientific analysis of reality, which makes us aware of the opposition in the world between the exploiting classes and the exploited, we opt for socialism. We see the process which is unfolding in Mozambique as a class struggle, which is the only way to create a new society free from all exploitation of man by man. . . . We reject every attempt to make ideological use of the faith by means of ethical or moral concepts that are closely tied up with the bourgeois idea of man and of the world. As believers, it is in the revolutionary process that we make real the fraternity announced by Jesus of Nazareth. . . . We cannot give our support to any kind of reactionary or reformist attitude or activity on the part of the Church.

The statement approved the government's nationalization of schools and medical facilities.[55]

No other missionaries voiced support for FRELIMO in such strong terms. Many were pleased, however, with the termination of the Church's involvement in educational and medical administration. In their view, this would free them for more direct grass-roots apostolates and for more direct social action. Unhappily, the government's restrictions on the Church soon rebuffed this expectation.[56]

Some missionaries could not accept the limitations on their customary apostolates or the pressures of their new lifestyle: real privation, confinement, and lack of privacy. Many withdrew voluntarily. The number of foreign priests and religious fell from 2,081 in 1975 to 681 in 1982.[57] For the missionaries who remained the enforced change of lifestyle made for serious stress. With time, however, they learned to rely more completely on God and to be content with their poverty. Their proximity to one another in the towns brought them into closer friendship and cooperation. Some used their enforced "idleness" to do valuable tasks that they might otherwise have neglected, such as translating the Bible into local languages. The idleness also gave them the opportunity to think together about their spiritual attitudes and about dealing with pastoral demands in their new situation. A contemplative convent in the Nampula diocese became a focal point for more intense personal prayer and reflection. From such exercises emerged a basic decision to stay in Mozambique, no matter what difficulties missionaries might face.[58]

The bishops were the Church's official spokesmen. Still entirely Portuguese, they issued a pastoral letter in August 1974 when FRELIMO's takeover was assured. Entitled "The Church in an Independent Mozambique," this reversed many of their previous positions. They welcomed independence as the proper status of the Mozambican people. They were pleased that independence would end numerous oppressions and injustices, including racism. They admitted, with reservations, the Church's complicity in colonial inequities. They offered help with social development, especially with work for which Church personnel were qualified.

They seemed to expect a continuing role in the schools. The new, just social order must involve "the whole man"; it needed conversion of heart, and therefore had a religious dimension. They urged freedom for the Church to do its work. They made no mention of FRELIMO's Marxist leanings and showed no awareness of what the party's religious policies would be.[59]

With two Mozambicans in their ranks, the bishops spoke again in a Christmas message of 1975, after FRELIMO had actually taken power. While this message followed the same lines as the earlier pastoral, it was more generous in praising the people who fought for independence. It also declared that the government's dismantling of familiar Church institutions should not frighten Catholics but should stir them to seek new forms of presence and service.[60]

The bishops issued additional pastoral letters and several "communiqués" for Catholics in the following years. They also sent several memoranda to government on issues that troubled them. After October 1976 only two of the bishops were Portuguese.[61]

In these further statements, the bishops protested forthrightly against the whole array of measures that interfered with preaching, teaching, and administration of the sacraments. These included the takeover of schools and school-compounds, seizure and closure of churches, prohibition of new construction, damage to church buildings and furnishings, restrictions on movement of church personnel, confiscation of residences, disregard for the needs of religious community, interdiction of the religious activities of laity and of voluntary associations, indoctrination of youth, monopolization of young people's time, barriers to their contact with the Church, prohibition of baptism to persons under eighteen, interrogation of church personnel and laity, harassment of church members, and censorship of Church publications.

Although the bishops congratulated the regime for its efforts to provide social services, they also pointed out the shortcomings of these efforts. Chronic shortages of foodstuffs and household commodities, they said, were hurting many people. Shortages of supplies and inadequate staffing were hampering medical services. In addition, authorities were sending citizens to "reeducation" camps merely for disagreeing with the party's views. While the bishops' statements apparently included no explicit complaint about the arbitrary power of SNASP, they did comment on the deplorable condition of the camps and the long delays in judging detainees' cases.[62]

At first the bishops tended to claim the Church's rights by using the concept of "two spheres" as Leo XIII had done in *Immortale Dei*. Later they relied on Vatican II's *Dignitatis Humanae*, stressing that the religious liberty both of individuals and of groups was a human right. Human dignity was likewise the ground on which they criticized the government's failings in the economic and social field and its repression of political freedom. Here they added that the restrictions of both religious and civil liberty were against Mozambique's constitution.[63]

The bishops emphasized Catholics' moral obligation to join in the country's socioeconomic development in accordance with Vatican II. Although they several times admitted the Church's past failures, they did so as a somewhat cursory gesture.[64] They did not comment on the weaknesses of Marxism as a theory or its nonapplicability to the Mozambican situation. Some diocesan bulletins and some overseas periodicals about the missions, however, pointed out that the historical record of the Soviet Union and other Communist countries foreshadowed serious difficulties for religion and human rights in Mozambique.[65]

Bishop Vieira Pinto had returned from Portugal. Apart from the bishops' joint statements, he put out several documents of his own. Although he did not disagree with his brother bishops, his writings were more analytic, nuanced, subtle, and irenic. He welcomed independence enthusiastically. He paid glowing tribute to those who had fought for it. He generously praised the FRELIMO regime's accomplishments. He spoke of the country as now being led by a "revolutionary vanguard" and prophesied a brighter future. He deplored the Church's historical transgressions. He accepted five criticisms of religion and the Church as basically true. These were the Church's collaboration with colonialism, religion's divisive impact on the populace, the "barrenness" of religion in the social field through exaggerated "otherworldliness," the Catholic Church's privileged position, and its consequent complicity with Portuguese wartime atrocities. He criticized the regime only indirectly, by calling for full fidelity to its own watchwords: unity, work, and vigilance. Although he recognized and reprobated FRELIMO's atheism, he hoped for better mutual understanding between believers and unbelievers. He showed familiarity with the Marxist-Catholic dialogue which Vatican II had initiated and was optimistic that this would lead to less troubled Church–State relations in Mozambique. Vatican II, in his view, highlighted a new kind of presence for the Church as a "liberating ferment" in society. It must evangelize, mainly through the hierarchy, and it must animate, mainly through the laity. The country's constitution ensured religious freedom; Christians must take their civic responsibilities seriously and bear witness to the faith in this way. Catholics must find new ways of carrying on the Church's work and of living the gospel in a socialist-oriented society.[66]

Vieira Pinto's statements gave Catholic clerical and lay leadership a deeper understanding of the political situation and of the theological and spiritual outlook they needed in order to deal with it. But they did not change FRELIMO's understanding of the Church's position or its attitude toward the Church. He was misled in his hopes for dialogue and better Church–State relations, perhaps because he was drawing upon only conciliatory Marxist writers like Roger Garaudy who were far from the mainstream of political Marxism-Leninism.

The bishops' major protest to government evoked an angry rebuff. Machel had asked the churches for their observations on his regime. But when the government invited the bishops, in December 1978, to discuss the questions and complaints they submitted to the president, it took the offensive. This was the meeting that provided the substance of *Tempo*'s attack on the Church. The government's spokesman lectured the bishops on the Church's complicity in Portuguese colonial exploitation, its ties with invading troops and the slave trade, and its racism, contempt of African culture, endorsement of forced labor, and relative indifference to the work of education with which it was entrusted. He cited the Concordat, the Missionary Agreement and the Missionary Statute, and the Church's resultant subservience to the Portuguese government. He cited the hierarchy's earlier support of the colonial regime and its opposition to the liberation movement, its silence about military atrocities against civilians, and its failure to protest even against the Portuguese army's desecration of churches.

He attacked personally the indigenous bishops who were present. He accused them of allowing the Portuguese seminaries to colonize their minds, of keeping cowardly silence during the liberation struggle, and, when the struggle was won, of laying their own claims inside the Church for promotion of black men to bishoprics. FRELIMO itself protested this idea because its own outlook was nonracial: it was not looking for a church that was Mozambican only in the color of its skin.

The bishops had requested government to explain cases of police action against church personnel. By way of answer, the spokesman charged several priests and religious with homosexual or heterosexual misconduct, financial fraud, and neglect of official duties. He offered to explain these charges publicly in the localities where the culprits were working.

He even intimated that one priest who was present was living with a married woman and had fathered a child by her.

The spokesman then berated the bishops for many of their criticisms and complaints. They were using a double standard, charging FREL-IMO with faults they were silent about when the Portuguese ruled. FRELIMO acknowledged some of these faults, but could correct them only gradually because of conditions bequeathed by the Portuguese. Its reeducation camps, for example, were old colonial jails which were indeed wretched and unsanitary. The bishops were appointing themselves interpreters of the constitution, and their explanations of the clauses they cited were wrong. Church personnel were repeatedly acting illegally. The spokesman ended by giving the bishops a comprehensive statement of the regulations outlined earlier that were to control religious activities.[67]

While the bishops together dealt with government on a national scale, the dioceses sought dialogue with local authorities. Individual bishops did this either alone or working with their pastoral councils. The process took long periods and enormous patience, but it sometimes mitigated Church–State tensions in some places. Even in the early years, too, the party's dynamizing groups often chose Catholic catechists or lay leaders for civic positions, presumably because they had integrity and relevant skills. Sometimes these people were even chosen for government jobs. Missionaries were of two minds about this development. True, such people could bring Christian principles to bear in society. Still, party pressures endangered their very faith. In the view of missionaries who favored the involvement, the opportunity to serve the public good justified the risk.[68]

While the Church made these efforts to change government attitudes, it also worked out new pastoral strategies for itself. The laity shared with priests and religious in this project. Consultations in the dioceses led to a National Pastoral Assembly at Beira in September 1977 which laid down the main lines of the Church's subsequent pastoral action. The new strategy included, as a key feature, the development of small Christian communities. Catholics organized themselves into small local groups that met frequently for prayer, reflection, discussion, instruction, and mutual help. For the most part they met without a priest, but these meetings might include a Liturgy of the Word. The groups chose their own leaders and their ministers for community tasks which did not require priestly ordination: readers, eucharistic ministers to bring Communion, and directors of the catechumenate. If feasible, the bishop or the parish priest commissioned the ministers at a special ceremony.[69]

The clergy thus accorded lay people wider responsibilities than in the past. The new system did make it necessary to *train* the people whom the communities chose, both in theology and in the ways that human beings interact in structured groups. Despite government pressures, several catechetical training centers—for example, at Anchilo and Guiuia—continued their work, offering short residential courses for lay ministries. Even though the training was of good quality, one observer noted that the centers could not cater to enough people, so that many ministers were not adequately prepared. Some priests also trained ministers through informal instruction. Community leaders in rural areas traveled considerable distances, at great inconvenience, to keep in touch with priests in the towns. Government sometimes detained and interrogated community leaders. Because it was suspicious of the communities as potentially subversive, it kept watch on them and tried to find out who belonged and what they discussed.[70]

To overcome the obstacles to training priests, the bishops tried several ways of organizing the seminary program. One way was to give part-time evening courses to young men who had daytime jobs. The results were not altogether satisfactory. The Church tried, too, to encourage sacramental marriage for its members and to instill Christian values into family life. It saw this as a way to carry on the religious formation of youth in the face of government's obstruction. In March 1976 the Bishops' Conference established a Commission for Justice and Peace. Its functions included inquiry for the conference into specific violations of human rights—for example, a study of FRELIMO's "reeducation centers," presented to the bishops in 1978. It also assisted the conference in its publication of documents related to social questions, and developed programs to familiarize Catholics with the Church's social doctrine. The Church put out some publications. These included diocesan bulletins and three modest mimeographed magazines. Their circulation was limited. Government censorship sometimes gave rise to difficulties.[71]

The bishops made clear to government the Church's willingness to cooperate in national development. But the government was reserved about the Church's participation; it was no more open to accepting help from Church people who had supported liberation than from those who opposed it. Early on, priests and religious did communal manual labor in agriculture and public works, but this was more of a symbolic gesture than a substantive contribution. Later, some helped organize cooperatives or instructed in scientific farming, but thus risked being accused by authorities of fraud in handling project funds. Some did medical work, but thus risked being blamed for failures that arose from bad management by government officials or from the disastrous national economy. Some taught in schools, although the prohibition of religious instruction and activities, along with the government's mandate to teach Marxism, troubled their consciences.[72]

Despite the Church's new strategies, the number of openly practicing Catholics dropped by as much as two-thirds. In the view of some clergy, however, not all the nonpracticing members truly abandoned their faith. Instead, they had made a judgment that open loyalty would cost them and their families more than God would expect of them; they would return when times got better. Observers also claimed that the depth and vitality of Christian commitment greatly increased among those who remained publicly Catholic. The new lay leaders gave time and energy generously. They risked political harassment, interrogation, detention, and discrimination in education and employment. The rank and file of the small communities were also generous; the bonds of mutual help were closer. The growth of lay leadership was striking. The "radical" decision to involve the laity in the planning process was a remarkable step for a hitherto "conservative" Church. It should have a powerful influence on the Church's future shape and operations.[73]

From 1981 onward, the government's attitude toward the Church softened somewhat. Immigration authorities more readily admitted new personnel for such occupations as teaching and health work. Personnel going home on leave could stay away longer. Government was more willing to permit foreign financial assistance for the Church. Although the stringent regulations on religious activity remained in force, officials were more lenient in applying them. Thus, in some places, authorities did not hinder the baptism of children, and missionaries could more readily get permission for weekend ministries in rural areas.[74] By 1988, the tensions between Church and State had subsided even further but had not disappeared. Catholics were openly attending Church in large numbers. Children were receiving religious instruction at church compounds. Joaquim Chissano, who became president in October 1986 after Machel died in an airplane crash, made a point of visiting the Vatican in 1987 before he visited Moscow, and Pope John Paul II visited Mozambique in September 1988.[75]

It was not clear why the government's attitude changed. Perhaps the dioceses in their negotiations with local officials had convinced them of the Church's sincere commitment to social development. Perhaps government was conciliating the opinion of its own people who were becoming disillusioned with the revolution's achievements and unhappy with its pressures on the Church. Perhaps, because it was then seeking foreign assistance to overcome the setbacks caused by flood and drought, it was trying to present a more favorable image to potential donors in the West. The Holy See, in fact, offered aid. Or perhaps FRELIMO's leaders were confident that their antireligious campaign had been effective enough to permit small concessions; that if they kept youth away and indoctrinated them with Marxism, the Church would die of suffocation.

## CRISIS AND GROWTH

Even though FRELIMO's doctrinaire and aggressive Marxism did seriously obstruct the Church's pursuit of its mission in Mozambique, the encounter also contributed substantially to the maturing of the Church and thus, one may hope, to its greater effectiveness in the long term.

When the encounter began, the Church was more severely handicapped than it was in most other sub-Saharan countries. The Portuguese colonial regime had been particularly oppressive and unenlightened, and Portugal's government had seemed totally oblivious to the "winds of change" blowing through Africa, although other European powers had begun accommodating to them as early as the 1950s. The Concordat, the Missionary Agreement, and the Missionary Statute seemed to identify the Church with the regime. Only Portuguese were bishops. They did little if anything to incorporate Catholic social doctrine into their instruction of the faithful; nor did they invoke it in judging the government's policies. While the Church did play a part in secular development through its schools and health services, it was not clear that this work paid sufficient attention to the people who most needed assistance, the indigenous population. Despite the new orientations of Vatican II, moreover, the Church remained clerical; layfolk, apart from catechists, were largely passive. One bishop, it is true, perceived clearly the incompatibility of Portugal's colonial policies with the Church's social thinking, and a good number of missionaries shared his perception. Bishop Vieira Pinto tried to make this thinking better known, and he and many missionaries urged the hierarchy to pressure the regime toward ending its injustices and oppressions. Unfortunately these efforts made little headway.

FRELIMO's successful push for independence and its adoption of

Marxist ideology roused the Church's social consciouness in several ways. The assumption of political power by indigenous radical nationalists moved the Holy See toward very rapid replacement of the Portuguese bishops with Mozambicans. At the same time, the new rulers' commitment to Marxist policies forced the new bishops, inexperienced though they were, to give social questions a central position in working out their pastoral strategies.

In dealing with these questions they faced something of a dilemma. On the one hand, as Mozambicans they were sympathetic with FRELIMO's critique of colonial injustices and supportive of government action to correct them. On the other hand, they could not accept the party's ruthless antireligious program and could not endorse its subversion of civil liberties or its adoption of economic policies that undermined productivity and aggravated the privations of the poor.

The bishops dealt with their problems in several ways. In pastoral letters and similar documents, they commented on public events in light of the Church's social teaching, especially the teaching of Vatican II. They protested frankly not only the government's measures against the Church but also its infringements of citizens' rights and its failure to meet citizens' needs; one might suggest that they had learned from the shortsightedness of their Portuguese predecessors not to be silent in face of injustice. The bishops tried at the same time, through dialogue with government, to ease the restrictions on the Church's activities and to mitigate the harmful effects of some government actions on the people. They urged the faithful to participate in the country's socioeconomic development, and offered the Church's institutional assistance in this effort.

Additionally, in order to continue their sacral ministries in the face of governmental obstruction, the bishops reshaped the Church's approaches to its pastoral tasks. Especially notable here were the consultation of the laity in a National Pastoral Assembly, and the promotion of the small Christian communities in which layfolk assumed responsibility for local leadership and for ministries that did not require the sacrament of Holy Orders. As a corollary to these measures, the bishops established programs to train the laity in both leadership and ministry. Although the clergy may have initially seen the new leadership role of the laity as a pragmatic adjustment to abnormal difficulties, in time they came to appreciate it as an appropriate application of Vatican II's ecclesiology. It should be added that neither bishops nor clergy confined their pastoral concerns to social issues and the ramifications of Marxist ideology. They

also devoted attention to such matters as marriage, family, biblical translation, culture, and Church vocations.

While FRELIMO's Marxist-Leninist religious policies led to a drastic
decrease in the Church's manpower, they also tended to increase the
relative weight of those clergy and religious who fitted better into a
critical period of transition. The missionaries who withdrew from Mozambique under pressure of frustration in their apostolate and hardship
in their new lifestyle tended to be people who were nostalgic for the
prerevolutionary order. The men and women who stayed were people
who tended to be more flexible. They adjusted more easily to austere
living conditions, better understood the urgency of political and social
change, and were readier for innovative approaches to ministry.

The government's persecution of religion powerfully affected the responses of the laity as well. It did deter many from open religious practice. But it also drew goodly numbers to more active roles in Church
affairs. This was especially true in the small communities. At the same
time, the programs of instruction for community leaders and ministers
led to better-informed religious practice.

The Church's initiatives in the social field were not without cost. They
entailed risk and required courage. Critical public comment by the bishops or others on government policies could prompt more severe restrictions on the Church's ministries. It did, in fact, provoke the government's
venomous attack at the meeting of December 1978, which included personal vilification of bishops who were present. Government-controlled
media took steps to undermine the Church's credibility. Clergy and religious found themselves charged with subversion, embezzlement, and
immorality. Lay leaders were watched, harassed, and interrogated by
security agents.

To say that the encounter with Marxism awakened the Church's social
consciousness is not to say that the Church's response had no shortcomings. For the most part, the bishops' public pronouncements were rather
narrow in scope; although they touched other human needs and freedoms, they focused most sharply on religious and ecclesiastical liberties.
Their pastoral letters seemed directed only to an elite. Bishop Vieira
Pinto's letters were more comprehensive and reflective than those of the
bishops' conference, but they may have conceded more validity than was
warranted to FRELIMO's positions. And they, too, could have been appreciated only by sophisticated readers. The bishops sensibly avoided a
direct and fruitless debate with government over the validity of Marxist
theory; but they might usefully have made greater efforts to let the faith-

ful at the grassroots know about the theory's failings. On this point, however, it is true that government's restrictions on the Church's use of mass communications made such efforts extremely difficult.

One particular issue in the bishops' approach to government was controversial. On several occasions they urged government to negotiate peace with the MNR even though the MNR's brutal tactics were totally foreign to Catholic social ideals. Their urging led to the suspicion that they viewed the MNR with some favor. More likely, they saw a negotiated peace as the quickest way to end the havoc the MNR was inflicting, especially on the helpless, poverty-stricken folk in the countryside. However well-intentioned the bishops' urging may have been, only time would tell whether it could help restore people's personal security and let them carry on their ordinary daily pursuits without fear.[76]

There is no intention here to suggest that only an encounter with Marxism could have bestirred social awareness in the Mozambican Church as it began to take charge of its own destiny. Other scenarios could have led in the same direction. If FRELIMO's revolution had been nationalist without being Marxist, for example, the new indigenous hierarchy would almost certainly have become more active than their predecessors in public discussion of policy and in promoting economic development. Vatican II's emphasis, too, on the Church's duty to engage "the modern world" would have filtered down to Mozambique, though slowly. There is no intention to suggest, either, that social concern and lay responsibility are the only important marks of a maturing Church. Well-rounded maturity has many other facets: these include, among other things, more solid spiritual formation of Catholics, more consistent internalization of divinely revealed insights and norms, and the fuller inculturation of faith and practice which is so critical in Africa. The Church in Mozambique still faces a broad and lengthy agenda, but its response to the challenge of Marxism marked an important step in its growth to full maturity.

## NOTES

1. See Thomas M. Henriksen, "Marxism and Mozambique," *African Affairs*, 77 (October 1978), 442; Munslow, *Mozambique*, pp. 9–11, 53–55, chap. 5.

2. See Munslow, *Mozambique*, pp. 7–8, 44–45, 63–64.

3. See ibid., pp. 26–27, 60–61, 69–71, 76, 79, chap. 9.

4. See ibid., pp. 85, 89, 96–97, 109–10, 119–20, 129.

5. See ibid., pp. 121–27.

6. See ibid., pp. 64–66, 69, 72–76, 126, 133–37.

7. See ibid., pp. 81–88, chap. 11; Edward A. Alpers, "The Struggle for Socialism in Mozambique," in Rosberg and Callaghy, eds., *Socialism in Sub-Saharan Africa*, pp. 280–90; Marina Ottaway, "The Theory and Practice of Marxism-Leninism in Mozambique and Ethiopia," in Albright, ed., *Communism in Africa*, pp. 120–22.

8. See Iain Christie, *Machel of Mozambique* (Harare: Zimbabwe Publishing House, 1988), pp. 3, 8–16, 24–25, 44, 59; "Mozambique: A Church in a Socialist State in a Time of Radical Change," *Pro Mundi Vita Dossiers*, Africa Dossier n.s. 3 (January–February 1977), 4.

9. See Munslow, *Mozambique*, pp. 136–38, 154–56; Ottaway, "Theory and Practice," in Albright, ed., *Communism in* Africa, p. 125; "Mozambique: A Church," 12; Christie, *Machel of Mozambique*, pp. 129–30.

10. See Alex Vines, *Renamo: Terrorism in Mozambique* (London: Center for Southern African Studies in association with James Currey, 1991), pp. 15–31 on Rhodesian and South African support, and pp. 87–90 on targets and terrorist tactics. See also Munslow, *Mozambique*, pp. 166–67; Ottaway and Ottaway, *Afro-Communism*, p. 94; "Mozambique," *Africa South of the Sahara, 1988* (London: Europa Publications, 1987), pp. 701–702; this source will henceforth be cited as "'Mozambique,' *Africa South 1988*." See also John R. Saul, "Development and Counterdevelopment in Mozambique," in Edmond J. Keller and Donald Rothchild, eds., *Afro-Marxist Regimes: Ideology and Public Policy* (Boulder, Colo.: Lynne Rienner, 1987), pp. 128–29.

11. See Munslow, *Mozambique*, pp. 161–62; Ottaway and Ottaway, *Afro-Communism*, pp. 73–74.

12. See Ottaway and Ottaway, *Afro-Communism*, pp. 74–75, 83, 92, 94; "Mozambique: A Church," 9-10.

13. See Ottaway and Ottaway, *Afro-Communism*, pp, 75, 86–90: "Mozambique: A Church," 8.

14. See Ottaway and Ottaway, *Afro-Communism*, pp. 93–95; "Mozambique," *Africa South 1988*, pp. 706–708: "Africa and the European Community: The Second Lomé Convention," *Africa South of the Sahara, 1980–81* (London: Europa Publications, 1980), p. 60; L. Adele Jinadu, "Soviet Influence on Afro-Marxist Regimes: Ethiopia and Mozambique," in Keller and Rothchild, eds., *Afro-Marxist Regimes*, pp. 248–49; "Mozambique: A Church," 11.

15. See "Mozambique," *Africa South 1988*, p. 708.

16. See "Mozambique: A Church," 10; "Mozambique," *Africa South 1988*, pp. 705–708; Henriksen, "Marxism and Mozambique," 453; Ezio Sorio, "Depois da autocrítica, o quê?" *Alem-mar* (Lisbon), 26 (April 1981), 11.

17. See "Mozambique," *Africa South 1988*, p. 709.

18. See Ottaway and Ottaway, *Afro-Communism*, pp. 91-92; "Mozambique," *Africa South 1988*, pp. 701, 706, 709; James H. Mittelman, "Marginalization and the International Division of Labor: Mozambique's Strategy of Opening the Market," *African Studies Review*, 34 (December 1991), 95.

19. See "Mozambique," *Africa South of the Sahara, 1980–81* (London: Europa Publications, 1980), p. 712; this source will henceforth be cited as " 'Mozambique,' *Africa South 1980–81*"; see also "Mozambique," *Africa South 1988*, p. 720; "Mozambique; A Church," 7; Ottaway and Ottaway, *Afro-Communism*, p. 95; Munslow, *Mozambique*, p. 168; Henriksen, "Marxism and Mozambique," 451.

20. See Munslow, *Mozambique*, p. 169; Ottaway and Ottaway, *Afro-Communism*, p. 95; "Mozambique: A Church," 7, 25.

21. See Munslow, *Mozambique*, pp. 169–70; "Mozambique: A Church," 8.

22. See Munslow, *Mozambique*, p. 157; Ottaway and Ottaway, *Afro-Communism*, pp. 79, 82; Ottaway, "Theory and Practice, in Albright, ed., *Communism in Africa*, pp. 126–27; Piero Gheddo, "L'ésperienza 'Socialista' in Mozambico," *Monde e missione* (Milan), 108 (November 15, 1979), 603.

23. See Ottaway and Ottaway, *Afro-Communism*, pp. 77–79; Henriksen, "Marxism and Mozambique," 445–46; "Meeting Criticizes Party Work," *AIM Information Bulletin* (Maputo), No. 61 (July 1981), 4–5; "Party Work among the Masses," ibid., Supplement to No. 64, 1–7; "Mozambique," *Africa South 1988*, p. 701.

24. See Munslow, *Mozambique*, pp. 151–53; Ottaway and Ottaway, *Afro-Communism*, pp. 81–82; Ottaway, "Theory and Practice," in Albright, ed., *Communism in Africa*, pp. 128–30; Henriksen, "Marxism and Mozambique," 443; "Mozambique: A Church," 6; Vines, *Renamo*, p. 9.

25. See Ottaway and Ottaway, *Afro-Communism*, pp. 83–84; Gheddo, "Ésperienza 'socialista' in Mozambico," 593, 596, 602; Henriksen, "Marxism and Mozambique, 457; "Mozambique: A Church," 6–7.

26. The Constitution is outlined in "Mozambique," *Africa South 1980–81*, pp. 707–708; on the judiciary, see p. 710. See also Ottaway and Ottaway, *Afro-Communism*, pp. 83–85; "Mozambique: A Church," 5. On the parallel structure and overlapping functioning of party and state, see Jens Erik Torp, L. M. Denny, and Donald I. Ray, *Mozambique, São Tomé, and Príncipe* (New York: Pinter, 1989), Part I, pp. 63–79. In Munslow, *Mozambique*, pp. 178–79, is a list of the leaders in the party and the state as of 1982; the list clearly indicates how extensively membership in the two groups overlapped.

27. See the Resolution of this section, "Party Work Is Weak Among the Masses," *AIM Information Bulletin*, No. 61 (July 1981), Supplement, passim; "Resolução de trabalho ideologico do Partido sobre estilo e metodos da actuação," *Noticias* (Maputo), July 6, 1981, pp. 2–3; Saul, "Development and Counterdevelopment," in Keller and Rothchild, eds., *Afro-Marxist Regimes*, p. 119; *Africa South 1988*, pp. 702, 706.

28. See "Mozambique: A Church," 8, 12; and the following places in *AIM Information Bulletin*, No. 61 (July 1981), 15, 19, 20; No. 64 (October 1981), 29, 31, 32.

29. See Ottaway and Ottaway, *Afro-Communism*, pp. 170–73; Henriksen, "Marxism and Mozambique," 448; Jinadu, "Soviet Influence," in Keller and

Rothchild, *Afro-Marxist Regimes*, p. 244; *AIM Information Bulletin*, No. 64 (October 1981), 26; "Mozambique," *Africa South 1988*, pp. 705–706.

30. See Munslow, *Mozambique*, pp. 166–67; Ottaway and Ottaway, *Afro-Communism*, pp. 93–94; "Mozambique," *Africa South 1988*, pp. 703–704, 706–707; "President of Mozambique Asserts South Africa Still Assists the Rebels," *The New York Times*, September 18, 1985, p. A-10; "South Africa Admits Breaking Mozambique Pact," ibid., September 20, 1985, p. A-7.

31. See R. Pattee, "Mozambique," *New Catholic Encyclopedia* 10:57–58; "The Church in Mozambique: The Colonial Inheritance," *IDOC Documentation Service Bulletin* (Rome), Nos. 7, 8, 9 (July–September 1979), 16–19.

32. For the substance of the documents, see "Government Policy and the Church in the Portuguese Territories in Africa," *Pro Mundi Vita Bulletin* (Brussels), No. 43 (1972), 23–24; For the texts, see "Inter sanctam sedem et rempublican Lusitanam conventiones," *Acta Apostolicae Sedis*, 32 (June 1, 1940), 217–33, 235–44; "Accord missionaire entre le saint siège et la république portugais (7-V-1940)," *Angola* V, ed. Antonio Brasio, C.S.Sp. Spiritana Monumenta Historica, Series Africana (Pittsburgh: Duquesne University Press, 1971), pp. 678–87, and "Législation missionaire portugais (6-V-1940)," ibid., pp. 792–817.

33. See "Mozambique: A Church," 3, 27n31. According to Sorio, "Depois da autocrítica o quê," 13, the FRELIMO regime confiscated 4,237 schools at all levels, 141 social centers, and 202 health centers. FRELIMO's accusation appears in "The Church in Mozambique: The Colonial Inheritance," 21. On literacy, see Munslow, *Mozambique*, p. 63.

34. See, for example, "Mozambique: A Church," 21–22; Luis Afonso da Costa, "Another Year of Agony! . . . With No Hope of Resurrection," *IDOC Communication* (Rome) 72/299/002 (August 16, 1972), mimeographed; idem, "In Vietnam as in Mozambique, Angola, and Guinea-Bissau," *IDOC Bulletin*, No. 3–5 (January 1973), 5–6.

35. See "Mozambique: A Church," 22n24; "À propos des massacres du Mozambique," *Documentation catholique*, 70 (October 7, 1973), 847.

36. See "Mozambique: A Church," 21–22.

37. See the following documents in *Documentation catholique*, 71 (May 5, 1974): "Communiqué du sécrétariat du diocèse de Nampula," 415; "Un impératif de conscience," 419–21; "Communiqué du sécrétariat de la Conférence Épiscopale de Mozambique," 421; "Répenser la guerre," 413–17; "Note du Ministère Portugais d'Outre-mer," 422; "Renouvellement et réconciliation de l'homme au Mozambique," 422–25; "Communiqué des évêques et des supérieurs d'instituts missionaires," 427; "Communiqué de la Conférence Épiscopale," 428.

38. See "First Meeting of Black Priests," *IDOC Bulletin* No. 25 (November 1974), 4.

39. See "Mozambique: A Church," 22n24.

40. Interviews with an official of a religious congregation, Rome, March 1982. See also "L'Église et les territoires d'outre-mer portugaises," *Documentation catholique*, 71 (February 3, 1974), 111–14.

41. In an undated document which argued in effect that the Church should not support the liberation movement, Archbishop Custódio Alvim Pereira of Lourenço Marquès mentioned only in passing the idea that international Communism sometimes supported revolutions. See "Prise de position de l'archevêque de Lourenço Marquès," ibid., 71 (May 5, 1974), 426.

42. See "Mozambique," *Africa South 1980–81*, p. 710.

43. See Christie, *Machel of Mozambique*, p. 68; J. Heijke, "Socialism and the Church in Africa," *Exchange* (Leiden), 10 (December 1981), 36–39.

44. See "Mozambique: A Church," 25–26; Gheddo, "Ésperienza 'socialista' in Mozambico," 606; "O Papel da igreja católica em Moçambique," *Tempo* (Maputo), No. 448, May 13, 1979, p. 40; "The Church in Mozambique: The Colonial Inheritance," 12.

45. See "Mozambique: A Church," 25; confidential report of a missionary in Mozambique to his Superior-General, August 1, 1980, typescript.

46. For these restrictions on the Church and its personnel, see "Mozambique: A Church," 26; Gheddo, "Ésperienza 'socialista' in Mozambico," 606–607; "The Church in Mozambique: Colonial Inheritance," 11, 45–46; interview with a Vatican official, March 1982; confidential report of a missionary in Mozambique to his Superior-General, June 26, 1980, mimeographed; confidential report of a missionary, August 1, 1980.

47. See "The Church in Mozambique: The Colonial Inheritance," 41–44; Gheddo, "Ésperienza 'socialista' in Mozambico," 612; interview with an official of a religious congregation, March 1982; interview with Vatican officials, March and April 1982.

48. See "The Church in Mozambique: The Colonial Inheritance," 43.

49. See ibid., 32–39, 42–43, 59.

50. See Bishop Manuel Vieira Pinto, untitled report on the diocese of Nampula, December 1, 1980, paragraph 20, mimeographed; "Moçambique: Uma igreja como as demais?" *Alem-mar*, 25 (October 1980), 27; Natale Costalunga, "Marxismo e missione in Mozambico," *SEDOS Bulletin* (Rome), No. 82/18 (December 1, 1982), 351.

51. See "Les Chrêtiens du Mozambique: Une foi à l'heure de l'épreuve," *Service de presse protestante romande*, No. 7, May 7, 1979, at IDOC International's office in Rome; this carries IDOC document No. 32966. Also "Mozambique: Churches Nationalized as Maputo Cracks Down," *AACC News*, July 1979 (IDOC document No. 33144); "Mozambique: Les églises protestantes se disent pleines d'espoir," *Informations catholiques internationales*, No. 496, July 1, 1976, 29–30 (IDOC document No. 08357).

52. See "O Papel da igreja católica em Moçambique," *Tempo* (Maputo), No. 447, May 6, 1979, pp. 25-40, and ibid., No. 448, May 13, 1979, pp. 37-40; "Religião a submissão do homen," ibid., No. 372, November 20, 1977, pp. 56–63; "A igreja em Moçambique hoje; Entre o colonialismo e revolução," *Noticias*, July 27, 1979, p. 1; "Uma aliança de quinhentos anos contra e povo moçambicano,"

ibid., July 28, 1979, p. 1; "Uma igreja incapaz de encontrar o seu lugar en historia," ibid., July 29, 1979, p. 3.

53. See "A New Church in an Independent Mozambique," *Documentation SEDOS*, 75 (July 14, 1975), 516–17 (IDOC document no. 03255); interview with a Vatican official, April 1982; "Mozambique: A Church," 25, 28; "The Catholic Church in Mozambique: The Colonial Inheritance," 28–29.

54. See "First Meeting of Black Priests," 3–6; "The August 1975 Meeting of USAREMO," *IDOC Bulletin*, Nos. 41–42 (March–April 1976), 9–10.

55. See "Mozambique: A Church," 36–37. For the full text of the statement, see "Fathers of Burgos Support the Mozambican Revolution," *IDOC Bulletin* No. 37 (November–December 1975), 10–11. During the war of liberation the Burgos Fathers in Beira helped FRELIMO agents conduct clandestine study sessions on the Front's program; see Munslow, *Mozambique*, p. 119.

56. See Gheddo, "Ésperienza 'socialista' in Mozambico," 606, 608.

57. I calculated these statistics from "Mozambique: Problems, Options and the Responses of the Church," *International Fides Press Service*, December 4, 1982, p. NE519.

58. See "Moçambique: Uma igreja," 30; "O Caminho do povo e da igreja," *Alem-mar*, 27 (February 1982), 14; "Inside Mozambique," *Tablet* (London), 232 (July 1, 1978), 625; Vieira Pinto, untitled report on the diocese: paragraphs 22, 26; report of a missionary, August 1, 1980.

59. See "L'église dans un Mozambique indépendant," *Documentation catholique*, 71 (October 20, 1974), 873–78.

60. See "Christmas Message of the the Bishops to the Church in Mozambique, December 1975," *IDOC Bulletin*, Nos. 41–42 (March-April 1976), 11–12.

61. "Mozambique: Problems, Options," p. NE519, indicates that the bishops issued nine important messages in the previous seven years; I was not able to find all of these. But see "Mozambique: A Church," 30–31, 34, on the bishops' letter of June 6, 1976, the first anniversary of independence; "Communiqué de la Conférence Épiscopale du Mozambique," May 1977, *Documentation catholique*, 74 (June 19, 1977), 574–75; "Testemunhar a fé em liberdade," December 3, 1978, published by the Conference, mimeographed; "Mozambique: La vie chrêtienne dans la moment actuelle," April 1980, *Agence internationale fides*, June 28, 1980, pp. NF375-385; "Appel aux communautés chrêtiennes en faveur de la paix," January 5, 1983, *Documentation catholique*, 80 (September 4–18, 1983), 857–858. An appendix of "Testemunhar a fé," p. 6, lists five memoranda to government: "Igreja e sociedade, entregue a Presidencia da Republica em janeiro 1977"; "Memorandum sobre problemas sociais, entregue a Presidencia da Republica, a 29 dezembre de 1977"; "Exposição do Conselho Permanente da CEM ad Senhor Ministro do Interior sobre a liberdade religiosa, a 8 augusto de 1978"; "Adidamento a exposição ad Senhor Ministro do Interior, sobre a situação da igrega em Lichinga, a 11 de septembre de 1978"; "Memorandum sobre as restrições a liberdade religiosa no pais, entregue a Presidencia da Republica a

3 de dezembre de 1978." "The Church in Mozambique: The Colonial Inheritance," p. 2, mentions a memorandum sent to the president on November 11, 1978; page 3 lists 21 points from the latter. I have not found the text of any of these memoranda.

62. See, for example, the cautions which the bishops expressed in "A Igreja na revolução moçambicana" (March 29, 1976), cited in "Mozambique: A Church," 15n3; their representations at a meeting with Machel on January 31, 1976, ibid., 34; the list of their complaints in "The Church in Mozambique: The Colonial Inheritance," 3; "Testemunhar a fé," passim.

63. Contrast "L'église dans un Mozambique indépendant," 874–75, with "Testemunhar a fé," 2–3, and with "La vie chrêtienne dans le moment actuel," p. NF377.

64. See, e.g., "Testemunhar a fé," 4; "La vie chrêtienne dans le moment actuel," pp. NF378, NF383.

65. See "The Church in Mozambique: The Colonial Inheritance," 35–39.

66. Bishop Manuel Vieira Pinto, "The Church in an Independent Mozambique" (published in "the first days of July 1975"), *IDOC Bulletin*, Nos. 41–42 (March–April 1976), 2-9. Among other documents of Vieira Pinto were: "Repenser la guerre," cited earlier, "L'église et le temps" (homily on the first anniversary of independence, *Spiritus*, 66 (1977), 65–78; "Ateismo e religião: Fé e revolução" (Christmas 1978), mimeographed.

67. See "The Church in Mozambique: The Colonial Inheritance," passim.

68. See Vieira Pinto, report on the diocese, paragraphs 18–19; idem, "Ateismo e religião," paragraph 27; "Mozambique: A Church," 37–38; "Moçambique: uma igreja," 27; "O Caminho do Povo et da igreja," 14; Gheddo, "Ésperienza 'socialista' in Mozambico," 612; Conferencia Episcopale de Moçambique, "Testemunhar a fé," paragraphs 14-16.

69. See "Mozambique: Problems, Options," pp. NE519–20; Gheddo, "Ésperienza 'socialista' in Mozambico," 609.

70. See Vieira Pinto, report on the diocese, paragraphs 6–8, 20; report of a missionary, August 1, 1980. Sorio, "Depois da autocrítica o quê," 11-12; "Moçambique: Uma igreja," 30; "Aide-memoire del'incontro SEDOS sulla presenza missionaria in Mozambico," October 11, 1983, p. 2, mimeographed.

71. See Sorio, "Depois da autocrítica o quê," 14; "La vie chrêtienne dans le moment actuel," paragraphs 20–24; "Mozambique: Problems, Options," p. NE520; Vieira Pinto, report on the diocese, paragraphs 13, 20; report of a Regional Superior in Mozambique to his superior-General for the years 1974–1980, mimeographed: interview with a Vatican official, April 1982. On the Justice and Peace Commission see *Rapport de la rencontre Pan–Africaine sur la justice et paix. Roma, Lesotho du 29 mai au 3 juin 1988, Rapports des Commissions Justice et Paix, Annexe XII, Mozambique*, pp. 42–56. According to page 47 the Commission was established in 1986, but the context makes it clear that this is a typographical error and that the Commission was operating earlier. The Annexe

summarizes a series of pastoral appeals for peace in Mozambique from 1983 to 1987, pp. 51–56.

72. See report of a missionary, August 1, 1980; Bishop Manuel Vieira Pinto, memorandum "A Minho reflexão apos encontro e a reunião de trabalho com o Ministro Oscar Monteiro en 15 do mes corriento," July 15, 1981, paragraph 8, mimeographed; "The Church in Mozambique: The Colonial Inheritance," 7; John Emmanuel, "Marxist Mozambique," *Tablet*, 234 (May 17, 1980), 474; "Roman Catholics and African Politics," *Pro Mundi Vita Dossiers*, Africa dossier 7/8 (March 1979), 19n3.

73. Interview with a Vatican official, April 1982; see Sorio, "Depois da autocrítica o quê," 13–14; "O caminho do povo," 14; Gheddo, "Ésperienza 'socialista' in Mozambico," 608–609.

74. See Sorio, "Depois da autocrítica o quê," 11–12; "Aide-memoire del'incontro SEDOS," 2; Vieira Pinto, report on diocese, paragraphs 19–21, 25.

75. See "In Marx's Garden: Atheism Wilts, Faith Blooms," *The New York Times*, May 10, 1988, p. A-4; "Pope Asks Mozambique to Work with the Church," ibid., September 17, 1988, p. A-3; "Mozambicans Greet Pope with Frenzy," ibid., September 19, 1988, p. A-3.

76. Ultimately, in 1988, with the approval of the government, representatives of Protestant and Catholic Churches in Mozambique began informal conversations with MNR representatives in Nairobi, and these finally led, in October 1992, to a formal peace agreement between the government and the resistance movement. For an account, up to early 1991, of the complicated maneuvers leading to this result, see Vines, *Renamo*, pp. 120–32.

# 6

# Marxism and the Church in Madagascar

MADAGASCAR'S COLONIAL BACKGROUND was different from Mozambique's. The potential impact of Marxism on the Church's mission was less obvious and less immediate. And the Church itself was further along the road to maturity.

## GEOGRAPHICAL AND HISTORICAL BACKGROUND

Madagascar is an island in the Indian Ocean, about 250 miles from Africa's southeastern coast. It is large, with an area of about 250,000 square miles. At its center is an extensive high plateau. A coastal plain surrounds this. The climate is tropical and semitropical. Drought and tropical storms recurrently wreak havoc on parts of the island.

The population was ten million in 1985, mostly an amalgamation of Malaysian and Negro stock. The former was more perceptible on the plateau and the latter among the *côtiers* ("coastal dwellers") of the lowlands. Although there were eighteen tribal groups and some inter-ethnic tensions among them, the country used a single national language, Malagasy (Malgache). French was also widely spoken. While cultural parallels with the continent were readily discernible, Malagasys had a strong sense of their distinctive identity.

About 85 percent of the people lived in rural areas. The largest city was Antananarivo, the capital, situated on the plateau, with a population in 1985 of 662,000. Six other cities had populations of more than 40,000. Rapid migration from the countryside to the cities was under way.[1]

The island's economy was mostly agricultural. The people produced such crops as rice, coffee, and sugar. They raised cattle (zebus), sheep, poultry, and other livestock. Forests were extensive. The country had not yet explored its mineral resources. The French colonial regime developed scarcely any industry. At independence, then, Madagascar faced the classic problem of dependency; it earned foreign exchange by exporting primary commodities at very unstable prices, and spent its earnings on high-priced manufactures.[2]

Europeans became seriously involved with Madagascar only in the early nineteenth century. By this time the Merina people on the plateau had achieved sovereignty over the whole island and imposed their language on the other groups. Madagascar was therefore already on its way to becoming a nation. It strongly resisted colonization, twice waging war against the French.[3]

After France won full control in 1896, Malagasy nationalism remained strong. Nationalist societies sprouted; local revolts recurred. In 1947 the regime ruthlessly put down a major insurrection, with a death toll that allegedly reached eighty thousand.[4] Some of this nationalism was strongly touched by radical strains which actually arose from the French connection. Malagasys who fought in the French army during both World Wars stayed on in France as students or workers, and thus came into contact with the French Left. In this milieu they blended socialist and Communist ideas with their nationalism. Between the two wars, Communists in France were expanding their following into the colonies; in 1929 it was two French Communists who led a nationalist march on the governor's residence in Antananarivo. Communists were also active under Madagascar's Free French regime during World War II, helping Malagasy nationalists with trade union organization. Although the early nationalists played no direct role in post-independent Madagascar, their radicalism was part of the island's political atmosphere.[5]

De Gaulle's government granted Madagascar autonomy within the French community in 1958 and independence in 1960. The country's first president was Philibert Tsiranana, a political moderate who maintained close ties with France and kept his distance from China, Russia, and the Eastern bloc. He also established economic links, but not formal diplomatic relations, with South Africa. For some ten years he remained popular with his compatriots. By 1970, however, internal rivalries were dividing his party, the economy was getting worse, and opposition was rising against his pro-Western stance, his dealings with South Africa, and his concessions to France.

Public discontent with Tsiranana broke into the open in 1971. Government's use of force against riots in the south provoked university and secondary students around the capital to organize a strike in May 1972.

A Maoist political movement had a hand in this development. Rioting erupted. Unemployed youth joined in the action. At least thirty people died. Thereupon the president handed over full powers to the commander of the army, General Ramantsoa.[6]

Ramantsoa tended to be apolitical, but his regime began to encounter new troubles late in 1974. On February 5, 1975, he handed over power to his Minister of Internal Affairs, Lieutenant Colonel Richard Ratsimandrava. Six days later Ratsimandrava was assassinated. A Military Directory, composed of officers in the security forces, then assumed control. Its most influential member was Ramantsoa's Foreign Minister, Lieutenant Commander Didier Ratsiraka. In June, the Directory named him head of state. The electorate ratified the Directory's decision through a referendum held in December.[7]

Didier Ratsiraka was born in 1936. He was a *côtier* and a Roman Catholic. Educated first at the Jesuits' Collège St. Michel in Antananarivo, he went on to the French Naval College in Brest; later he attended the École Supérieure de Guerre. For part of his naval career he served as military attaché at the Malagasy Embassy in Paris. Nothing in his background clearly indicates how his political thinking acquired its Marxist coloration. As Ramantsoa's Foreign Minister he renegotiated Madagascar's cooperation agreements with France. He won the withdrawal of French security forces from the island. He established diplomatic relations with China, the Soviet Union, and other Communist countries, and broke the country's connections with South Africa. He withdrew the country from its membership in the franc zone. He also brought it into the OAU.[8]

While the Directory was still running the country in early 1975, Ratsiraka drafted a program for reform and circulated it "for discussion." It carried weight because the leaders of various groupings sensed the need for such a program and no one else had produced one. Ratsiraka's program became *La Charte de la Révolution Socialiste Malagasy*, the *Red Book* (*Boky Mena*). He published it for the general public in August. Shortly after coming to power he drafted a second document, a new constitution. Later, in 1978, he outlined and established new economic structures in a collection of laws called *La Charte des enterprises socialistes*.[9] The referendum that ratified his election as president also asked the voters whether they approved the *Red Book* and the new constitution. They did so resoundingly. Thereafter, he repeatedly cited this assent as evidence that his regime was doing nothing more than executing the will of the people.[10]

## RATSIRAKA'S PROGRAM

Because Ratsiraka made the *Red Book* an official statement of his program, it provides a starting point for looking at his policies. Its style was direct and uncomplicated but repetitious; its rhetoric was radical. The book's central idea was that in 1975 Madagascar was beginning a new era, a socialist revolution. It was emerging from merely formal independence to real independence. It would become a self-reliant society, a society dedicated to the development of "the whole man and every man," a just society ending the exploitation of man by man, and an egalitarian society where everyone would have a fair share of wealth, of social services, and of cultural opportunities. Its socialism would not follow foreign models, however, but be rooted in the country's own traditional communal ideals and structures.[11]

A key structural feature would be decentralization, ending the tight centralism inherited from the French. The change would entail revitalizing the traditional local community, the *fokonolona*, which would be juridically structured as a *"fokontany."* This community would have responsibility for running its own affairs. All members over eighteen years of age would take part in its deliberations. This community as such, moreover, would have a voice in the next highest level of organization, the *firaisampokontany* (subprefecture), which would in turn have a voice in the *fivondramkontany* (prefecture), and so on. At each level a general assembly would make policy decisions, and an elected executive committee would look after everyday management. The assemblies would receive periodic reports from their respective executive committees and could dismiss the committees at any time. To make sure that a handful of better-educated people would not overwhelm the simple folk in the *fokonolona*, government would promote adult literacy and access to formal education, and would arrange brief training courses at the local level in ideology and the management of village affairs.[12]

Ratsiraka insisted, however, on always maintaining national unity. To this end, the new structures would operate on the principle of "democratic centralism." This principle would allow free discussion of any issue at any given level until a decision was reached by majority vote; then discussion and opposition would cease. Ratsiraka's constitution mandated observance of this principle by the *fokonolona* and the other "territorial collectivities." The decisions of higher echelons would bind lower echelons. But higher echelons would consult lower echelons before making decisions, and would report to the lower ones on their discussions and activities.[13]

The *Red Book*'s socialist economics required nationalization of important industrial and financial enterprises and those involved in international commerce. These enterprises were exploitative; they belonged mostly to foreigners, sometimes associated with local compradore bourgeoisie. Cooperatives would handle internal distribution of commodities. There was need to develop quickly the indigenous cadres to run the newly nationalized institutions. To keep them under control, workers would share in management through structures parallel to the *fokonolona*. The country must aim at early self-sufficiency in basic needs; it would accept foreign aid only if this did not compromise independence.[14]

In the early stages, Madagascar would make agriculture the base and industry the motor for building its autonomous economy. Its abundant agricultural potential would first provide food for its own people and then furnish raw materials for export in order to accumulate capital for developing light and heavy industry. Industry would stimulate other kinds of economic growth when it reached its "take-off" point.[15]

To begin with, an agricultural revolution was needed. The *Red Book*, however, did not call for collectivization; instead, it wanted to promote cooperatives—which fit the country's communitarian traditions. Using cooperatives would avoid cutting lands into parcels too small for economic cultivation, and would make it easier to employ modern agricultural methods. Government could more readily make available seeds, fertilizers, draft animals, machinery, and credit; farmers would not be paying high rentals and interest to rich entrepreneurs. Under a selective land-reform program, government would confiscate the property of absentee landowners or of people who did not take specific measures to protect the soil. It would then distribute this land to the peasants, under certain restrictions. The program did not condemn private property as such; it condemned its abuse. Government would respect private ownership as long as it was not contrary to the revolution's objectives.[16]

The *Red Book* called for the establishment of a new international economic order to ensure Madagascar's economic and financial independence. The government's opening to the Communist countries, the book explained, was partly aimed at diversifying the country's economic relations and lessening its dependence on France and the West.[17]

The rest of the *Red Book* sketched particular political and social initiatives linked with its central ideas. Government would make primary and secondary education universally available. It would multiply schools, especially in rural areas, and offer free tuition. It would adapt the curriculum to Malagasy culture (but it saw the practical value of skill in French language). It would decentralize higher education by setting up new centers for particular disciplines away from Antananarivo.[18] The book called for health services better suited to the people's needs, particularly in the countryside. Government would improve old facilities and build new ones. It would speed up and decentralize the training of medical personnel. It would emphasize preventive medicine.[19] The book also called for improving transport and other elements of infrastructure, for providing houses, and for stimulating employment.[20]

To mobilize manpower for the program, the *Red Book* proposed a system of national revolutionary service. Such service, lasting from twelve to eighteen months, would be compulsory for young people who completed "the cycle of their regular studies." Their work would be mainly civil, although they would receive some military training in the Forces Armées Populaires. The armed services themselves, however, would have a social mission that would include literacy training, technical aid to the *fokonolona*, agricultural extension, rural medical service, and construction of public works and housing.[21]

But more than new structures and procedures were needed; it was necessary to change people's mentality and awaken a new civic spirit. In addition to the new educational system, ideological formation outside the schools would promote this change. The *Red Book* also looked here at the mass media and the need for a policy on "information." The press, radio, and television must educate the public, explain the reasons for the revolution, and inspire the people to join it.[22]

More of Ratsiraka's program was incorporated in his draft constitution. This did not follow the models of East or West. The president was chosen by direct popular election for a seven-year term. The Supreme Revolutionary Council (*Conseil Suprême de la Révolution*, or CSR) was to assist him, as "the guardian of the Malagasy Socialist Revolution." The president named two-thirds of this council's members at his own discretion, and chose the other one-third from a list given him by the National Assembly. The "Government" ran the state's administration under the president's direction. He named the members of the Council of Ministers and presided over their meetings.[23] The National Popular Assembly, elected by universal direct suffrage, was the "supreme delegate of the people's legislative power." Its term was five years. The High Constitutional Court had seven members, two named by the president, two by the CSR, two by the assembly, and one by the government.[24]

The president had extensive executive powers; he also had legislative powers when the assembly was not in session and during a state of emergency. The legislative powers were especially important, because the National Popular Assembly's ordinary sessions could total no more than 120 days a year. But he could use these powers and many executive powers only if the CSR concurred. If he passed an ordinance between sessions, it was effective immediately, but ordinarily he had to ask the next assembly session to ratify it. He could seek the High Constitutional Court's opinion on the constitutionality of any law before he promulgated it; if the court ruled a given clause unconstitutional, he could refrain from promulgating either the offending clause alone or the entire law.[25] In certain circumstances the assembly could vote no confidence in the government. The president then had to appoint a new government. If this failed to win the assembly's confidence, he could dissolve the assembly and order new elections.[26]

The Constitution's Title II, "Fundamental Rights and Duties," listed socioeconomic rights along with classic civil rights, and sometimes echoed socialist catchwords. It provided for "Freedom of expression, press and assembly . . . when these are exercised in accordance with the objectives of the Revolution, the interests of the workers . . . and with a view to strengthening the new democracy for the advent of a socialist state." "No one can be pursued, arrested or detained except . . . according to forms prescribed by law." No one can be punished under a law passed *ex post facto*. "The law guarantees the right of private property, notably for family residence, for useful furnishings . . . and for economic exploitation of . . . an artisinal character." "The workers have the right to participate in the management of enterprises, under conditions fixed by law." But the citizen's exercise of all rights was conditioned on fulfillment of his duties: "No right or freedom can be invoked by a citizen who has not fulfilled his duties toward the collectivity." And "no right can be invoked in order to obstruct the State in its work of instituting a socialist order."[27]

Ratsiraka believed that a pluralist system of political parties was divisive. In his view, a person had to be either for or against the revolution. Those against were enemies of the people, trying to frustrate their will. They therefore had no title to participate in public affairs. People who were for the revolution should not fragment it by setting up partisan organizations; they should unite their efforts.[28] But he perceived strong resistance to his idea, so he settled for less than the single-party system he wanted. In 1975 he banned parties but allowed the old ones to exist as "revolutionary associations." He then formed his own group, AREMA, the Avant-Garde de la Révolution Malgache, and pressured the five others (later they became six) to join a single National Front for the Defense of the Revolution (FNDR) for the election of the National Assembly in 1976. The Front supported a single list of candidates; AREMA won 112 of 137 seats. Four of the other six parties had some kind of Marxist connection. MONIMA, the Mouvement Nationale pour l'Indépendance de Madagascar, was a radical socialist grouping. Vondrona Socialista Monima, which broke off from it in 1978, was Marxist-Leninist. AKFM (a Malagasy acronym for the Parti du Congrès de l'Indépendance de Madagascar) had been formed in 1959 by the pastor of the most fashionable church in Antananarivo. Although it was made up largely of Protestant Merina bourgeoisie, it professed Marxism and was clearly pro-Soviet. MFM (Mouvement pour la Pouvoir, or "pouvoir aux petits,") was on the extreme left and was characterized as "Maoist." Though small, it had a following among the volatile unemployed youth of the capital.[29]

Despite its name, AREMA was not a close-knit, elite, vanguard organization on the Leninist model. It neither was a parallel government, nor claimed to rule in the name of the proletariat. Ratsiraka did not want to turn away the multitudes who believed in what he was trying to do. Nominally, AREMA was structured from the bottom up; each organizational level was elected by the level below. Even though the party did not have a powerful politburo at the top, Ratsiraka dominated it, under cover of democratic centralism.[30]

### IMPLEMENTATION OF RATSIRAKA'S PROGRAM

Such were the theory and structure of Madagascar's revolution. How did it unfold in practice after 1975?

To initiate the new era, Ratsiraka changed the country's name to Democratic Republic of Madagascar. The name was a hairbreadth away from "*People's* Democratic Republic," the style favored by other countries when they opted for a Marxist-Leninist identity.[31] He quickly set up the governmental structures he had envisaged. By mid-1977 he had created the Supreme Revolutionary Council, conducted elections for the National Popular Assembly, established the High Constitutional Court, and brought the *fokonolona* into operation.[32] In 1978 the *Charter for Socialist Enterprises* arranged for worker participation in management. Organizations of the workers in each enterprise elected representatives to deal not only with issues such as compensation, welfare, safety, and discipline but also with such matters as programs of investment, review of accounts, and the application of public policy to some economic sectors.[33]

The new government nationalized banks, insurance companies, shipping firms, the oil refinery, minerals, cinema, and the biggest foreign trading company, the Société Marseillaise de Madagascar. It went ahead with the establishment of agricultural cooperatives, in some cases handing nationalized plantations to peasants so organized. It worked out a development plan running from 1978 to 2000.[34]

But economic performance fell far short of the program's objectives. Productivity expanded marginally at best. Industry, commerce, and mining lacked managerial and technical personnel to replace departed foreigners. Shortfalls in agriculture and restrictions on imports deprived some industries of needed raw materials. Corruption was rife among the local bourgeoisie who were managing these enterprises. Farmers tended to work only for their family interests. Government did not give them persuasive motivation, clear guidance, or adequate training for running cooperatives. Incentives for production were insufficient: official prices for produce were too low; collection of crops for shipment was poorly managed; consumer goods were not reaching the countryside; supplies of seeds and fertilizers were short. Drought and cyclones complicated all the other problems.

Slack activity in industry reduced employment. Low industrial and agricultural output led to scarcity of basic commodities and high prices. Reduced exports diminished receipts of foreign currency. Some of these receipts, moreover, had to be spent for importing the country's staple food, rice. Meanwhile, well-connected people were bringing in badly needed materials and selling them at black-market prices. Foreign debt rose. Madagascar had to seek help from the International Monetary Fund in 1980, 1982, and 1985. The IMF's stringent conditions compelled government to impose even greater austerity on the masses.[35]

The deteriorating economy provoked widespread discontent. People were demoralized. Alcoholism was on the rise. Unemployed youth turned to crime and prostitution, or swelled the ranks of urban drifters. Sporadic rioting occasioned some deaths. Armed bands of thieves, the *daholo*, systematically stole cattle and other livestock from the peasants. They sometimes raided villages and took away crops, money, and other properties. In the opinion of many, well-to-do and influential men controlled and protected the bandits. The gendarmerie did not pursue the bandits very zealously, either because they were in collusion with them or because they believed that the robbers' patrons would frustrate prosecution. Local folk in some areas reacted with vigilantism, punishing even petty thievery with instant death. More generally, however, insecurity drove many peasants from their farms, thus further diminishing agricultural production.[36]

Malagasy society was marked by some social stratification. A Merina aristocracy dated from precolonial times. Modernization under the French gave rise to a kind of bourgeoisie: civil servants, professionals, and businessmen who lived in relative wealth and comfort. Although industry employed too few people to develop an industrial proletariat, the young people streaming into the cities came close to filling this role: jobless, living in poverty and frustration. But the revolution did not inspire class warfare. Government did not prosecute or persecute the aristocracy or the bourgeoisie. Ratsiraka saw a difference between the "compradore bourgeoisie," who were allied with imperialist exploiters, and the "national bourgeoisie," who were victims of colonial exploitation like everybody else. In his view these people were on the side of the masses; they were mainly government functionaries who were not proprietors and did not command large resources. In fact, however, such people became a "new class." They enjoyed generous perquisites and used their influence and inside knowledge to negotiate lucrative deals.[37]

It was not clear whether Ratsiraka decentralized much real power to the *fokonolona*. According to some observers, he tried to impose central planning on the rural economy, and the peasants responded by noncooperation. According to others, he gave the *fokonolona* more responsibility than rural people could manage and thus contributed to agriculture's poor performance.[38]

Neither the government nor AREMA set up any monopolistic youth movement. But the party did maintain centers for instruction in the principles of Marxism-Leninism, and government did attempt some indoctrination. Radio and the press fed the public a steady diet of ideology. School syllabuses, the national youth service, and training programs for the *fokonolona* shared in this task. But the short-term impact was uncertain. According to one young university lecturer who had passed through the system, these efforts had not affected his own outlook very much. He had taken these elements of the various programs as things students had to get through without necessarily accepting them.[39]

The regime tightly controlled radio and the press. Censors once forbade a newspaper to print an extract from the government's own Official Journal, because it made public the possibly inflammatory fact that government had raised the gendarmerie's salaries; they also delayed for three months publication of the Catholic bishops' 1981 pastoral letter. Censors monitored the importation of foreign publications, too. They banned *Jeune Afrique* for years, but admitted the radical *Afrique-Asie*, which even got some of its revenue from running the government's official advertisements.[40]

Although the regime's educational program certainly expanded school enrollments, the quality of education appeared to decline. In one case, according to a critic, twenty of twenty-five teachers staffing a secondary school were only school-leavers doing their national service. Students in government schools were weak in French language even though this was still essential for success in university and for the better jobs. By contrast, private schools, at least Catholic schools, maintained reasonably high standards of instruction. Health care did not improve much, if at all; chronic shortages of drugs and equipment, most of which had to be imported, hampered medical services.[41]

Facing acute financial need, Ratsiraka eased somewhat his hostile stance toward the West. But he continued his warm relations with Communist countries, particularly the Soviet Union, China, and North Korea. Russia was the main supplier of arms, payment for which took a large share of Madagascar's foreign exchange. Russians instructed the army and the navy. Koreans also instructed security forces, most notably a militia called "Youth Awareness," recruited among the unemployed; this was reminiscent of the Korean-trained Youth League in Lesotho and the Fifth Brigade in Zimbabwe. Chinese medical teams staffed some hospitals. The French-owned but quasi-government newspaper, *Madagascar Matin*, gave a good press to these countries' technical-assistance projects. Bookshops in the capital offered attractive and inexpensive books published in the same countries. The shops themselves appeared to be centers for other kinds of contact. These nations, however, did not respond to Madagascar's need for large loans, nor were they among the country's main trading partners.[42]

At various times Ratsiraka announced the discovery of plots against the regime. Detentions and interrogations followed. The plots may have been real or they may have been fictitious—publicized in order to strengthen the president's hand at moments of crisis. A formidable investigative agency, the Direction Générale de l'Information et de la Documentation (DGID), certainly held some detainees for long periods without trial, and allegedly sometimes used torture. But Madagascar seemed freer of such abuse than most dictatorships of the left or the right.[43]

HISTORY AND DEVELOPMENT OF THE CATHOLIC CHURCH IN MADAGASCAR

Before discussing the ways in which the Ratsiraka regime's policies touched the mission of the Catholic Church, we will say something about the Church's history, structure, and work in Madagascar.

Catholic missionary efforts in the sixteenth century failed to establish anything permanent. Anglicans began successful evangelization on the plateau in 1820, and acquired a strong position among the Merina aristocracy. For many years thereafter, the Merina rulers obstructed Catholic missionary activities. These early frictions gave rise to tensions between Catholics and Protestants which lasted until very recent times. Although Catholic evangelization began to take hold in the 1850s, the government's expulsion of French missionaries during the two Franco-Malagasy wars again got in the way.[44]

Nevertheless the Church grew, both on the plateau and among the côtiers. In 1985, it had almost 2.3 million members, 23 percent of the population. Protestants were slightly less numerous, about 3 percent of the people were Muslims, and somewhat more than 50 percent followed traditional religions. The Church had seventeen dioceses and eighteen active bishops, fifteen of whom were Malagasy. Priests numbered nearly 700, of whom 30 percent were indigenous. There were nearly 400 religious brothers and 1,900 sisters.[45]

By 1975, when Ratsiraka came to power, the Church had moved further along the road to maturity than in most African countries. As it grew, its bishops had taken several exceptionally forward-looking initiatives. In 1936, long before national episcopal conferences became common, they began to meet and consult together on matters of island-wide relevance. They began, fairly early, to think about inserting the Church more firmly into local culture. They saw the need to prepare indigenous leadership so that local people could assume management of their own church; the first Malagasy was named bishop in 1939. The bishops also talked about making Catholics familiar with the Church's social doctrine and about promoting social awareness and action among the faithful. They published joint statements. They acted together to apply new pastoral orientations, although follow-up sometimes took many years to become effective.[46] While the Church as such took no part in the nationalist movement, the bishops stated in 1934 that there was such a thing as a "just nationalism." In 1948 and again in 1953, they declared that the Malagasys' desire for independence was legitimate.[47]

The bishops were concerned, in the 1930s, to counter the influence of

Communists, who were then active in France and its colonies through the Confédération Générale du Travail (CGT) and similar agencies. To this end they promoted what could be called "Catholic Action," based on the principles of Christian democracy. They backed the setting up of cooperatives and Christian trade unions, and sponsored sessions for the social formation of lay activists and the clergy. They envisaged, in 1934, the creation of an Action Populaire Malgache to think, train, and act in the social field. This project finally took shape, however, only in 1952, as the Centre Nationale d'Action Sociale, based in the capital but with branches in the dioceses. In addition, they tried to focus the Church's social service activities; for this purpose they established Sécours Catholique Madagascar, which later became Caritas Madagascar–Bureau de Liaison d'Action Sociale et Caritative (CM-BLASC).[48]

For a local election at Antananarivo in 1956, Catholics organized themselves and ran a successful contest against a Marxist-leaning party. The bishops then decided, however, that the Church should not take an active role in party politics—apparently because this event aroused hostility. The colonial government expelled a French missionary who helped organize this electoral effort. It may be added that in 1962 Tsiranana's government expelled another missionary who was involved with Christian trade unions.[49]

## THE STATE AND THE CHURCH'S MISSION

Against this historical background we return to the points at which Ratsiraka's regime touched the Church's mission. The *Red Book*'s socialism did not imply hostility to religion. In fact, the book listed "freedom of religion" among the "socialist principles on which the state was founded." "Religions are ideological imports," it said, "but we accept them if they are not contrary to the objectives of the revolution, but are contributing to the moral development of society. The fact is that the Malagasy people's fundamental values are founded in a certain primacy of the spiritual. For us, development and economic growth are not ends in themselves; they are at the service of the social and cultural progress of the Malagasy man." The constitution listed as a fundamental right "freedom of religion. . . . Cults may organize and function freely in conformity to law." This was not the classic phrasing of Communist constitutions, guaranteeing the "freedom to believe or not believe."[50]

According to informed observers, Ratsiraka remained a Catholic. He seemed unaware, however, that recent documents of the Holy See and the Malagasy bishops heavily emphasized social justice and humanistic values and that one of these documents provided his own thematic phrase: "development of the whole man and of every man." He told a journalist in 1977: "We confront a paradoxical situation, where the Christian religion rejects socialism." He then asked: "Isn't socialism the very foundation of the Christian religion?" "If religion consists in saying that the exploitation of man by man must cease, that people should enjoy at least a minimum standard of living, that they have dignity, that they can build a human and fraternal society, then I don't see how religion would be against the objectives of socialism." He could conceive of a Christian's being a militant for "our" socialism. If one used an arbitrary kind of definition, Ratsiraka would call himself a monotheistic Marxist, a believing Marxist.[51]

There were almost no frictions between Madagascar's socialist government and the Catholic Church concerning the Church's religious or social functions. Government did not interfere with worship, evangelization, religious instruction, baptism, the employment of foreign missionaries, the recruitment of indigenous priests and religious, the organization of lay movements and societies, or the operation of medical services. There was a problem, however, touching the Church's role in education.

Actually, this problem dated back to colonial days. The Christian churches conducted all the island's schools until 1896. Then the "school question," linked with French anticlericalism at the turn of the century, spilled over into the colony. Secularists insisted that only state-supported, religiously neutral schools be permitted to function—the so-called *école unique*. Believers, chiefly Catholic, wanted to operate schools in which they could teach and foster their own religion. They wanted government to recognize and subsidize these schools—the *"école libre."* In practice, parallel school systems came into being: one secularized, tuition-free, government-supported; the other with a religious identity, financed by student fees, and tolerated by government. The colonial governor introduced state schools to Madagascar in 1896; his successor, in 1905, extended France's Combes Law to the colony. Enrollments in state schools then rose; those in Church schools fell but remained substantial. On the issue of government recognition, the Church schools entered a kind of limbo, where they remained for decades.[52]

The *Red Book* said two things that touched private schools: the revolution aimed ultimately at free schooling for everybody; and the whole nation would take charge of education. These, however, were long-term objectives. In the meantime, government would assist and control private schools and would define their place in an educational system directed toward building a socialist society. The second statement seemed to open the possibility of government's giving official recognition to private schools.[53]

In 1976 the Minister of Education, a Catholic, organized a seminar as a step toward preparing a statute for private education, but nothing more was done until 1977. Meanwhile, officials in the education service were urging rural communities to open state schools even where church schools were already operating. They argued that private schools were undemocratic, exploited the poor by charging fees, and should be suppressed or left to die. Poor rural children were transferring from the Church schools, thus forcing many of these to close. At about the same time, the ministry was arranging short refresher courses for teachers; the officials who ran these often attacked religion, believers, and denominational education. Concerned Catholics wondered who and what was behind these developments, whether the regime approved them or whether radical politicians and bureaucrats were pursuing them as personal projects.[54]

A commission for reorganizing the school system met for several weeks in December 1977. Its agenda included the question of a statute for private schools. But a mere four of its sixty members represented private education. Only on the night of its final session did the commission take up the issue of a statute—and then solely because the private-school representatives insisted. The commission concluded by accepting the principle of such a statute only until the state took over all education.[55]

The government finally promulgated a statute for private schools in July 1979. This provided that such schools be integrated into the national system. It thus assured a place for them. To protect against profiteering by private entrepreneurs, it established professional qualifications and prescribed the formalities for opening schools and getting authorization to teach. Although the statute did not end all possibility of friction, it held much less potential for harm than the earlier situation. Informed Malagasy Catholics saw the statute as promising a better future for their schools.[56] At the national bishops' meeting in 1984, a commission reported that children were returning to the Church's primary schools because they had met with negative experiences in state schools. And Cardinal Razafimihatrata reported an encouraging statement by the prime minister; he had called together the heads of the Christian churches to say, among other things, that the government was counting on the education and formation that the churches were giving.[57]

Two Church initiatives related to the schools began before Ratsiraka took power. First, Catholic parents in the diocese of Fianarantsoa set up an association to assume responsibility for all the schools in the diocese. The parents volunteered when the bishop said, in 1972, that he could no longer finance the schools. The system included a secondary school, St. Francis Xavier College, and primary schools which enrolled thirty thousand pupils and were staffed by eight hundred teachers. A committee of parents, teachers, and one diocesan representative was in charge of each school. The association looked after finance, administration, and curriculum. Although teachers received less pay than in government schools, they stayed because they found their work rewarding. Parents willingly paid fees both because they were ensuring a religious formation for their children and because the children were performing better on examinations than pupils in public schools. Parents also distrusted the marxizing tendencies in the public system. While they did not reject socialism, they wanted it to have a Christian perspective. They therefore arranged annual training sessions to refresh teachers' understanding of Catholic educational ideals and Catholic social doctrine. Other dioceses had similar but less powerful organizations.[58]

A second initiative related to the educational curriculum. In 1974, before Ratsiraka's revolution, the Ministry of Education developed a secondary-school social science syllabus with a strongly radical bias. For example, under the heading of "America in Crisis," the syllabus presented teachers of history and geography with readings on the Pentagon and the American System; Economy and Militarization; Stagnation and Recession; Detroit, Capital of Unemployment; Ten Million Secondary Students on Drugs; and Harlem and the Cancer of America. To restore balance to teaching this material, a competent Catholic scholar with the pseudonym "Hugues Indrianala" published a series of quality textbooks that covered the syllabus more objectively. His books neither condemned nor lauded capitalist societies or the revolutionary societies of China, Cuba, and Vietnam. They did point out, but more temperately than Western critics, such failings of the Soviet Union as economic weakness and civic repression. These books won wide acceptance in the schools.[59]

## THE CHURCH'S RESPONSE TO MARXIZING TENDENCIES

Apart from the question of schools, the revolutionary government's Marxist tendencies touched the Church only in general and indirect ways. The Church was concerned, however, that stronger Marxist influences might lead to serious confrontation. Partly for this reason and partly because positive social engagement was an element of its own mission, it became more active in promoting social teaching and social action. It was also concerned that the regime's failures were making life more difficult for citizens. The bishops and other articulate Catholics, therefore, often faulted particular decisions, developments, and tendencies as unjust and harmful. Their comments sometimes struck sensitive political nerves. We will look, therefore, at various elements of the Church's response: bishops' initiatives, the use of organization, and particular undertakings of clergy, religious, and activist laity.

The Malagasy Church had advantages in approaching its task. It had earlier developed an active bishops' conference. It had already begun to promote social action based on the Church's social doctrine. It had recognized quite early the validity of the nationalist claim to independence. It had elevated local clergy to the episcopate. It had seen the need for relating faith to culture and had promoted research aimed at inculturating its pastoral work. By the 1970s, moreover, documents of Pope John XXIII, Pope Paul VI, Vatican II, and the Synod on Justice in the World updated social teaching and linked it more closely with gospel values. They also offered a better understanding of contemporary social problems and possible solutions.[60]

The bishops voiced their response to Malagasy socialism most fully in a series of their conference's documents. Although they published some of these before Ratsiraka took office, these early pieces treated the social role of Christians comprehensively, and so furnished a foundation for later statements; they referred to Marxism because it was already in the atmosphere. While Tsiranana was still in power, the bishops issued a pastoral letter entitled "The Church and Development in Madagascar." This appeared on March 25, 1972, the fifth anniversary of Paul VI's *Progressio Populorum*. On December 7 of the same year, at the end of their regular meeting, they published a second letter, dealing with the situation that arose from Tsiranana's fall. Addressed to Catholics, this proposed to answer the questions: "What do the bishops think of the events the country is living through? . . . What do they think of the many difficulties that confront us at this moment?" On December 25, 1973, they put out a third letter, which was a promised follow-up on their first; it was called "The Church and Politics."[61]

A National Synod which included lay representatives met in October 1975, after Ratsiraka had published his *Red Book*. Following the Synod, the bishops issued a document that summarized and approved that meeting's conclusions. In November 1977, after their own annual assembly, they put out a "declaration" to the faithful. After a National Meeting of Priests in October 1978, they formally approved orientations, some of them social, which the meeting had developed. In July 1980, Cardinal Razafimahatrata issued a letter of his own, "The Engagement of the Christian in the Life of the Nation," reflecting on twenty years of independence. Finally, at the conclusion of their meeting in November 1981, the bishops wrote a letter entitled "The Conduct of the Christian in Public Life."[62] As the bishops turned out this series of pronouncements, the number of Malagasys among them grew from six of sixteen in March 1972 to fifteen of eighteen in October 1978.

A review of these documents' main lines will suffice for our purposes. The bishops agreed that Madagascar in the 1970s should assert its independence more effectively than it had in the 1960s. Such independence related to politics, economics, and culture. The country should work out its own kinds of institutions, suitable to its own traditions. The aim should, indeed, be the development of "the whole man and every man." Men, however, needed one another; no man could become fully human except through the help he gave and received in society. Truly human development, too, implied growth in spirit as well as in mind and body.

The Church was obliged to promote this kind of development. God's dealing with the Israelites was an archetype of "liberation." Jesus' mission, too, was liberation: from the oppressions men inflict on one another and from the egoism and sinfulness lying behind oppression and social disorder. The Church had to witness to this mission—through its members and through their work for development. Social and political participation was an obligation of Christians; it was even a kind of vocation, a response to a call for men to cooperate with God. The Church's preaching of charity was mere babbling unless Catholics worked for justice and the common good. In all this activity, however, the growth of persons was primary; economic and political progress were only means, not ends; they were subordinate to personal growth. Special concerns in human development were respect for man's dignity as God's image, assurance of basic human rights, and just distribution of society's tangible and intangible benefits. The Church, in fact, should examine its own conscience to discover and correct injustices in its dioceses, parishes, schools, and other institutions.[63]

The laity, primarily, should participate directly in material development. The clergy should support them, mostly by helping them apply gospel values to the work at hand. There was no room for clericalism; the clergy should not give orders or directives; they should encourage the laity to take up their own proper responsibilities. The clergy should not, moreover, become directly involved in politics. If unusual circumstances seemed to require this, they should first consult the presbyterium of their respective diocese to get their bishop's approval.[64]

The Church had no prescriptions for social structures or processes, proposed no ideology, and could endorse no political party. It offered only general principles, based on revelation and its traditional teachings. In 1972 the bishops had taken their position on political parties and on the clergy's staying out of politics, and they held to this consistently. But they also pointed out that politics necessarily affected the Church's work at some points, such as education, and that the Church should then try to protect its own interests.[65]

The pastoral of March 1972 dealt rather extensively with the linkage between "liberation" and socioeconomic development; the commentary on the priests' meeting did so more briefly. The bishops did not give "liberation" the directly political connotation it had in Latin America. They told of God's liberating activities among the Israelites. They recalled that Jesus liberated more fully and that, following him, we had to liberate our brethren. The impact of his redemptive mission, however, was interior; it touched our hearts and gave us our internal freedom, freedom from the egoism that was at the root of social disorder. Once we ourselves were freed, we could participate fully in freeing other people from the alienations imposed by unjust social structures. In this task we were to *remain* free, as Jesus was. We were not to be co-opted by partisans of the right or left. Spiritual liberation, as the bishops saw it, moved Christians to work for liberation in the temporal order, but did not determine the line of action they should take. The bishops said nothing about liberation's being linked with social analysis, and they undertook no critique of social structures on the Marxist pattern.[66]

Virtually all the bishops' documents, when they looked at what had to be done, called attention to the major failings and shortcomings of Malagasy society—a catalogue that did not change very much. Unemployment was rising, joblessness was driving young people into alcoholism, drug abuse, crime, and prostitution. Shortages of basic commodities and inflated prices imposed hardship on the poor. Incompetent administration in government and business was partly behind the economic stagnation. The use of position and influence for personal enrichment made this situation worse. Corruption filtered downward, as subordinates took their lead from superiors, using whatever means they could to benefit themselves. There was a form of "moral underdevelopment." Brigandage in the countryside threatened the livelihood of the rural poor and drove them away from their farms. People were becoming demoralized and indifferent. Government had lost its credibility by manipulating public information. It had muzzled criticism and freedom of expression. Freedom, it was true, brought risks for government, but wise policy would show more confidence in the people.[67]

The bishops almost never faulted Marxism directly. Malagasys are skilled, however, at making points by indirection. The cardinal, for example, in his 1980 letter, queried the "excessive submission [*inféodation*] to new ideologies which lead the people and even officials to lay all our evils at the door of imperialism-colonialism or of anyone else but themselves." His use of the word *inféodation* echoed ironically Marxists' use of "feudalist" as a derogatory epithet. He commended Ratsiraka's policy of openness in all directions, but then went on: "After five years of experience, however, some people express the fear that this policy is leading only toward a new domination over the country and a new dependence." He observed later that the Malagasy values that were so prized in the 1970s had now disappeared from view, and then he asked: "Does someone want to take from us what makes us Malagasy in order to replace it with a certain internationalist philosophy without spiritual values, without national values, and without traditions?" He thus reminded readers that imperialism could come from East as well as West and that this kind of imperialism threatened the values closest to the nation's heart.[68]

With reference to the Church's sacral mission, the bishops' only comments concerned the hostility of some officials to religion itself, and questions about the schools. Their 1977 letter protested "surreptitious efforts to undermine . . . the dimensions of man that transcend the economic and political. They attempt to smother all religious belief in people's consciousness." "Fishers in troubled waters" were employing "all kinds of maneuvers to paralyze confessional schools and finally to make all religious education impossible." The bishops then related their critique to the basic philosophy of the revolution itself. True, Christians must work for economic and social liberation. But "to build the revolution on the principle that man is an end in himself, the only artisan and moving force of his own history, is to prepare the way for . . . totalitarianism which will sacrifice the human person to the myth of Collective Progress." "We reject every kind of revolution which tries to truncate man's truth, dignity or divine sonship." "Marxism, under whatever form it presents itself, winds up by making man no more than a machine for collective production."[69]

The bishops' general stance toward the revolution, then, was one of openness but caution. An interviewer in Rome sought the cardinal's reaction shortly after Ratsiraka was installed and his *Red Book* accepted as the revolution's official charter. The charter, the cardinal replied, had no official interpretation, so politicians could read it their own way. The hierarchy considered its socialism acceptable; it was humanistic; it respected persons and individual freedom. While the situation held dangers, and those in responsible positions had to be watchful, it also offered people a share in building the nation; it was an invitation for the Church to play a role through the action of the faithful. Christians should take the opportunity offered them.[70]

The danger the cardinal cited lay in the ambiguous ideology of the charter. It did reflect some Marxist-Leninist ideas, though they were not very well integrated; it used Marxist catchphrases. Danger lay, too, in the presence of some openly Marxist politicians in government, people who would try to make their own interpretations effective in running public affairs. There was also danger in the country's openness to agitation by the many personnel from Communist powers. For these reasons the bishops were wary, made complaints, and voiced warnings. But they were not reasons for rejecting the revolution itself. The bishops aimed not at countering a Marxist revolution but at making a non-Marxist interpretation of the revolution prevail, offsetting attempts to make it aggressively hostile to religious belief and practice.

If few Catholics actually read the bishops' letters, most heard about them from priests and other community leaders. Political elites, even if they were unfriendly, were attentive. The AKFM's party newspapers reacted bitterly to the 1977 letter. One of them charged that it was against the constitution's prohibition of counterrevolution and that the authors should lose their rights as citizens. Governments had fallen after bishops' letters in 1972 and 1975, and some people half expected the same thing to happen after the cardinal's 1980 letter. The letter surely reminded the president, who was a shrewd balancer of political forces, that the country had a large and alert Catholic constituency.[71]

Catholics other than the bishops were also responding to Marxist currents in Madagascar. At a general level, there were the National Synod and the National Priests' Meeting. These considered, among other things, the roles of laity and clergy in social development and political life. Although formation in Catholic social doctrine had been going on for decades, these meetings underscored its need and gave it new impetus. Layfolk and clergy should know not just the fact that the Church was against Marxism; they should also know why. They should know, too, why and how the Church was backing the struggle for social justice. Clergy competent in the social sciences were urged to share their knowledge with their confreres and the faithful. The bishops mandated the Justice and Peace Commission to look into injustice and social conflict, to explain social issues, and to prepare a program of instruction. Layfolk established a Centre d'Études, de Documentation et d'Information sur le Développement (CEDID), to analyze the country's development, conduct sociological surveys which would help toward pastoral planning, assist in the social formation of Catholics, and train leaders for social development. At a considerably later juncture, Fr. Sylvain Urfer established a similar but better-equipped institution in Antananarivo. Called Foi et Justice, it had its own large collection of books on social development, along with facilities both for study and for conferences.[72] The national seminary taught social doctrine as part of both moral theology and ethics. Many sisters' congregations treated this as part of religious formation. Seminarians and young sisters were intensely concerned for social justice. The bishops approved the engagement of religious in the affairs of the local *fokonolona*.[73]

The movement toward social formation, however, fell short in some sectors. Earlier links with the trade unions were not maintained. Contact was tenuous with Catholic young people caught in the flood-tide of urban migration. In the university at Antananarivo, the chaplain worked well with the students he could reach but had difficulty making others aware even of his presence; the chaplaincy center was small and not easily accessible to students. At Fianarantsoa enrollments were smaller, the center attracted students as a congenial place for studying and socializing, and the chaplain could more easily reach them in a pastoral way.[74]

Several publications offered instructive material. Some study groups used Fr. Louis Rasolo's pamphlet, "Finoana sy Fivoraran-karena" (Faith and Development), which reviewed general social principles, sketched current social philosophies, and related all this to the *Red Book*.[75] A bimonthly (later quarterly) for the clergy, *Aspects du christianisme à Madagascar (ACM)*, often treated social issues. Some of its pieces were quite sophisticated. Relying on *Octogesimo Anno*, the authors were open to socialism and avoided anti-Marxist polemics, but cautioned against naïveté in dealing with Marxists.[76] The editors presented a convenient, schematic

"Manuel de doctrine sociale" in 1982.[77] The weekly *Lakroan'i Madagasikara*, usually called simply *Lakroa*, carried a regular column, "Coin d'Elèves." One contributor, Fr. Emil Takidy, published a series of these columns as a textbook for upper secondary or university classes, *Introduction à la philosophie politique*.[78]

*Lakroa* itself offered social formation at a popular level. This was a national newspaper sponsored by the bishops' conference. It ran four to eight pages, partly in Malagasy and partly in French. Its circulation was about twenty thousand. Reportedly, many non-Catholics read it because they trusted it more than the government-controlled press. Typical issues carried official statements of the bishops, news of local and universal churches, reports of secular events, regular columns and features, book reviews and editorials. *Lakroa* often criticized domestic social situations, usually by indirection. It countered Marxist propaganda circulating in other media. For example, it pointed out the imperialist thrust of the Communist powers the government was courting. It faulted the Soviet invasion of Afghanistan. It corrected the standard Soviet version of Russian and Western involvement in World War II, and explained the Soviet Union's oppressive postwar activity in Eastern Europe. It reviewed a Russian dissident's book on the workings of *Nomenklatura*, dealing with the maintenance of the USSR's bureaucratic "new class." It explained how Mao's rigid ideology blocked development in China. But it also explained how international (First World) banking practices were devastating the Third World.[79]

A second popular publication was the monthly *Isika Miankavy* (We as a Family). It was sponsored by FTMTK, the Young Christian Farmers, and had a circulation of twenty-one thousand. Written in Malagasy, it treated farming, animal husbandry, civic training, and Christian formation, and it reinforced a skeptical outlook on the Malagasy scene which was typical of FTMTK's members.[80]

Editing these two newspapers took special skill because the law forbade criticism of government, and the state closely controlled the media. Editors had to submit their copy for censors' approval. When newspapers appeared with blank spaces, readers knew that censors had killed a story, but if a paper went to press three times with blanks, government could suspend its publication entirely for six months. Editors therefore had to voice their criticisms deftly.[81]

Government radio stations allowed the churches time for religious broadcasting, but censorship operated here also, so the work was delicate; broadcasters had to submit their scripts twenty-four hours in advance. A

Catholic priest associated with *Lakroa* did use this opportunity to give a Catholic social viewpoint and for correcting opposing views and insinuations.[82]

Several Catholic lay organizations contributed substantially to positive social action. Such was the FTMTK (Malagasy initials), which sponsored *Isika Mandavy*. This organization was linked with the international Mouvement de la Jeunesse Agricole et Rurale Catholique (MIJARC). In 1982 its members numbered about twenty-five thousand in the age bracket of sixteen to thirty-five. It aimed at the development of rural life in the perspective of faith, but it dealt also with agricultural and management techniques and home economics. Its triennial national assembly laid down lines of action on which the members would focus their efforts; the programs from 1972 onward all called for promoting the country's development. At the regular local meetings, members began with reflection on their everyday problems and led to considerations of faith. Their frequent discussion of concrete realities gave them a solid grasp of principles inspired by the gospel and a hardheaded practicality. Their experience also made them skeptical of ideology and authority; politicians and bureaucrats found it hard to mislead them.[83]

At least one priest tried to infuse the concepts of "small Christian communities" into the *fokonolona*. But while the bishops and religious superiors encouraged priests, brothers, and sisters to participate actively in the affairs of this institution, they paid little attention to the "small Christian community" idea—which could have provided a vital structure for continuing pastoral ministries if ever a hardline Marxism came to prevail.[84]

## THE CHURCH'S SOCIAL ACTION

Fulfillment of the Church's mission entailed promoting social action as well as social thought. From its early years, the Church in Madagascar provided various services, notably health care: clinics, hospitals, and leprosaria. Looking toward organization of such ministries, an appendix in the bishops' 1972 pastoral listed norms for undertaking social projects. Among other things, planning should enlist the participation of local people without regard for their church affiliation; projects should be modest in scale and should fit with government plans; their financing should include a local contribution. To facilitate the Church's coordination of projects, they should pass through the diocesan pastoral council and through BLASC.[85]

In 1982 some local observers believed that the state's involvement in development tended to limit the scope of voluntary agencies' activities.[86] Nevertheless, Catholic medical services operated as in the past. FTMTK was both animating rural life and giving technical assistance. Some missionaries and lay volunteers conducted specialized training projects. One of these was the Centre Artisinale de Promotion Rurale (CAPR) at Fianarantsoa. Here, in a large but ramshackle workshop, young men received three years of training in carpentry, iron work, and masonry. In a nearby residential compound they also cultivated a garden to provide much of their own food. While training, each young man *made* a complete set of tools for himself which he took with him when he returned home. The trainees thus went away with a capacity for financial independence and with useful skills for their local community. They could earn a living as artisans and, at the same time, work their own farms.[87] Similar but simpler programs were conducted elsewhere. Some of these aimed at preparing *moniteurs* who could teach their skills to apprentices later on.[88] An overseas Catholic agency conducted a nutritional program for forty thousand preschool children and health education for their mothers.[89]

CM-BLASC was the national coordinator of the Church's developmental activities. Its mandate was to raise the social consciousness of Catholics and to form and inform them; to animate, assist, coordinate, and follow projects; and to ensure dialogue with funding agencies and government. BLASC tried to get local communities involved in planning projects and gave them technical advice, helped design projects, evaluated proposals, and prepared these for submission to sponsors. Many projects were directed at improvement of local infrastructure, such as water supply, bridges on rural roads, community centers, and facilities for clinics. The "Caritas" section of the agency provided help in disasters such as drought and flood, and made funds available to Catholic agencies for everyday charitable needs.[90]

The Church's social concern showed some ecumenical linkage. In 1980 the Church joined the mainline Protestant churches in the Christian Council of Churches in Madagascar (FFKM). Given the long history of Catholic–Protestant tension, this was an historic step, opening the way for readier cooperation. The council's member churches issued a joint statement in April 1982 in which they criticized many aspects of the country's social situation, similar to criticisms leveled by the Catholic bishops.[91]

Later, in fact, the Church's membership in the FFKM involved the bishops in an activist political role about which some Catholics had mis-givings. When serious political unrest came to a head in 1991, threaten-ing Ratsiraka's tenure as president, the FFKM began by mediating between his government and the *forces vives* that opposed him, and ended by giving the latter the powerful support that led to his defeat in 1993.[92]

## ENCOUNTER AS CATALYST

The Malagasy Church's encounter with Marxism in the 1970s and 1980s did not effect a jump start toward maturity as in some sense it had for the Church in Mozambique. Instead, the encounter effected a nudge forward in a process that was already well under way. By 1975, when Ratsiraka's policies made Marxism an issue, the Church in Madagascar had moved further beyond the status of "missionary church" than most of the local churches in sub-Saharan Africa.

Even though it still needed personnel and financial help from abroad, its episcopal leadership was Malagasy and it had a substantial nucleus of indigenous priests and religious. It had already taken steps, too, toward inculturation, notably in its catechesis. Significant numbers of layfolk carried their religious motivation into the domain of temporal affairs, and were willing to accept burdensome responsibilities in so doing. Insti-tutions for social development such as the parents' association in Fian-rantsoa, FTMTK, CAPR, and BLASC were already operating. The editorial staffs of *Lakroa*, *Isika*, and *ACM* were turning out intelligent, instructive, and informative publications well suited to their respective readers, even though their circulation was much smaller than one could hope. As early as the 1930s, the missionary bishops, in response to the Marxist tendencies of the French Left, had undertaken to foster a lively social awareness among Catholics. Their successors, caught up in the new wave of social concern stimulated by Vatican II, had continued this tradition in their pastoral letters of 1972 and 1973.

The effect of the encounter with the Marxist leanings of Ratsiraka's regime might be seen as roughly analogous to that of a chemical catalyst: it gave some impetus to the maturing of the Church, but did not itself enter into this reaction—at least not very intimately. In considerable part this was because Ratsiraka's theories, as set forth in the *Red Book*, in-clined more toward eclectic social democracy than toward systematic, orthodox Marxism-Leninism, and they were not hostile to religion or the Church. The absence of a vanguard party on the Leninist model further diminished anxiety. Some uneasiness could arise, however, from three features of Ratsiraka's constitution: its concentration of power in the office of president, its insistence on democratic centralism, and the justification this provided for repressing dissidence. The large presence of technical assistants from Marxist countries could also be worrisome. Most troubling of all was the evidence which surfaced, especially in connection with education, of a more hostile Marxism among unidentified bureaucrats. While the bishops were cautious, therefore, about Ratsiraka's policies and programs, they were not antagonistic to his socialism: They simply tried to make sure it would not be officially interpreted in a Marxist sense. Apart from any concern about Marxism, one other aspect of Ratsiraka's revolution troubled the bishops: the fact that it was ineffective and even counterproductive in bringing the benefits of development to the people at large.

Government policy toward the schools was the only issue on which there was a semblance of confrontation between the Church and the regime. And here, while Marxist sympathies appeared to be at work among some Education Ministry personnel, the hostility the Church encountered did not spring exclusively from Marxist leanings; it had roots also in the anticlericalism that was part of the French colonial heritage. And in any case the ultimate approval of a statute for the *écoles libres* of voluntary agencies was a small victory for the Church.

The encounter with Marxism, then, nudged the Malagasy Church mainly by intensifying its interest in fostering a knowledgeable social concern among Catholics. This interest had some influence on the agenda of the National Synod and the National Meeting of Priests, both of which, in turn, gave new stimulus to cooperation among and between laity and clergy. The encounter also gave some orientation to the Church's social concern. Thus the bishops' letters after 1975, the National Synod, and the National Meeting of Priests all took account of marxizing political tendencies in a nonpolemical way, and, at the same time, stressed the urgency of laboring positively for the social equity that was the proclaimed objective of Marxism's promoters. Organizations like FTMTK and the parents' association directed some specific programs to issues raised by Marxist sympathizers, and numerous contributions to the Catholic press aimed at correcting standard distortions of Marxist propaganda.

None of this is to suggest, however, that the Church in Madagascar could be complacent about the fulfillment of its mission. The work of any local church is never done. Its response to Marxism did little to advance the sacral dimensions of its mission. The infiltration of Western secularism threatened religious perspectives as seriously as Marxism ever had done. The Church still needed to bring home the moral urgency of social obligation to some strategically situated Catholics who seemed not to be listening—for example, those members of the "new class" who were profiteering at the expense of the nation.[93] It needed also to make sure that social awareness became not a transitory preoccupation but a permanent part of the Catholic mindset among clergy and laity alike, if only because Madagascar's struggle for development and social justice would clearly continue for a long time to come.

## NOTES

1. The figures for ethnic distribution and urban dwellers are from "Madagascar," *Africa South of the Sahara 1988* (London: Europa Publications, 1987), p. 621. This source will henceforth be cited as " 'Madagascar,' *Africa South 1988*."

2. See ibid., pp. 616–19.

3. See ibid., p. 610; Hubert Jules Deschamps, "Madagascar, History of," *Encyclopaedia Britannica*, 15th ed., 1974, Macropaedia, 11:278–79.

4. See Mervyn Brown, *Madagascar Rediscovered: A History from Early Times to Independence* (Hamden, Conn.: Archon Books, 1979), pp. 259–60, 268, 270–71; "Madagascar," *Africa South 1988*, p. 610.

5. See Brown, *Madagascar Rediscovered*, pp. 260–62, 265, 270–71.

6. See ibid., pp. 270–71; Robert Archer, *Madagascar depuis 1972: La marche d'une révolution* (Paris: Éditions Harmattan, n.d.), pp. 54–57; "Madagascar," *Africa South 1988*, p. 611.

7. See Archer, *Madagascar Rediscovered*, pp. 95–101, 132; "Madagascar," *Africa South 1988*, pp. 611–12; Simon Malley, "À coeur ouvert avec Didier Ratsiraka," *Afrique-Asie*, No. 151 (December 26, 1977–January 7, 1978), 31–32.

8. See Archer, *Madagascar depuis 1972*, pp. 74–75, 84–90, 125–26; "Madagascar," *Africa South 1988*, pp. 611, 614.

9. *La charte de la révolution socialiste malgache tous les azimuts, 26 août 1975* (Tananarive: Imprimerie d'Ouvrages Éducatifs, 1975) (henceforth cited as *Red Book*). Repoblika Demokratika Malagasy, *Lalampanorenana* (Antananarivo: Transoprintim Pirenena, 1979) (henceforth cited as "Constitution"). Repoblika Demokratika Malagasy, *Charte des enterprises socialistes* (Antananarivo: Imprimerie Nationale, 1979) (henceforth cited as *Enterprises*).

10. See Archer, *Madagascar depuis 1972*, pp. 138, 151; Malley, "À coeur ouvert," 32.

11. See *Red Book*, pp. 9, 11, 13, 15, 17, 26–27; Malley, "À coeur ouvert," 32–33.

12. See *Red Book*, pp. 15–16, 18, 29–36, 71–73, 103; Malley, "À coeur ouvert," 32.

13. See *Red Book*, pp. 34–36; Constitution, article 102.

14. See *Red Book*, pp. 26, 48–50, 52–53, 61–62, 67–70, 97.

15. See ibid., pp. 50–54, 62–63.

16. See ibid., pp. 38, 55–60.

17. See ibid., pp. 24–26.

18. See ibid., pp. 71–82.

19. See ibid., pp. 91–92, 94–95.

20. See ibid., pp. 98–101.

21. See ibid., pp. 24–26.

22. See ibid., pp. 9, 47–48, 71–73, 81–85, 88.

23. See Constitution, articles 46–47, 49, 55, 58, 60–61.

24. See ibid., articles 65, 67–89.

25. See ibid., articles 53–54, 56, 62, 64, 69, 74–75, 77, 81–82, 92–93, 95.

26. See ibid., articles 78, 80.

27. See ibid., articles 12–18, 22–31, 37–42.

28. See Malley, "À coeur ouvert," 34–35.

29. See "Madagascar," *Africa South 1988*, pp. 612, 626; Archer, *Madagascar depuis 1972*, pp. 43–44, 57, 123n1, 192–99; Maureen Covell, *Madagascar: Politics, Economics and Society* (London: Frances Pinter, 1987), pp. 60–62, 104–106; Malley, "À coeur ouvert," 34.

30. See Covell, *Madagascar*, pp. 119–22; Malley, "À coeur ouvert," 34–35.

31. See Archer, *Madagascar depuis 1972*, p. 159.

32. See Malley, "À coeur ouvert," 32.

33. See *Enterprises*, passim. This volume contains several laws, ordinances, decrees, and related documents. The most comprehensive is "Ordonnance 78–106," pp. 11-35. "Decree 78–134," pp. 51–59, deals with the Council of Orientation; "Decree 78–135," pp. 61–68, with the Management Committees; "Decree 78–136," pp. 69–92, with the participation of workers; and "Decree 78–137," with labor disputes.

34. See "Madagascar," *Africa South 1988*, pp. 612, 619; Archer, *Madagascar depuis 1972*, p. 158; "Nos espoirs déçus: La situation actuelle de Madagascar par un malgache," *Chine-Madagascar* [Lille], No. 181 (February–March 1981), 14.

35. See Covell, *Madagascar*, pp. 63–69; "Madagascar," *Africa South 1988*, pp. 612, 616, 619–20; "Nos espoirs déçus," 14-16; "Madagascar à l'heure de la auto-critique," *Chine-Madagascar* [Lille], No. 183 (June–July 1981), 20–21; René-Claude Andriamaja, "Lettre ouverte aux députés malgaches," *Chine-Maduré-Madagascar* (Lille), No. 201 (February–March 1985), 14–16; Rasediniarivo, "Billet malgache: Securité, revitaillement, et justice," ibid., No. 202 (April–May 1985), 16; Felix Rabemora, "Dix années de socialisme à Madagascar," ibid., No. 204 (September-November 1985), 16 (this is Part 1 of a two-part series).

36. See "Madagascar," *Africa South 1988*, p. 613; "Nos espoirs déçus," 15; "Madagascar à l'heure," 20; Rasediniarivo, "Billet malgache," 16-17; Rasediniarivo, "Chronique hebdomadaire: Cas typique de zones enclavés," *Lakroan'i Madagasikari* (Antananarivo), December 13, 1981, p. 1 (henceforth cited as *Lakroa*);

André Rasolo, *L'Expérience socialiste à Madagascar* (Thesis for the third cycle, University of Aix-en-Province, Marseilles, 1978), p. 228.

37. See Archer, *Madagascar depuis 1972*, pp. 17–19, 137; *Red Book*, pp. 65–66; Malley, "À coeur ouvert," 34–35; Rabemora, "Dix années de socialisme à Madagascar," Part 2, *Chine-Maduré-Madagascar*, No. 205 (December 1985–January 1986), 16; interview with Fr. Rémy Ralibera, of *Lakroa*'s editorial staff, May 1982.

38. See "Madagascar," *Africa South 1988*, pp. 613, 616; Archer, *Madagascar depuis 1972*, pp. 140–141, 143–147.

39. See Covell, *Madagascar*, p. 121; Rabemora, "Dix années de socialisme," Part 2, 15; Rasediniarivo, "L'école catholique à Madagascar aujourd'hui," *Maduré-Madagascar* (Paris), No. 168 (July 1978), 339–40; interviews with Fr. Ralibera; with Fr. Michel Razafindrabe, Catholic chaplain at the National University of Antananarivo, May 10, 1982; and with two confidential informants, May 1982.

40. See "Nos espoirs déçus," 16; Rabemora, "Dix années de socialisme," Part 2, 15–16.

41. The statistics in "Madagascar," *Africa South 1988*, p. 624, are only for 1984, and they are very incomplete. See "Madagascar à l'heure," 20; "Nos espoirs déçus," 15; Rabemora, "Dix années de socialisme," Part 2, 14–15; interview with confidential informant, May 1982.

42. See "Madagascar," *Africa South 1988*, pp. 614–15; "Madagascar à l'heure," 20; Rabemora, "Dix années de socialisme," Part 2, 16. See also "Madagascar Kills 20 in a Sect," *The New York Times*, August 3, 1985, p. 3; Judy Kimble, "The Lesotho Coup," *West Africa*, February 3, 1986, p. 235. In *Madagascar Matin* (Antananrivo) see: "La R.D.M. s'associe à la joie des coréens" who were celebrating Kim Il Sung's seventieth birthday, April 15, 1982, p. 1; "Lénine et son rôle dans l'édification du socialisme," April 23, 1982, p. 1; "Livres soviètiques remis par Ambassadeur Moussatov à la BN," April 26, 1982, p. 3; "Les nouveaux médicins chinois acceuillis par des vivats à Manitsy," April 28, 1982, p. 1; "La R.D.M. décore plusieurs coréens (techniciens et pilotes)," May 4, 1982, p. 1.

43. See "Madagascar," *Africa South 1988*, pp. 612–13; Rabemora, "Dix années de socialisme," Part 2, 17; Covell, *Madegascar*, pp. 71, 131. Interview with Fr. Ralibera; with Fr. René-Claude Andriamihaja, a member of *Lakroa*'s editorial staff, May 1982; with a confidential informant, May 1982. The interviewees agreed that there were not many political prisoners.

44. See Jesuit Conference on Africa and Madagascar, *JECAM 1976: Jesuit Response to the Challenge of Mission in Africa and Madagascar Today* (Washington, D.C.: Jesuit Missions, 1976), pp. 35–36. "Madagascar," *Africa South 1988*, p. 610.

45. See *Catholic Almanac 1988* (Huntington, Ind.: Our Sunday Visitor Publishing Division, 1987), p. 351; "Madagascar," *Africa South 1988*, p. 626; "The Church and Christians in Madagascar Today," *Pro Mundi Vita Dossiers*, Africa Dossier 6 (July–August 1978), 3; "Rencontre nationale des prêtres" Part 2, *As-*

*pects du christianisme à Madagascar*, 17 (September–October 1979), 144. This journal will henceforth be cited as *"ACM"* (until 1972, it was entitled *Ami du clergé malgache*).

46. See Jean Marie Aubert, "L'église catholique dans le nord de Madagascar: Inculturation et structures pastorales," *ACM* n.s. 1 (July-September 1985), 118–22, 127; Joseph Greco, *Vingt-cinq ans de pastoral missionaire: recueil des principales ordonnances et directives pastorales des réunions des évêques de Madagascar (1931–1957) et quelques décisions de Saint Siège* (Issy les Molineaux: Imprimerie St. Paul, 1958), 12, 179-186, 201; Marc Spindler, "Évolution de la théologie à Madagascar," *ACM* 19 (September–December 1984), 341.

47. Some Catholics, priests and laity, were among the early nationalists; see Brown, *Madagascar Rediscovered*, pp. 259–60; see also "Church and Christians," 32; Conférence Épiscopale de Madagascar, *L'Église et le développement à Madagascar*, Pastoral letter, March 26, 1972 [Fianarantsoa: Imprimerie St. Paul, 1972], paragraph 60; Pierre Lupo, *L'Église et décolonisation à Madagascar* (Fianarantsoa: Librarie Ambozontany, 1974), pp. 47–48, 53, 60, 66.

48. See Aubert, "L'église catholique," 119-22; Victor Sartre, *"Rerum Novarum* et les syndicalistes chrétiens à Madagascar," *ACM*, n.s. 4 (October–December 1991), 174–75; *Rapport générale sur CM-BLASC*, Antananarivo, May 17, 1992, pp. 1-2, mimeographed.

49. See "Church and Christians," 33; Sartre, *"Rerum Novarum* et les syndicalistes chrétiens," 178.

50. See *Red Book*, pp. 19, 37–38; Constitution, article 39.

51. Interview with Fr. Andriamihaja; see also Malley, "À coeur ouvert," 33. The phrase "the whole man and every man" appears almost verbatim in Pope Paul VI's *On the Development of Peoples* [encyclical letter *Progressio Populorum*," March 26, 1967] (Boston: Daughters of St. Paul Editions, n.d.), paragraphs 14 and 42.

52. See Rémy Ralibera, "L'enseignement privé à Madagascar a désormais son statut," *Chine-Madagascar*, No. 174 (October 1979), 13-14.

53. See *Red Book*, p. 75.

54. See Rasediniarivo, "L'école catholique à Madagascar aujourd'hui," 339–41; "Ou va l'enseignement à Madagascar," *Chine-Madagascar*, No. 169 (October 1978), 17–19.

55. See "Ou va l'enseignement," 19.

56. See Ralibera, "L'enseignement privé," 15.

57. See "Assemblée Plénière 1984," *ACM* 19 (September–December 1984), 325–26.

58. Interview with a member of the parents' association, Fianarantsoa, May 15, 1982. See also "Church and Christians," 19.

59. See the series *Civilisation du monde contemporain. Série histoire-géographie-instruction* (Papagile de la Grande Île, 1975). This was published by BEP-OTEP (Bureau d'études des programmes—Organ technique d'élaboration des pro-

grammes). See Hugues Indrianala, *Civilisation des pays du tiers monde*. I. *Présentation générale et approche critique* (1979). II. *Algérie* (1979). III. *Madagascar* (1980). IV. *Vietnam* (1980). *Civilisation des pays socialistes*. I. *Fondements historiques et idéologiques* (1980). II. *Union Soviètique* (1979). III. *Chine* (1979). IV. *Cuba* (1979). *Civilisation des pays capitalistes*. II. *États-unis d'Amérique*. (1982). III. *Japon* (1982). These were all published at Fianarantsoa by the Librarie Ambozontany. See also the same author's *Le socialisme à l'épreuve du sous-développement* (Fianarantsoa: Librarie Ambozontany, 1981).

60. See Aubert, "L'église catholique," 115, 118–119; Spindler, "Évolution de la théologie à Madagascar," 341.

61. See Conférence Épiscopale de Madagascar, *L'église et la développement à Madagascar*; "Lettre des évêques de Madagascar à tous les catholiques de l'île," *ACM*, 14 (January–February 1973), 18–26; Conférence Épiscopale de Madagascar, *Lettre des évêques de Madagascar sur l'église et la politique*, Pastoral letter, December 15, 1973 [Tananarive: Imprimerie Catholique, 1974].

62. See "Synode nationale de l'église à Madagascar," *ACM*, 16 (January–February 1976), 209–37. "Déclaration des évêques de Madagascar," November 23, 1977, *Maduré-Madagascar*, No. 167 (April 1978), 289–91. "Rencontre national des prêtres," October 7-15, 1978, *ACM* 17 (July–August 1979 and September–October 1979), 105–25, 129–65. Cardinal Victor Razafimhatrata. "L'engagement chrétien dans la vie du pays," *Chine-Madagascar*, No. 179 (October–November 1980), 13–18. "Déclaration des évêques de Madagascar aux chrétiens de leur église et à tous les hommes de bonne volunté," November 22, 1981, *Lakroa*, February 14, 1982, pp. 2–3.

63. See *L'église et développement*, paragraphs 3, 10–11, 13, 15–19, 21–22, 26–29, 34, 42–44, 48–50, 52–55, 63; *L'église et la politique*, paragraphs 21–22, 27–31, 38–39, 44, 55–56, 60, 64, 66–67; "Synode national," paragraph 17; "Rencontre des prêtres" (first part), paragraphs 11–12, (second part), paragraph 15.2; Razafimahatrata, "L'engagement," 15–16; "Déclaration des évêques," November 22, 1981, p. 2.

64. See *L'église et développement*, paragraphs 53–54, 56–57, 59–60; *L'église et la politique*, paragraphs 20–22, 27–31, 34, 41, 45–52; "Rencontre des prêtres" (first part), paragraphs 13–14, (second part), paragraphs 13.5, 14.

65. See *L'église et développement*, paragraphs 42, 58; *L'église et la politique*, paragraphs 35–36, 38, 40–42, 45–53; "Rencontre des prêtres," (second part), paragraph 14.

66. See *L'église et développement*, paragraphs 42–48; "Rencontre des prêtres," (first part), paragraph 11; Raymond Saint Jean, "Problèmes et perspectives de synode national," *ACM*, 15 (September–October 1976), 351–52.

67. See *L'église et développement*, paragraphs 11, 25–26, 31, 38–39, 49; *L'église et la politique*, paragraphs 54–57, 66; "Déclaration des évêques," November 23, 1977, 290–91; Razafimahatrata, "L'engagement," pp. 14-15; "Déclaration des évêques," November 22, 1983, p. 2.

68. See Razafimahatrata, "L'engagement," 14-17.

69. See "Déclaration des évêques," November 23, 1977, 291.

70. See "Church and Christians," 9.

71. See "Remous autour d'une lettre," *Maduré-Madagascar*, No. 169 (September 1978), 353–354; "Nos espoirs déçus," 16.

72. See "Le Centre 'Foi et Justice,'" *Chine-Maduré-Madagascar*, No. 223 (June-August 1989), 20.

73. See "Assemblée plénière de la conférerence épiscopale de Madagascar, nov. 19–27, 1974," *ACM*, 15 (January–February 1975), 14–15; "Synode national," 215–32; "Rencontre des prêtres" (first part), 108; (second part), 157–58; "Church and Christians," 23; interview with Fr. Louis Rasolo, rector of the Jesuit scholasticate, May 1982.

74. See "Church and Christians," 33; interviews with Fr. Razafindrabe; with Fr. Giustino Bethaz, chaplain of the University students at Fianarantsoa, May 1982.

75. See Louis Rasolo, *Finoana sy Fivoaran-Karena* (Fianarantsoa: Transoprinty Masindary Paoly, 1979).

76. See, for example, "Synode national de l'église de Madagascar," (compterendu), *ACM*, 16 (March–April 1976), 247, 254–56; M. Sales, "Praxis marxiste et discernement chrêtien," *ACM*, 17 (November-December 1979), 165–83.

77. See "Manuel de doctrine sociale de l'église," *ACM*, 18 (March–April 1982), 225–257, and (May–June 1982), 257–89.

78. See Émil Takidy, *Introduction à la philosophie politique* (Antananarivo: FOFIPA, 1980), mimeographed.

79. See, for example, the following items in *Lakroa*: (On domestic affairs), Belanto, "Jongle ou tentation anarchique," December 13, 1981, pp. 3–4. "Quelques réflexions après le discours du Président Ratsiraka en 10 janviei," January 17, 1982, p. 5. "Du bon usage des structures," March 21, 1982, p. 3. Rasediniarivo, "Toamasina II: Cas typique vécu réel des paysans malgaches aujourd'hui," (suite) April 18, 1982, pp. 5–6. (On foreign relations), Aimé Ravelimana, "Afghanistan: Zanatany Sovietika," March 14, 1982, p. 4; also April 18, 1982, p. 3. Aimé Ravelimana, "L'histoire nous interpelle," May 9, 1982, pp. 5–6; also May 16, 1982, pp. 5–6. "Et si cela arrivait pour l'île Sakhaline," May 9, 1982, p. 5. Jerasina, "Dernier chance pour socialisme," December 13, 1981, p. 4. Jerasina, "Aspects du socialisme dans l'Europe de l'Est," March 21, 1982, p. 3. "Il ne faut trafiquer histoire," May 16, 1982, p. 5; "Le coin des élèves" (about Mao), February 7, 1982, p. 3. About *Lakroa* itself, see Rémy Ralibera, "Madagascar 1986," *Chine-Maduré-Madagascar*, No. 209 (September–November 1986), 16–17; René-Claude Andriamihaja, "Avec les jésuites malgaches rédacteurs de LAKROA," *Chine-Maduré-Madagascar*, No. 213 (June–August 1987), 17–18; "Prêtre et journaliste à Fianarantsoa: Une interview du Père René-Claude Andriamihaja," *Chine-Maduré-Madagascar*, No. 227 (April–May 1990), 12–14.

80. Interview with Fr. Pierre Allain, promoter of MIJARC in Madagascar, May 1982. See "Church and Christians," 21.

81. See "Nos espoirs déçus," 16; Ralibera, "Madagascar 1986," 16; Andriami-haja, "Avec les jésuites malgaches," 18; Covell, *Madagascar*, p. 132; interview with Fr. Pierre Girard, responsible for the coverage of Madadgascar on Vatican Radio, March 1982.

82. Interview with Fr. Ralibera.

83. Interview with Fr. Allain. See "Church and Christians," 16–17.

84. See Yves Pleyber, "La force des pauvres en terre malgache," *ACM* 18 (November-December 1981), 168–71; "Problèmes psycho-pédagogiques," *Lakroa*, January 10, 1982, p. 5; "Assemblée plénière, nov. 19–27, 1974," 14–15.

85. See *L'église et développement*, 61–64.

86. Interview with confidential informant, May 1982.

87. Author's personal observation of CAPR, May 1982.

88. See, for example, Rasediniarivo, "Chronique hebdomedaire: Cas typique des zones enclavés," *Lakroa*, December 13, 1981, p. 1.

89. See Catholic Relief Services of the United States Catholic Conference, "Rapport annuel d'activités. Année 1981. République démocratique de Mada-gascar," passim, mimeographed. Interview with Fr. Roger Bisson, director of Catholic Relief Services in Madagascar, May 1982.

90. See *Rapport général sur CM-BLASC*, pp. 5–6, 17–26; "À baton rompue: Avec le Père Watine, aumonier régional de Caritas," *Lakroa*, February 7, 1982, pp. 2–3.

91. See "Inauguration of Christian Council of Churches of Madagascar," *International Fides Press Service*, February 23, 1980, pp. NE113–114; "Message du Conseil Chrêtien des Eglises de Madagascar," *Documentation catholique*, 79 (September 5–19, 1982), 836–38; the message was issued on April 11, 1982.

92. Pieces in successive issues of *Chine-Maduré-Madagascar* relate the main steps of the process that led to the ratification of a new constitution and to new elections for the presidency—which Ratsiraka lost; several of these contributions highlight FFKM's involvement in the process. See Adolphe Razafintsalama, "À Madagascar: La FFKM, Conseil des Églises, réunit les forces vives de la nation," *Chine-Maduré-Madagascar*, No. 230 (December 1990–January 1991), 13–15; idem, "Sous l'égide du F.F.K.M.: Les conséquences du Forum National," ibid., No. 238 (June–August 1992), 12–14; "À Madagascar: Chronique d'une révolu-tion," ibid., no. 234 (September–November 1991), 13–15; "À Madagascar: Après six mois de crise," ibid., no. 235 (December 1991–January 1992), 15; "À Mada-gascar: En attendant le référendum," ibid., No. 236 (February–March 1992), 19–20; "À Madagascar: Vers le référendum," ibid., No. 237 (April–May 1992), 15; "Nouvelles de Madagascar: Du référendum aux élections," ibid, No. 239 (September–October 1992), 23; Diogène Dumortier, "Madagascar au bord de la guerre civile: Une élection présidentielle laborieuse," ibid., No. 240 (December 1992–January 1993), 23; "Nouvelles de Madagascar," ibid., No. 242 (April–May 1992), 28; "Les élections législatives du 16 juin 93," ibid., No. 243 (June–August 1993), 17. For the misgivings of some Catholics, see "Assemblée plénière ordi-

naire de la Conférence Épiscopale de Madagascar, 6–14 novembre 1991," *ACM*, n.s. 4 (April–June 1992), 274–75, text of an intervention presented to the bishops by lay members of the Comité National d'Observation des Élections et de l'Éducation des Citoyens; "Considérations sur les evénements en cours à Madagascar," ibid., n.s. 4 (October–December 1992), 379–81.

93. In fact, later pastoral letters of the bishops' conference especially urged Christian decision-makers at high and intermediate levels of government and private enterprise to act in accordance with God's design for secular society. See "Le pouvoir au service de la société," April 21, 1985, *Documentation catholique*, 82 (August 4, 1985), paragraphs 3, 17; "Le redressement de la nation," November 29, 1987, ibid., 85 (May 1, 1988), paragraphs 5, 21, 26, 27, 30, 34.

# 7

# Marxism and the Church
# in Zimbabwe

UNLIKE MOZAMBIQUE'S AND MADAGASCAR'S, Zimbabwe's colonial background was British. And here Marxism was only one of several major social issues the Church had to confront.

### GEOGRAPHICAL AND HISTORICAL BACKGROUND

Zimbabwe is situated in south-central Africa. It is landlocked, bordered by Botswana, Namibia, Zambia, Mozambique, and South Africa. It lies mostly on a plateau, above 2,700 feet, but some of it is lower, especially in the basins of the Zambezi and Limpopo rivers. Its moderate climate attracted European settlers. About 20 percent of its land is suitable for commercial farming, while 60 percent is suitable at best for raising livestock. Rainfall is unreliable and drought is frequent. It has a variety of workable minerals, chiefly for industrial uses. Coal, along with water power from the Kariba Dam, furnishes ample energy. No petroleum has yet been discovered.[1]

Its population in 1987 was 8.6 million, of whom more than 95 percent were indigenous. These included several language groups. The largest of these, the Shona (or Mashona), outnumbered the second largest, the Ndebele (or Matabele), by four to one. The population at independence counted 223,000 people of European descent, many of them with South African connections, and 37,000 Asians and "Coloureds." Many Europeans subsequently emigrated, leaving only 100,000 in 1984.[2]

Zimbabwe's colonial history began in 1890 when Cecil Rhodes, holding a royal charter for his British South Africa Company (BSAC), moved northward from South Africa seeking gold. European settlers followed, but farming replaced mining as their main occupation. The territory was named Rhodesia in 1895. The BSAC's regime ended in 1922 when Great Britain granted the settlers a constitution as a largely self-governing crown colony.

There grew up a racially stratified society dominated by the whites. Legislation reserved specific tracts of land for the two races. The whites' land was more productive than the blacks' and proportionately more extensive. Laws and regulations protected white commercial interests against any black competition. Government provided more and better social services for whites. Blacks worked mainly on commercial farms and in mines or as domestic servants. Racial segregation was almost total.

World War II brought prosperity to the Rhodesian economy as demand for primary exports rose. Local industries, even in iron and steel, were established. The white population almost doubled between 1946 and 1958. In the view of several white political leaders, the expanding economy would need more skilled and reliable black labor and even a black middle class. They therefore took small steps to make conditions better for the black community. They improved schools, cleared the way for black apprenticeships in skilled trades, recognized trade unionism among blacks, and promoted black commercial farming. They also gave blacks the right to vote on a special electoral roll, and, in 1961, allowed limited black membership in the legislature.[3]

## RHODESIAN FRONT RULE AND THE UNILATERAL DECLARATION OF INDEPENDENCE

Such "liberal" policies made many whites fearful of "appeasement." In this atmosphere the hardline Rhodesian Front (RF) won the 1962 elections, and two years later Ian Smith became prime minister. His party then held absolute control of the legislature until the liberation struggle ended in 1980. The RF quickly moved to stem a rising tide of nationalism among blacks. It took measures to control the media, to stiffen penalties for "subversive" activities, and to authorize arbitrary detention of potential troublemakers. Smith dissolved nationalist organizations and detained or restricted virtually all their leaders.[4]

Because whites worried that the British government might attach conditions favoring blacks to ultimate decolonization, the RF in the 1962 elections urged that Rhodesia become independent of the "mother country" and master of its own fate. In subsequent negotiations, the RF would not accept Britain's insistence that black majority rule would be installed at some indefinite future date. In November 1965, therefore,

Smith announced the country's Unilateral Declaration of Independence (UDI).[5] He then struggled, vainly, for the next fifteen years to win British and international acceptance of his decision. He struggled also to perpetuate the subjugation of blacks which the declaration implied. From 1966 onward he faced armed resistance from the blacks.

## NATIONALIST STRUGGLE FOR LIBERATION

Rhodes had ruthlessly repressed Shona and Ndebele rebellions in 1896–1897, but in the 1920s a succession of new nationalist movements took shape among the blacks. While the settlers were quick to label these "communist," Marxism had no substantial influence among them. British and South African Communists had no success in infiltrating workers' organizations. Few if any blacks who enrolled in foreign universities became Marxist converts. Initially, moreover, the nationalists did not call for violent revolution. They wanted the peaceful establishment of equity: political participation, fair wages and land apportionment, educational opportunity, and decent living conditions. They sought these objectives within the existing system by petition, peaceful protest, and negotiation.[6]

Their attitude changed in the 1960s. In the face of government's refusal to make concessions, its imposition of more serious discrimination, and its tightening of security against dissent, black resentment grew. The nationalists became convinced that they could no longer work by peaceful means within Rhodesia's system. They still believed, however, that they could persuade the "mother country," Great Britain, to ensure the equity the white settlers were refusing.[7]

The nationalists began sporadic armed resistance in 1966. In 1972 this became well-organized guerrilla war, from bases in Mozambique and Zambia, and it continued for the next seven years. The war hit rural areas the hardest. The lives and property of white farmers became insecure. Guerrillas commandeered food and medicine from rural blacks; government forces herded many of these into "protected villages"; both sides intimidated them to prevent their helping the "enemy." Schools and health stations were closed down. Country roads became unsafe. Rural black folk fled to massive shanty towns in the cities or to refugee camps in Zambia and Mozambique.[8]

Meanwhile, factionalism was dividing the nationalists. For practical purposes two main organizations emerged: the Zimbabwe People's Union (ZAPU), headed by Joshua Nkomo, and the Zimbabwe African National Union (ZANU), headed by Robert Mugabe. Each group had

MARXISM AND THE CHURCH IN ZIMBABWE 145

its own guerrilla forces, the Zimbabwe People's Revolutionary Army (ZIPRA) and the Zimbabwe African National Liberation Army (ZANLA), respectively. But pressure from neighboring African countries compelled Nkomo and Mugabe in 1976 to form an alliance, the Patriotic Front, which held together until the end of the war. Mugabe, however, in order to preserve his own movement's identity, retained his organization's name with only the slightest modification: "ZANU(PF)."[9]

After numerous vain efforts to reach a settlement, proposals made at the 1979 Commonwealth meeting finally led Britain to convene a constitutional conference, involving Smith, Nkomo, and Mugabe, at Lancaster House in London. Negotiations dealt with a new constitution, with provisions for British aid to the country, and with arrangements for transition. The settlement provided for immediate black majority rule. Elections took place in February 1980 under British supervision. Britain then granted Rhodesia its independence as Zimbabwe. The new government took over in April.[10]

The constitution provided for a parliamentary system of government. A president was head of state, but his functions were largely ceremonial. The head of government was the prime minister. The legislature consisted of a Senate and a House of Assembly, with the latter holding dominant power. To protect the position of the white minority during a transitional period, a special "roll" of white voters would elect twenty assemblymen and (indirectly) ten senators. Even though British election officials obstructed Mugabe's campaign, his party won 63 percent of the vote and fifty-seven of the eighty unreserved seats in the Assembly, an absolute majority. ZAPU took 24 percent of the votes and twenty-nine seats, almost all from Ndebele areas. The election thus consolidated a division of the major parties along tribal lines, a situation that gave rise to serious problems in the years that followed. Ian Smith's RF, now renamed the Republican Front, won all twenty white seats.[11]

## ZANU's Marxist Leanings

Marxism emerged as an issue in Zimbabwe almost entirely because Mugabe and ZANU began leaning toward this ideology during the war and continued to do so after they came to power.

Robert Mugabe was born in 1924. He finished ten years of schooling with the Catholic mission. He then began teaching and at the same time completed secondary education and some private university study. He next took a degree at the University of Fort Hare in South Africa, and taught for four years in Rhodesia and four more in Ghana. Returning home in 1960 he became active in politics. He first held office in ZAPU, but then joined Ndabiningi Sithole in setting up ZANU. Smith's government detained him from 1964 to 1974; during his imprisonment, he earned two more degrees by correspondence from the University of London. A fellow teacher at Gwelo first sparked his interest in Marxism, and he read Marx's *Capital* and Engels's *Condition of the Working Class in England*. His experience in Nkrumah's Ghana made the ideology more appealing. He apparently began to think of himself as a Marxist during his detention.[12]

Shortly after Smith released him, he joined ZANU's leaders in Mozambique and became the organization's president in 1976. China, then countering Russia's backing for ZAPU, was helping ZANU with arms, training, and advice; Mozambique's FRELIMO was likewise supporting ZANU and influencing its strategy and ideology. Thus, while ZANLA was waging its war against Smith, it also began to indoctrinate Rhodesia's rural blacks with Maoist slogans.[13] ZANU's first congress in 1964 committed the party to a vague "socialism." The Central Committee, meeting under Mugabe's leadership in 1977, changed the commitment to "Marxism-Leninism," without making this more specific. Mugabe did say, in an interview at Maputo in 1978: "We can never apply Marxist-Leninist principles in the same way as they have been applied in the Soviet Union or in China or even here in Mozambique. These principles as we apply them must take into account our own local situations, our history and our traditions so that we end up with a system that is in accord with the inspirations of our own people." As the war approached its end, therefore, ZANU's choice of Marxism-Leninism was explicit but general. Later statements by ZANU and Mugabe would develop the party's ideology more fully.[14]

ZANU's 1980 election manifesto did not mention Marxism at all. It did refer to the party's "humanitarian philosophy" and spoke about a socialist economy in which "each and everyone works for others as he also works for himself." Mugabe often explained that nature has placed the world's natural resources under the dominion of all men together. "Our concept of socialism thus recognizes this phenomenon of collective ownership of the country's resources." These were to be used by everybody. This way of looking at things fitted African traditions. An earlier statement of the party's land policy relied on the same principle: "Land-hunger was one of the main objectives of the freedom struggle." "ZANU would dismantle white farms" in favor of a "new socialist arrangement." Peasants would be able to use the land through cooperatives.[15]

ZANU's 1984 congress was more explicitly Marxist. It declared that the party aimed at reconstructing the national economy "to assure the victory of socialism over capitalism"; it would establish a "socialist state . . . based on Marxist-Leninist principles but firmly based on our own experience . . . under the Vanguard Leadership of the workers, peasants and intellectuals."[16] In accordance with Mugabe's point about the ownership of nature's bounty, the party intended to "abolish capitalism," at least in the long run. Mugabe criticized capitalism because, among other things, it encouraged individualism and selfishness. Socialism would promote mutual concern, helpfulness, and sharing. The party would nationalize industrial, commercial, and agricultural enterprises, and bring them under control as parastatals or collectives or in some other way. Meanwhile, it would give the workers an increasing share in management and profits.[17]

Equality among men (and women) was another basic principle for Mugabe. ZANU would end division by class, race, and tribe. It would therefore end Rhodesia's longstanding racial discrimination in hospitals and schools. It would expand educational facilities for the black population. Academically superior schools which catered to whites would have to admit blacks. ZANU would also foster literacy among black adults who had had little or no schooling in their youth.[18]

Another ZANU leader, the Reverend Canaan Banana, linked the idea of mutual concern with humanism "which gives a central place to man, ensuring his welfare, happiness and independence." He recalled, as one might expect of a clergyman, that the *koinonia* of early Christianity was a "fellowship of equality and brotherhood" expressed in the sharing of goods; it was a "kind of classless collectivism, as opposed to capitalistic divisionism."[19]

To reshape society in accordance with the socialist vision, ZANU would become a vanguard party. Democratic centralism would control its internal functioning. Ultimately it would become the only party in the country.[20]

Not all these ideas were peculiar to followers of Marx, and Mugabe's acceptance of them did not necessarily make him an orthodox Marxist. At the very beginning of his regime, in fact, he clearly held other views on at least two points. Despite the party's declaration, he did not intend to nationalize private enterprise at any early date or perhaps ever. He reminded journalists several times during 1980 that Zimbabwe had inherited a system of private enterprise and he would not begin by taking it apart; he would use it as a base for a new society and would see what changes he would make in the course of time. "I don't think you will ever get a situation where everything belongs to the state." ZANU's election manifesto, moreover, did not envisage massive expropriation of land. Its government would, indeed, acquire land from the private sector for peasants with no land or poor land. But this would be "unused land or abandoned land, underutilized land or land used by absentee owners." Private agriculture would continue but would be restricted to efficient farmers.[21]

## ZANU's POLICIES AND PROGRAMS

As we look at how Mugabe's regime applied the party's principles, we can begin with the party's own organization. The 1984 congress adopted a new constitution that structured ZANU along classic Marxist-Leninist lines. The People's Congress held supreme authority but met only once every seven years. The Central Committee, with ninety members, ran the party in the meantime. The Political Bureau was the administrative organ of the Central Committee, and supervised governmental agencies through five Standing Committees. A congress resolution declared that "democratic centralism shall be the fundamental tenet in the internal functioning and administration of the party." Other resolutions likewise had a Marxist-Leninist sound: "It is now necessary for order, peace and good government that the supremacy of ZANU(PF) be asserted and that henceforth the policies of the Party shall be implemented by all without equivocation." "It is the settled . . . will of the people and their Party to bring about a one-party state in the fulness of time and in accordance with the policies and programmes of the Party." "To deepen . . . the ideological consciousness of the Party and to further fulfill its vanguard status a Chitepo College of Marxism shall be established and . . . run jointly by the State and the Party." Membership in the party would henceforth be more selective; candidates would have to complete a course in party ideology. Despite these provisions, however, ZANU remained a mass movement for mobilizing the electorate.[22]

A striking feature of Mugabe's initial conduct as prime minister was his effort at reconciliation. He undertook no reprisals against his black rivals or his white wartime enemies—even though he had once threatened criminal prosecution of Ian Smith. He invited Nkomo and three of his ZAPU colleagues to join his cabinet and gave two cabinet posts to whites. He retained General Peter Walls, the former head of the Rhodesian security forces, to supervise the fusion of ZANLA and ZIPRA guerrillas into an integrated Zimbabwean army.[23]

By way of social development, Mugabe's government vastly expanded the school system. It opened new schools, especially in rural areas, increased enrollments, reduced school fees, and accelerated teacher training. Primary school enrollments rose from 819,000 in 1979 to 2,260,000 in 1986; secondary enrollments, from 74,000 to 546,000. Government required private schools to admit at least 60 percent blacks, and it limited school fees in order to keep them within reach of black families. It also promoted adult literacy programs; these enrolled 250,000 people in 1984.[24] Government forbade racial discrimination in the admission of patients to hospitals. It proposed to set up 360 rural health centers within three years. Health care was free for people whose annual income was less than Z$150.[25]

To improve living standards and increase productivity among the black rural population, Mugabe's government began to develop "growth points" in the countryside. These were to have schools, clinics, water supply, electricity, and small industries. The plan was intended to bring more cash to these areas and to slow down urban migration. Government also encouraged agricultural cooperatives. It made credit available for them and for peasant farmers, and provided training and advice on crop cultivation and business management. These programs were implemented slowly, but they showed some success; small farmers' production of some crops in 1985 equalled that of the white commercial farmers.[26]

Mugabe's government was not hasty in working out its economic policies; it issued general guidelines only in February 1981 in a statement entitled *Growth with Equity*. The declared aim was to attain a "society founded on socialist, democratic and egalitarian principles." Past policies had been designed to establish "a sound economy but an inequitable economic order." The policies outlined in the statement were intended to preserve the economy's soundness but to remedy its inequities. Specific aims included promotion of rural development, fairer distribution of land and other resources, indigenous participation in ownership, increased employment opportunities, correction of the racial imbalance in jobs, improvement of infrastructure, expansion of social services for lower-income groups, democratization of the workplace and worker participation in making decisions, and resettlement of ex-combatants and people whom the war had displaced. Other aims were maintenance of a high growth rate (to benefit everyone), a stable balance of payments, self-sufficiency in energy, and conservation of natural resources.[27]

In September 1980, Mugabe's government sponsored an independent study of the economy when it set up a Commission of Inquiry into Incomes, Prices, and Conditions of Service. Headed by economist Roger Riddell, the commission had five white and four black members; two of its members were women. It reached its conclusions unanimously and presented them in June 1981. They touched on income distribution, wage differentials, job evaluation, taxation, land, foreign trade, price controls, housing, transport services, social security, grievance procedures, and trade union education.[28]

Although *Growth with Equity* and the Riddell Report showed serious concern for social justice and the problems of the poor, neither document leaned significantly toward Marxist solutions. The former envisaged the continuance of private enterprise in industry and commerce and welcomed foreign investment, especially investment aimed at increasing exports. Multinationals, however, had to comply with the United Nations Code for Transnational Corporations. In regulating taxes, prices, and repatriation of funds, government would keep in mind that investors had to make reasonable profits. Government itself would hold shares in some ventures.

The government followed the lines of *Growth with Equity* in permitting large white commercial farms to carry on. According to the Lancaster House Agreement, it could acquire land only by purchase, not by expropriation, and ordinarily only from *willing* sellers. While Britain at Lancaster House had vaguely promised help for government to buy land, Mugabe complained that he was not getting enough and threatened to ignore the agreement unless he got more. But government did not confiscate any land which was in actual use, and it repeatedly removed squatters who occupied land illegally.[29]

Government followed the Riddell Report by setting minimum wages for workers. This measure corrected the exploitation of many workers, but it also gave rise to unemployment, as middle-class families pared household staff and farmers reduced the seasonal hiring of local villagers. Government ended racial discrimination in hiring and required employers to arrange programs for upgrading the skills of black workers. To expand job opportunities it curbed overtime work. Employers who wished to reduce staff because of poor business conditions had to obtain government approval.[30] Government took modest steps toward workers' sharing in decisions when it encouraged the formation of committees to let workers take part in solving problems and improving conditions in workplaces, but this created confusion because trade unions thought it interfered with *their* dealing with workers' grievances. The unions, in fact, early confronted Mugabe with a serious crisis. A wave of strikes in the first months of independence slowed the economy just when increased productivity was critical. Government prosecuted union leaders and restricted the right to strike, and in order to ensure labor discipline it pressed the unions to join the newly founded Zimbabwe Confederation of Trade Unions.[31]

Government did not nationalize any commercial or industrial firms. Business people kept asking when the intended transition to socialism was going to take place. Mugabe simply reasserted the general intention without making it more specific.[32]

Although Zimbabwe's economy was fragile, its problems were not as acute as those in most African countries. The regime inherited an unusually balanced economy. The international sanctions imposed on the Smith regime during the war of liberation had actually strengthened some industries as they made up for shortages of imports. Agriculture suffered several years of drought, but commercial farmers survived and remained productive.

ZANU's intention to establish a one-party state had a powerful impact on security and civil rights. Although Mugabe insisted that he would install the one-party regime only if the people backed it, government and party agents seemed to be using coercion to achieve the objective. The government justified its use of force by pointing to real incidents of violence that threatened public peace. Tension between ZANU and ZAPU, Shona and Ndebele, continued. Some whites entertained hopes of ousting Mugabe. South Africa recruited former Rhodesian soldiers into a potential resistance movement for destabilizing Mugabe's government.[33] In 1980 ZANLA and ZIPRA forces, which had been brought together in camps to be fused into a national security force, openly fought each other. In September there were indications that General Walls was involved in plotting a coup d'état, and Mugabe dismissed him. In August 1981 sabotage triggered the explosion of an arms depot near Salisbury. In December a bomb ripped through ZANU headquarters at a time when Mugabe was supposed to be there. In June 1982 gunmen fired at the prime minister's residence. In July sabotage destroyed most of the air force's planes.[34]

Nkomo did not respond to Mugabe's early overtures for merging their parties. Mugabe transferred him from the Ministry of Home Affairs.

This angered Nkomo. Then security forces allegedly found arms hidden on ZAPU properties, and Mugabe dismissed Nkomo from his cabinet. In 1982 government charged two prominent ZIPRA leaders with treason; the court acquitted them; government immediately detained them again. Some ZIPRA veterans deserted the new army and reportedly joined comrades in the bush who had never gone to the camps after Lancaster House. Nkomo was alleged to control these forces. But ordinary bandits with no partisan connections were also at work.[35]

Meanwhile, dramatic incidents of violence were arousing widespread anxiety: highway robberies, raids on settlements, kidnappings, attacks on politicians, intimidation of party supporters, and murders of white farmers. The government responded to the rising disorder by using a special security force with an odd history. Mugabe brought in North Korean instructors in 1981 to train a special-services unit called the Fifth Brigade. When this move aroused suspicion, he explained that he wanted a force with more than military skills, a force trained politically to win the support of civilian populations.[36] Government now focused its attention mainly on the southwest, Matabeleland, Nkomo's stronghold. In early 1983 it sent the Fifth Brigade to suppress the "dissidents." The brigade, according to reports, operated ruthlessly. Deaths were numerous. Many of those killed were clearly not engaged in violence. People disappeared without explanation. Soldiers allegedly raped women and horribly mutilated some victims. Protests against the brigade's activities were voiced at home and abroad. The Lawyers' Committee for Human Rights, based in New York, reported that security forces had killed at least 1,500 people in 1983, carried on with arbitrary detentions and beatings into 1984, and abducted one hundred ZAPU leaders in 1985. The committee concluded that government was carrying on systematic repression of the Ndebeles. An earlier report by Amnesty International had made similar charges. The campaign against dissidents, it seemed clear, entailed repeated and serious violations of human rights.[37]

Curiously, Mugabe apparently believed that the national electorate would show its approval of the one-party state by choosing only ZANU candidates in 1985. He was wrong. ZANU did win 77 percent of the total vote and 63 percent of the seats on the "common roll." Despite all the contrary pressure, however, ZAPU retained fifteen seats, including all those in Matabeleland. And Smith's supporters won fifteen of the twenty "white" seats. Mugabe ended the whites' roll by constitutional amendment in 1987. Another amendment replaced the country's parliamentary system with a presidential structure, and Mugabe became president. The same year, after lengthy "on and off" negotiations, he finally persuaded Nkomo to merge ZAPU with ZANU and to accept a *de facto* one-party state.[38]

Mugabe's foreign policy was nonaligned. He established diplomatic relations with Eastern and Western countries. He delayed opening relations with the Soviet Union, however, because the Russians had backed ZAPU and not ZANU during the war of liberation. He remained on generally good terms with Britain and the United States, although particular incidents sometimes occasioned friction with both. The government made a major plea for foreign aid at the Zimbabwe Conference on Reconstruction and Development (ZIMCORD), held at Salisbury in March 1981; the Western powers responded generously. Despite South Africa's provocative conduct, Mugabe maintained an uneasy *modus vivendi* with his southern neighbor, for most of Zimbabwe's exports and imports had to pass through South African ports.[39]

The ZANU government's human rights record, apart from the operations in Matabeleland, was reasonably sound but not unblemished. The government showed respect for judicial independence by the nonpolitical appointment of judges to the Supreme Court, the High Court, and the Review Tribunal—which periodically reviewed cases of preventive detention. Even though government kept extending the Smith regime's highhanded Emergency Powers Act, it also, grudgingly, respected court decisions that restricted the workings of the act.[40] Early on, the government purchased the country's major newspapers from a South African syndicate, and these generally supported government positions. But they also published criticisms of ZANU policies, especially in readers' letters. For the most part, private publishers seemed not to experience serious interference. The government, however, did invoke the Emergency Powers Act during the troubles in Matabeleland and forbade newspapers to publish any details of "anti-terrorist" operations.[41] There were curbs on freedom of assembly, too. Authorities often forbade political rallies on the grounds that these endangered public order. This tactic mostly obstructed ZAPU's political campaigning in ZANU areas in 1985. The "party stalwarts" of both parties often prevented opposition meetings by straightforward physical intimidation as well.[42]

## HISTORY AND DEVELOPMENT OF THE CATHOLIC CHURCH IN ZIMBABWE

Before we examine ZANU's attitude toward the Catholic Church, we will review the Church's background. After several unsuccessful earlier attempts to lay a foundation for the Church, the Jesuits came in 1890, providing ministries for the first group of BSAC settlers. Religious sisters arrived two years later as nurses for this group. Under the company's protection, the missionaries then began to evangelize the native peoples. The company granted them land on which they established Christian villages. Here they gave young people religious training and elementary education, taught them farming and useful mechanical skills, and then allowed them to reside and maintain themselves. Schools and medical services became prime channels for bringing local people into the Church. The government granted modest subsidies for the schooling of Africans. The development of indigenous clergy was slow. The Church opened a major seminary in 1936 and ordained its first black priests in 1947. A congregation of indigenous sisters began in 1922; missionary congregations for women began accepting African members at about the same time.[43]

Meanwhile, the missionaries continued serving the white community, too. Apart from strictly religious ministries, they offered elementary schooling, and in 1896 what came to be St. George's College was opened at Bulawayo; the Dominican sisters established a convent school at Salisbury in the same year. Other sisters expanded medical facilities for white families. The Church's special concern for whites was an inevitable outgrowth of its initial history in Rhodesia.[44]

When Zimbabwe became independent in 1980, the Church comprised five dioceses and one prefecture apostolic. Three of its bishops were Zimbabweans. It was staffed by 323 priests, 102 religious brothers, and 912 sisters. Of these, 63 priests, 16 brothers, and 517 sisters were indigenous. It conducted approximately 50 hospitals and 240 schools at all levels; the schools taught 103,000 pupils. It was by far the largest single Christian church, representing about 37 percent of all Christians. The majority of the country's population, however, were still followers of traditional religions.[45]

## THE CHURCH AND SOCIAL ISSUES

The Church's social engagement was extensive: promotion of agriculture, vocational training, medical care, and elementary education for Africans. Two black laymen organized a Catholic Action Association in the 1930s to mobilize adults for self-help in producing "better homes, better hearts, and better harvests." A religious brother organized a successful credit union movement in the 1960s. Priests and religious sometimes intervened with government to correct particular injustices to blacks. Thus Father Burbridge, parish priest in a township near Salisbury in the 1920s, effectively pressed for better social services including the provision of suitable quarters for married couples and of adequate water supply in the township. He pressed, too, for fair treatment in courts and more humane conditions in prisons. In addition, he criticized the racial bar that ran through the whole society. Unfortunately, however, the closeness of other missionaries to the white community sometimes distorted their view of black-white relations.[46]

Despite the Church's involvement in social activity, it was slow in turning its attention to social theory and social policy. These concerns became more urgent in the 1960s. Nationalism among blacks and the intensified efforts of whites to keep their supremacy evoked the attention of Church leadership. When the Church began to deal with social policy, then, it focused first on questions of interracial and social justice, not on Marxism. The outbreak of warfare later added the questions of violent revolution and peace.

Bishop Lamont of Umtali in 1959 issued a pastoral letter on racial discrimination.[47] This was the first in a series of statements and actions by the bishops on related social questions. Among specific issues were the RF government's laws and regulations which obstructed the Church's freedom in ministering to blacks. Government was requiring special permission to open schools for blacks, and its limitations on the residence of blacks impeded the efforts of Church schools and hospitals to desegregate. The requirement that whites obtain authorization to live in black areas restricted the access of Church personnel to the people they were serving. The bishops protested in published statements and oral negotiations. They cited the Church's God-given freedom to teach and to serve, the immorality of racial discrimination, and the injustice of the economic and social conditions imposed on blacks. Their response in some cases was simply to ignore objectionable laws.

Most of the bishops' letters dealt with wider issues. They based their positions on papal teachings from Leo XIII to Paul VI and on the declarations of Vatican II and postconciliar synods.

*Peace through Justice* in 1961 sharply challenged the racist assumptions on which the RF based the constitutional revision of that year and the pervasive social injustice of the racist system.[48]

*A Plea for Peace* in 1965 condemned the declaration of independence. It protested especially against Ian Smith's claim that the declaration was in defense of Christian civilization. It urged blacks, however, to refrain from violence as this could do even greater damage to the common good.[49]

*A Call to Christians* appeared just before the whites were to vote on approving the 1969 constitution. It criticized clauses that worsened racial discrimination, tightened government control of the media, and made for dictatorship. The constitution's aim was not the common good but the consolidation of one group's privileges at the expense of another. The constitution was completely contrary to Christian teaching and should be rejected.[50]

*Reconciliation in Rhodesia* was issued for the 1974 Holy Year. It included comment on the political implications of reconciliation. The government had to end all its racist policies in order to ensure permanent peace. It had to ensure black political representation, equal job opportunity, land reform, protection of basic rights, and access to integral human development.[51]

The bishops published *The Road to Peace*, a "study document," in 1976. Its purpose was to help priests and people to reflect on the drastic social changes they were experiencing. The document discussed the reasons for Africans' challenge to the social order, their reliance on violence to correct it, and their questioning the relevance of Christianity to their life situation. It enumerated the rights that must be respected in order to establish peace, and pleaded with Christians to shun violence and to create a governmental system embodying justice and love.

In this document the bishops used for the first time some of the social criticism that became current after Vatican II. They gave more attention to how Africans saw their own situation. Africans did not want to be other people's clients; they wanted to be architects of their own development. Some were giving up Christianity because it was used to canonize injustice and was therefore an obstacle to their liberation. Others were asking for answers to their questions: Did not Christian belief require people to engage personally in changing society?

The bishops also introduced the concept of "institutional violence," the state's repressive action in defense of an unjust social order. And despite their plea for peace, they came just short of approving the use of arms against the Smith regime. "It is not possible to impose the obligation of pacifism on everybody." They stated the conditions under which the Church traditionally justified forcible overthrow of unjust governments and concluded: "It is not just for us to judge those who came to the conclusion that these conditions were fulfilled in Rhodesia." But they added that a good end did not justify evil means, so that one must always condemn the killing of the innocent, mutilation, torture, and intimidation.[52]

Apart from these formal documents, the Church was taking other steps to bring its social doctrine to Catholics' attention. Articles in Church periodicals regularly supported the bishops' positions. These were the *Shield*, read mostly by whites, and *Moto*, a monthly intended specifically for African readers. Smith's government suppressed *Moto* in 1974 as subversive.[53] In 1964, Church authorities invited Fr. Paul Crane of Claver House in London to lecture in the townships on the Church's social doctrine. Claver House was a center offering leadership courses for Africans from many countries.[54]

The Church had to make special efforts to make any impression on white Catholics. These numbered about 37,000 in 1977, about 6.2 percent of total membership. Many of them became increasingly irritated with the Church's repeated challenges to government measures linked with racial politics. Often they attacked the bishops' line as "Marxist." Accordingly, in 1972 the Justice and Peace Commission prepared a series of outlines for Sunday sermons and for parish discussion groups. The outlines explained the doctrinal basis for the Church's criticisms of government and defended the bishops' orthodoxy. At the same time, Fr. Richard Randolph, executive secretary of the bishops' conference, lectured on this topic at countless parish meetings. The Bishops' Conference Commission on Christian Formation in 1978 published seven booklets on "The Social Teaching of the Catholic Church." These laid out a full year's course, intended for upper secondary school and for individual and group study.[55]

The Church was also connected, but only indirectly, with a venture of individual scholars. In 1978–1980 the Justice and Peace Commission, along with the Catholic Institute of International Relations (CIIR) in London, put out a series of nine booklets entitled *From Rhodesia to Zimbabwe*. These analyzed Rhodesia's socioeconomic situation in a semi-popular style and suggested lines along which a future Zimbabwean government should build the new society, especially to supply the basic needs of its poorer members. The authors covered such topics as land, labor, unemployment, health, education, food supply, and community development. At least one contributor was a Catholic, Roger Riddell, who later headed the Riddell Commission.[56]

During these decades, too, the Church established several institutions intended to work toward a more just society. In 1964 the Jesuits opened a Centre for Leadership and Development at Silveira House, Chisha-

washa, directed by Fr. John Dove. Initially the Centre offered a program
of "civic education." It was responding to discussions in the townships
around Salisbury which indicated a need for people to know more about
the structures and workings of government and about capitalism, socialism, and communism. As time passed, the Centre added programs in
such things as commercial education, agriculture, dressmaking, child
care, and nutrition. Mugabe's two sisters were on the staff. The Centre
functioned throughout the war—doubtless under the close surveillance
of Smith's government.[57]

The Jesuits also established in 1964 the School of Social Work in Salisbury, directed by Fr. Edward Rogers. Although the school enrolled
whites as well as blacks, it aimed primarily at training blacks for social
work in urban conditions. It responded to new needs as they arose.[58]

The bishops, in 1972, set up the national Justice and Peace Commission. This initially undertook three tasks: to inform people's consciences
on issues of justice and peace, to obtain and disseminate information
about the country's social situation, and to investigate alleged injustices,
publish its findings, and take whatever corrective action was possible.
The commission had a powerful influence on events through its cooperation with the CIIR: This connection provided international circulation
for the commission's reports on the Smith regime's oppressive security
measures and on atrocities committed by the security forces. This publicity helped the nationalists to win international support. The government
detained four of the commission's key members in 1977, threatened to
try them, and finally deported them—a fate it ultimately imposed on
Bishop Lamont, too. Despite such harassment the commission kept
working and the bishops backed it.[59]

## THE CHURCH'S RESPONSE TO MARXIZING TENDENCIES

Marxist tendencies, some specifically antireligious, became prominent in
ZANU (and ZAPU) after 1975. Mugabe spoke of himself as a Marxist.
ZANU's Central Committee formally adopted Marxism-Leninism as its
ideology. ZANU and Mugabe were closely associated with Mozambique
and Machel. Chinese and Soviet Communists were helping ZANU and
ZAPU, whose guerrillas were indoctrinating the rural population. They
ridiculed Christianity and sometimes forced Christians to denounce the
"white Jesus." They called the missionaries "agents of imperialism," and
told African sisters that they were the "slaves of the whites." They kid-
napped the entire student body of a Catholic secondary school. They

forced rural schools, clinics, and churches to close. Guerrillas (of uncertain identity) killed several groups of missionaries in cold blood. Might not all this foreshadow an antireligious campaign in independent Zimbabwe like the one in Mozambique?[60]

The Church was concerned not just with the threat to religion. It could also fear that the nationalists would rule as arbitrarily as other Marxist-Leninist governments had, suppressing human freedom, replacing the old exploiting class with a new one, and stifling the economy just when it needed to grow.

The bishops' statements during these years sometimes adverted specifically to the Marxist danger. *A Plea for Peace* indirectly warned against Soviet agitators: "godless forces of great world powers that insidiously foment disorder and solicit . . . the allegiance of dissatisfied millions."[61] *The Road to Peace* spoke of Marxism more extensively. Although it sometimes echoed the language of liberation theology, it kept a greater distance from Marxism than some liberation theologians were doing. The document explained how three strands of thought endangered peace: atheistic Communism, individualistic liberalism, and extreme nationalism. Communism attracted some Christians despite the hardships Communist governments imposed on the Church. Although Marxism posed appropriate questions for Christians to reflect on, it regarded all religion as alienation and illusion; religion had to be eliminated either by suffocation or by active persecution. True Marxists rejected the very idea of God, not just a bourgeois caricature of him as some people claimed. Marxism, further, rejected morality drawn from any concept beyond man and beyond class; it justified any means to support the party cause.

This criticism did not imply, however, that Christians must fight commu*nists*, they must fight commun*ism*—insofar as it was directed against God and the Church. The way to fight it was by doing away with its causes and offering an alternative. Aggressive anticommunists were often the ones who created the conditions on which the ideology thrived. Christians could accept some points in Marxist economics and sociology; they could not accept that God did not exist and that faith was the product of oppression. Service of the human cause was not man's final goal; the Christian could not give up faith in God and seek liberation through atheism.[62]

Other Church programs, projects, and agencies did not criticize Marxist theory so directly. Neither Silveira House nor the School of Social Work engaged in confrontation with Marxism. Both helped their students to understand various social philosophies and to weigh their strengths and weaknesses. The Justice and Peace Commission paid little attention to linkages between Marxism and the nationalist movement. Although the booklets in *From Rhodesia to Zimbabwe* used some insights associated with Marxism, they were actually based on conventional sociology and economics, and leaned toward Western European socialism. Given the Marxist currents in the liberation movements, the booklets' significance lay in offering a positive, non-Marxist program for Zimbabwe's new social order. In 1983 the Justice and Peace Commission undertook a multifaceted program to awaken social consciousness, entitled "Education for Justice."[63]

One initiative, however, dealt specifically with the possibility that the nationalists would bring Machel's religious policies to Zimbabwe. A symposium on "The Church and the New Order" was held at Driefontein in May 1977. The participants were bishops, men and women religious superiors, directors of priestly and religious formation, and representatives of the National Council of Priests; just under one-third of the participants were Africans. The group looked at the Church's situation in Mozambique and what might happen under an aggressively secularist government in Rhodesia. The participants asked how the Church should act in the existing situation to make itself helpful and credible; how it should operate under a new, radical regime; and how it should prepare to work in such an environment. Their replies were sympathetic to the people seeking liberation and assumed that they would win.

Reviewing the existing situation, the participants observed that some guerrillas were antireligious and anti-Christian and were persecuting the Church. But government security forces were also arousing fear. The war was disrupting communication and travel, and preventing priests from visiting congregations. The Church was too priest-centered; in future it should rely more on lay leaders and train them better for their responsibilities.

Looking to the future, the participants expected that they might lose control of institutions, might be under financial constraint, might lack vehicles and other tools, might have to do manual labor, and might be legally restricted in ministries. They concluded that some privations could be a blessing; a simpler lifestyle could make the Church more credible. They also listed suggestions for living under such constraints, some of which touched on such specifics as reservation of the Blessed Sacrament. At a more general level, religious instruction should stress the concept of Church as community rather than as organization. It should aim at greater maturity in faith. It should present social doctrine, paying some attention to "African socialism" and countering Marxist indoctrination. The Church should encourage extraliturgical, Bible-oriented worship in local communities. It should retrain Church personnel, preparing them for loss of status and other changes; update their knowledge of socialism; and teach them how to build community, share responsibility, and train trainers. Each diocese should have an emergency team to help the bishop develop plans to handle political contingencies.[64]

## ZANU AND RELIGION

During the war, Mugabe made some moves to reassure Church authorities. He told an interviewer in 1978 that the party would not interfere with the churches in any way. ZANU (and ZAPU) in most cases denied responsibility for attacks on missionaries. They blamed isolated bandits or claimed that government forces staged the attacks to discredit the nationalists. In some cases they penitently admitted that guerrillas were perhaps involved owing to lapses of discipline.[65]

After independence, ZANU's Marxist commitment continued to puzzle Church leaders. Looking for answers, they could begin with the person of Mugabe. Some priests and religious knew him well; some had spoken privately with him during and after the war. He had been a serious Catholic at least until 1975; his convictions had drawn his fiancée to join the Church. While he seemed to have discontinued regular church attendance by 1980, his religious and social outlook remained basically Christian. His policy of reconciliation was an example of this. Inside the party he tended to reach decisions by consensus and not to impose his own will. The Marxist ideas he favored were not the ones that threatened religious and other human rights. As many informed Catholics saw it, then, he was not going to impose an atheistic, authoritarian, totalitarian regime. They judged, too, that he was in full control of the party and that more radical leaders were not likely to oust him and introduce a rigidly Marxist rule.[66]

In his public statements after the war, Mugabe recalled that the ZANU election manifesto recognized religious belief as a basic freedom and promised not to interfere with the churches' spiritual work. In a press interview he called Zimbabwe "a Christian country." He thanked the Catholic Church unreservedly for its help during the war. It refused to accept Smith's racism. Its exposure of the regime's inhumanities won international support for the liberation movement. It let freedom fighters know that people inside the country agreed with them, so they were not struggling alone. He thanked the Church, too, for its earlier contribution to development through its educational, medical, and other social services. He asked the Church to cooperate with his regime in continuing development and making society more equitable.[67]

But because Mugabe and and other officials understood that the churches were wary of Marxism, they insisted that this ideology reflected Christian ideals. Socialist principles called for the equality of man in society and communal ownership of the country's resources and means of production along with equal sharing of the benefits produced. Egalitarianism was more in line with Christianity than individualism, greed, and selfishness. This morality was higher than capitalism's. The papal encyclicals condemned the impoverishment of people by selfish entrepreneurs. Although Marx did write some unpalatable things, he supported freedom of religion.[68]

Banana, who was president, used a more theological approach in seeking church support for development. He questioned an excessively otherworldly view of religion. This view distinguished too sharply between body and soul, here and hereafter; it was too concerned with individual salvation and neglected the social implications of serving God. The churches should work to establish justice and should use social analysis to find the roots of injustice.[69] These ideas echoed *Gaudium et Spes* and showed traces of liberation theology. As time went on, however, Banana would use liberation theology more explicitly, in a version that many Catholics would question. He overlooked the centrality of divine revelation and set aside any interest in values transcending time and in life transcending death. He told an interviewer in 1986: "I encourage churches to ensure that their members behave first and foremost as Zimbabweans; in other words allegiance to the church must be subordinated to our allegiance to Zimbabwe."[70]

Some leaders broached the question of public criticism by the churches. The Minister of Justice in effect invited the Justice and Peace Commission to keep serving as watchdog in the new society; socialist as well as capitalist societies could give rise to injustice. Banana similarly asserted that government was open to criticism, but advised the critics to be objective and to acknowledge government's achievements. He warned the churches not to be used by the country's external enemies; the government would flush out clergymen who were hiding in sheep's clothing. Mugabe himself said that he would close down any church that preached against his government. Government would allow churches to worship as they pleased, but they should stick to worship and leave politics alone.[71]

The comments of ZANU's leaders showed small understanding of Marxism. They paid little or no attention to Marx's theorizing about economics, class formation, and the historical movement toward revolution, or to Lenin's elaboration of Marx's ideas. Instead, they accepted simplistic clichés about the promotion of humanitarian values. They did not really appreciate, either, *why* the churches were wary. Although Mugabe acknowledged that Marxists in some countries had labored to annihilate religion, he claimed that there was good reason for this: religion in those countries was allied with oppression. But other Marxist countries gave the Church freedom to develop—for example, Bulgaria and Poland![72]

On balance, despite their ambiguities, the public statements of ZANU's leaders were reassuring. They seemed to identify their Marxist ideology with humanitarian concerns for justice, equality, and democratic participation, and seemed not to envisage any conflict with the churches. Informed clergy and laity believed, moreover, that Marxist-Leninist indoctrination was not making any deep impression on people. As late as 1982, there appeared to be few if any Marxists even among university staff and students. Observers did not note any flow of radical pamphlets, posters, or other publications or any evidence of Marxist thinking among the masses.[73]

Nor did the regime's early policies and activities show any hostility to the Church. It did not take over mission schools or impose oppressive regulations on them. It provided the same general kinds of financial assistance as the settler regime had done. It asked the churches, in fact, to help set up new schools and expand old ones. It accepted the "right of entry" to public schools, allowing church personnel to give religious instruction to pupils of their respective denominations. Although the Minister of Education intended to have schools instruct pupils at all levels in Marxist ideology, he was very slow in developing the syllabuses for this purpose.[74]

Government allowed the churches to keep their medical facilities, and even undertook to pay their staff salaries and to underwrite the costs of maintenance, drugs, and medical supplies. It did not fully succeed in this undertaking, however. By 1983, voluntary hospitals were finding it hard to meet expenses.[75]

Local party officials in some areas did make known their hostility to religious practices. This discouraged people, especially men, from identifying themselves as Christians and kept them from church attendance. But when a high government official was asked about a practice of calling local party meetings on Sunday mornings, he answered that this was not party policy; ZANU had instructed its officials to hold their meetings on Saturdays, precisely to avoid interference with church attendance. Some clergy believed that men were really spending their time in beerhalls and thus staying away from church.[76]

The government's steps toward reconciliation and development were steps that the Church could readily endorse. The government's early achievements in making education more available, in ending racial discrimination, and in improving job prospects of blacks were creditable. The Church could be and was concerned, however, about secular policies touching justice, human rights, and the general welfare; the economy still left many people in dire poverty while others enjoyed abundant prosperity. Mugabe's determination to establish a one-party state was worrisome, because such states tended to become arbitrary and oppressive and could not be changed except by violence. And the security forces were brutally harassing innocent people in the southwest.

### The Church's Response to ZANU's Policies

After ZANU came to power, the bishops' statements did not, for the most part, speak explicitly of Marxism or address particular social issues or criticize government. Their first statement, *Welcome Zimbabwe*, in April 1980, promised the Church's help in nation-building. It said nothing about the government's claim to be Marxist-Leninist, but showed some concern about relations between Church and State. It recalled that the two institutions were both at the service of men but were autonomous in their own spheres. The Church was not bound to any political party or system. It was, instead, the moral conscience of the nation, safeguarding the values of human persons. It must always be free to preach the faith and to make moral judgments even on political matters when basic human rights or the salvation of souls so required. The statement, then, was laying the foundation for any claim the bishops might have to make in the future against FRELIMO-style pressures on the Church.[77]

The bishops issued no statement at Christmas 1980. Fr. Randolph filled the gap, however, with a long article in the *Zimbabwe Herald*, "The Catholic Church and the New Zimbabwean Society." He affirmed the Church's approval of many national aims as articulated by leading political figures. Propaganda labeled many of the leaders as atheistic Marxists, whereas they were practicing Christians or held views compatible with Christianity. The Church agreed with the morality implied in their public statements. In its aim to correct the plight of the poor and oppressed, Marxism was parallel to Christianity, but it was concerned only with the here and now and with the realization of an earthly utopia. Christianity aimed at the integral development of man here in preparation for his final destiny hereafter. The Church approved the building of a new society which would attend to both the material and the spiritual advancement of man, and it had helped the cause of human rights, especially from 1969 onward. Randolph reviewed the ways in which the Church was assisting government, and he looked to a future in which the Church and the State would continue their mutual cooperation.[78]

On the first anniversary of independence in 1981, the bishops urged continued efforts at reconciliation.[79] In November 1982 they issued *Our Way Forward*, in which they exercised their function as moral critic. While praising the government's accomplishments, they cautioned against several developments that threatened justice and equity. One was the legal immunity of security officers for unlawful acts. Another was a hankering for wealth which led officials to corruption, nepotism, and ostentatious living. A third was a tendency in the dominant party to intimidation of the minority. The bishops rejected laissez-faire capitalism and approved "the socialization of certain means of production," but they saw danger when a state owned the means of production and was run by a few leaders through a centralized bureaucracy. The impersonal state thus controlled the lives and labor of workers and peasants, subjecting them to the same alienation and exploitation as capitalism did.[80]

The bishops' Easter message in March 1983 complained about the conduct of the Fifth Brigade in the southwest. They thus provoked a bitter reply, to which we will return. In January 1984 they issued *Socialism and the Gospel of Christ*, in which they intended to "shed some further light on the socialist path our country has chosen to follow." Because some forms of socialism did not agree with Christianity, believers had to inspire Zimbabwe's version with Christian vision. This socialism meant equality, equitable distribution of land and social services, fair wages, self-reliance, cooperation in production, and reconciliation. The asocial behavior of influential people, unfortunately, contradicted ideals of social justice and created a credibility gap between the authorities and ordinary citizens. Conversion was necessary. People needed spiritual vision to use material goods properly. The bishops could not agree with those who adopted atheism with their socialism. Such people seemed to think they had to eliminate God in order to liberate man. But faith in God was not opium; it freed men from enslavement to material possessions. And class strife was not a positive force for social change. "If this is 'scientific socialism' we cannot accept it." The bishops welcomed leaders' assurances that they would use only persuasion, not force, in integrating people into the new order.[81]

The uproar at Easter 1983 began with something the Justice and Peace Commission did. In February the commission presented the government with a report on the security situation and drought relief. Investigation by the commission had turned up evidence of serious human rights abuses in the southwest. Government did not react publicly. Then at Easter the bishops spoke about security in this area. They praised the government's efforts at reconciliation and catalogued the brutal misdeeds of dissidents. It was difficult to deal with these, and government had to maintain public order even by military means. But the methods used had degenerated into brutality and atrocity; the bishops had given evidence to government that people were being maimed and killed. The "indemnity" regulations led some security personnel to think they were above the law. The mass media were not informing the public about killings, rapes, house burnings, and the cutting off of food supplies. The government should set up a judicial commission to establish the truth and recommend action.[82]

Minister of Information Shamuyarira issued a stinging reply. Reconciliation did not apply to the dissidents, who were linked with South Africa in trying to destroy Zimbabwe. While Justice and Peace had submitted some evidence, the bishops had not. The army had brought peace to the area; people were relieved. Government would make an investigation, but would not use a judicial commission. The plea for "ethnic rights" was reactionary, reflecting South Africa's bantustan system, and had been issued at the urging of foreign interests. The bishops and the Bible would not protect the people from armed gangs. The Church and some of the statement's signatories had once collaborated with the colonialists.[83]

Shortly afterward Mugabe himself lashed out at the bishops. Speaking to the Heads of Denominations, he first complained about criticism from foreign journalists, nongovernmental organizations, and churches. He then turned to the bishops' statement "sermonizing my government on our military operations in Matabeleland." He wondered why the Church and its clerics had never criticized ZAPU's atrocities. What were the "ethnic rights" of minorities? Were the bishops opposed to national

unity? Their evidence that government was hiding atrocities was hear-
say; the government would have to verify it. False evidence did not become true just because bishops presented it. The bishops were casting
doubt on the government's commitment to human rights, but government leaders' commitment to these rights had once put them in prison
and later moved them to armed struggle. "Surely these credentials give
us a better title than our 'holier than thou' critics to sermonize on this
kind of commitment." The Church had to demonstrate the virtues of
humility, honesty, and objectivity.[84]

The bishops spoke again shortly thereafter on Zimbabwe's third anniversary of independence. Although they were conciliatory they did not
retreat. They again accepted government's duty to protect its people
from the dissidents, even by force. They condemned violence "by whom-
soever committed." They reaffirmed their entitlement to speak on political matters which touched personal rights and the salvation of souls. But
they also welcomed the prime minister's assurance that government
would investigate their allegations and follow up with whatever action
was necessary. The public controversy ended with this document.[85]

For some years the bishops seemed reserved in their personal relations
with the regime, and friendly officials were reportedly puzzled by their
tendency to keep at a distance from public authorities.[86] But they apparently maintained this attitude in order to keep their freedom. Bishop
Lamont, who had been most outspoken in support of the liberation
struggle, wrote to the *Herald* in January 1981, asserting that the Church
must keep independent of every political party. Fr. Randolph made the
same point in early 1982: "the Church must refuse to be made an agent of
the Government in implementing party political policies, whether their
ideologies be capitalist or socialist."[87]

A pamphlet published by ZANU in 1987 disagreed with this declaration of ecclesiastical independence. Entitled "Society and the Church," it
was explicitly a piece of theological reflection along President Banana's
line. It took Latin American liberation theology as its base. Christian
theology in Europe, it said, had provided the theological foundation for
state oppression, and in the missions it was racist and imperialist. The
hierarchy and orthodoxy were defenders of the colonial order. Even after
Zimbabwe's independence, churches' adaptation was purely opportunis-
tic, aimed at preventing further change. The ending of colonial rule was
only the first stage of the revolutionary process; ZANU would go further, installing a socialist order which would do away with the injustices
of capitalism. But the churches were saying "thus far and no further."

There was need to liberate theology from its narrowness. In Latin America and South Africa, revolutionary priests found their true vision and vocation in Marxism, which looked deeply into the causes of oppression and sought a cure. Revolutionary theology would justify itself by helping the people fight for their democratic rights and human dignity. The churches were well placed for this task. Their vocation was to change the existing order.[88]

The pamphlet looked like an attempt to bring the churches around to unreserved support of the party and its Marxist identification. Fr. Oskar Wermter responded with a measured critique in *Moto*. The Catholic bishops, he recalled, had protested injustice for twenty years before independence, and thirty Catholic missionaries had died during the war because they saw their place as being with the people. Church workers were still *doing* what other people were *talking* about, helping development in remote areas. If the Church should not have been identified with past regimes, it should not be identified with the present one either. The pamphlet assumed that the party was the people. But were the party's intellectuals sure that they never let self-interest prevail over the common good? that their record entitled them to look down on the Church? Poor folk might have a different answer. The Church was more than an auxiliary doing the same thing as the State. It had a different purpose: bringing people face to face with the ultimate meaning of their lives. ZANU's pamphlet, moreover, showed ignorance about the Church's teaching on capitalism and private property. While Wermter appreciated the party's effort to define its relationship with the Church, he regretted that it knew so little about the Church's doctrine on social justice. The pamphlet sounded like an ultimatum, the party's last word to the Church. He would rather consider it a beginning.[89]

Church personnel other than the bishops were less reserved about personal contact with officials, and took the initiative in seeking fuller understanding of what ZANU stood for. During the first few years of independence, government speakers, including the prime minister and the president, were invited to address the Salisbury clergy, the National Association of Diocesan Priests, the sisters' conference, and the Justice and Peace Commission.[90]

The Church responded generously to government's request for help with reconstruction and development. The Commission for Social Service and Development (CSSD) of the bishops' conference collated information about Church-sponsored projects, related these to government plans, and found money for them, mostly from overseas Catholic agencies. CSSD's work enabled the Holy See's representative to pledge US$10.8 million at the ZIMCORD meeting. The largest sums went into rehabilitating schools and medical facilities: Z$2.5 million for education, Z$2 million for health, Z$1 million for families and agricultural rehabilitation, and Z$1 million for vocational and technical training, especially of ex-combatants.[91] The Church's contribution involved personnel, too: priests, brothers, and sisters. Catholic secondary schools were especially important in rural areas, because the settler regime had not put government schools in these places. Some Catholic missionaries joined the staffs of new public schools in the countryside instead of staying with Church schools.[92]

Silveira House and the School of Social Work added new programs. Silveira House devised a short course for reorientating ex-combatants to civilian life, particularly female ex-combatants who faced more difficult problems. At the request of Mrs. Mugabe, who headed the national women's movement, it trained women for grass-roots leadership. In agriculture it helped cooperative groups with technical advice on preparing land for planting, ordering inputs, caring for crops, harvesting, and marketing; and with arranging finance through revolving loans. In 1982 the project was reaching thirty thousand farmers in nine regions.[93] In 1986 the institution served a curious additional function. Herbert Ushewokunze, secretary of ZANU's political commissariat, used Silveira House as temporary quarters for Chitepo College, the party's center for ideological training of its cadres. The lectures, by Ushewokunze and some university dons, followed classic Marxist-Leninist lines. Silveira House staff lectured on subsidiary subjects. The program was suspended when Ushewokunze lost his party post later that year.[94]

The School of Social Work prepared administrators for government agencies dealing with social work, rehabilitation, manpower, and education. It also conducted short courses to meet new needs; it thus trained ex-combatants as paraprofessionals in rural social development; these were needed when government began to organize "growth points" in the countryside.[95]

The Zimbabwe Project also helped. The Bethlehem Fathers and the CIIR had begun the project mainly to assist refugees during the war. The Rhodesian Bishops' Conference was among its sponsors but it was ecumenical. After independence it helped people uprooted by the war to settle at home and rebuild their lives. Among other things, it helped its clients to form cooperatives for small manufacturing and commercial enterprises and ran programs to train ex-combatants in commercial subjects. Catholic institutions assisted the project in this undertaking.[96]

The Justice and Peace Commission continued to function. Although the government took no immediate reprisals against the commission for its critical report in 1983, it remained sensitive to criticism of its human rights record by the Church and the foreign press. Apparently as part of a deliberate effort at intimidation by Home Affairs Minister Nkala in May and June 1986, the police arrested the commission's acting director, Nicholas Ndebele, and its chairman, Michael Auret. They charged Ndebele with spying for an enemy nation and Auret with possessing "prohibited materials." When Mrs. Auret phoned Mugabe to protest, he made it clear that the hostility was not his and ordered their immediate release.[97]

In addition to sharing in the government's development efforts, the Church took steps to organize and animate its own laity. The Young Christian Students and Young Christian Workers were awakening their members to social responsibility. A new Catholic Youth Council helped develop skills, leadership, and spirituality among young people; youth responded to it warmly in some places. The bishops announced the formation of a Catholic Women's Organization to facilitate cooperation with its governmentally sponsored counterpart. Some effort was made to promote small, self-contained, Christian communities as the Driefontein Symposium urged, but this program did not work very well.[98]

The Church's effort at positive instruction in social doctrine appeared to falter after independence. Programs at the major seminary and the intercongregational center for training young sisters seemed not to have a firm definition and structure. Sometimes priests or religious lectured on socialist ideologies at meetings of clergy or sisters, but their explanations were often confused. Responsibility for preparing a school curriculum was not clear; nor was it clear how extensively the 1978 booklets on social teaching were being used. Some observers would have liked to see a simple catechism on social thought.[99] A Catholic bookshop at Harare in 1982 carried a small amount of relevant material. *The Light*, the archdiocesan newspaper in Salisbury, published helpful pieces on social teaching in English and Shona, but its circulation was small. *Moto* resumed publication after independence. Its editorials and correspondence represented a wide range of social views. Articles often dealt with social issues from a Catholic viewpoint; these varied in quality, but some were very perceptive.[100]

## MARXISM AS ONE FACTOR AMONG MANY

The predominant feature of the Church's maturing process in Zimbabwe lay in its preoccupation with social issues, and ZANU's Marxism was only one of these. Before independence, Church leaders focused first on the pervasive racism and social injustice in Rhodesian society and the horrible cost of the war of liberation. It tried, through the bishops' public statements and various programs, to convince its white members that the existing social system was unjust, and to show its black members that there was a sounder social theory than Marxism. At the same time it pressed government to correct injustice. The Justice and Peace Commission won international sympathy for the nationalist movement's struggle. Silveira House and the School of Social Work prepared blacks for effective community leadership and equipped them with skills that would contribute to socioeconomic development. The Church undertook only one exercise that focused on Marxism's potential threat to religion. This was the Driefontein symposium's consideration of the "worst case"—the establishment of a hostile Marxist government along the lines of FRELIMO in Mozambique.

After independence, when the Church became more attentive to ZANU's Marxist leanings, its response was in continuity with its earlier line of thought and action. The party's Marxism, especially as represented by its leader, Robert Mugabe, was notably ambiguous. The new government did not interfere with the Church's ministries or make any radical changes in the economy. There was, in fact, danger that it would perpetuate an oppressive division between the "haves" and the "have-nots," placing a "new class" of party leaders in positions of wealth and privilege. Although its respect for human rights and the rule of law was commendable in many ways, its pressure to establish a one-party state led to serious abuses in Matabeleland and perhaps foreshadowed more permanent oppression later on.

Evaluating the practical impact of ZANU's commitment to Marxism, then, the Church showed caution but not anxiety. It maintained its concern for integral human development as an objective of its ministry. It therefore contributed generously to socioeconomic development through existing and newly established institutions. It showed itself open to government measures that would curb the injustices of capitalism. It resumed its pressure for social justice and human rights under the new regime, and its preindependence advocacy and action on behalf of justice gave credibility to its postindependence stance.

The Church's response to social issues, then, contributed markedly to its coming of age in Zimbabwe, and ZANU's Marxism was a highly significant element in these issues. But the Church still faced a daunting agenda. There was need to accelerate the indigenization of its clerical leadership: the bishops and priests. There was need to draw lay Catholics to more active participation in its life and mission. There was need to develop a deeper understanding of Catholic doctrine and spirituality among the laity, particularly among the elite who were now so exposed to secular worldviews. Included here was the need for ongoing efforts to help them appreciate the Church's social ideals and to involve them in constructive social action. There was need, also, to take up the sensitive and perplexing task of inculturation. And there was still need to continue its extensive engagement in primary evangelization.

## NOTES

1. See "Zimbabwe," *Africa South of the Sahara, 1989* (London: Europa Publications, 1988), p. 1136; this source will be cited henceforth as " 'Zimbabwe,' *Africa South 1989.*"

2. See ibid., pp. 1136, 1141, 1148.

3. See ibid., pp. 1137–38.

4. See ibid., pp. 1138–39.

5. See ibid., p. 1139.

6. See the brief sketch of early nationalist movements in Patrick O'Meara, *Rhodesia: Social Conflict or Coexistence?* (Ithaca, N.Y.: Cornell University Press, 1975), pp. 91–106. See also André Astrow, *Zimbabwe: A Revolution That Lost Its Way?* (London: Zed Press, 1983), pp. 30–34.

7. See O'Meara, *Rhodesia*, pp. 107–13, 121–22.

8. See "Zimbabwe," *Africa South 1989*, pp. 1139–40; Ian Linden, *The Catholic Church and the Struggle for Zimbabwe* (London: Longman, 1980), pp. 271–72.

9. See O'Meara, *Rhodesia*, pp. 113–19; Astrow, Zimbabwe, pp. 93–94, 99, 102–108; "Zimbabwe," *Africa South 1989*, p. 1140; "Mugabe, Robert (Gabriel)," *Current Biography, 1979* (New York: H. W. Wilson, 1979), p. 269.

10. See "Zimbabwe," *Africa South 1989*, pp. 1140–41.

11. See Astrow, *Zimbabwe*, pp. 156–58, 186n49; Colin Stoneman and Lionel Cliffe, *Zimbabwe* (London: Pinter Publishers, 1989), pp. 32, 34–35. See the summary of the constitution in "Zimbabwe," *Africa South 1989*, pp. 1155–56; for the full text, see Albert P. Blaustein and Gilbert A. Flanz, *Constitutions of the World* (Dobbs Ferry, N.Y.: Oceana Publications, 1986), vol. 18.

12. See "Mugabe," *Current Biography*, pp. 267–69; David Smith and Colin Simpson, with Ian Davis, *Mugabe* (London: Sphere Books, 1981), pp. 16–18, 20–22, 54–57.

13. See "Mugabe," *Current Biography*, p. 269; Astrow, *Zimbabwe*, pp. 88–89; Linden, *Catholic Church and the Struggle for Zimbabwe*, p. 218. Interview with confidential informant, March 1982.

14. See "Zimbabwean Socialism," *Zimbabwe Catholic Bishops' Conference News Sheet*, No. 104 (1982), 104/11, mimeographed, referring to an interview with Mugabe by Sr. Janice McLaughlin. The Zimbabwe Bishops' Conference will henceforth be abbreviated "ZCBC." See also "ZANU Congress," *Moto* (August 1984), as reprinted in *Zimbabwe Pressespiegel* [Harare], 3 (August 1984), 2; this source will henceforth be cited as "*Spiegel*."

15. See "Zimbabwean Socialism"; Richard H. Randolph, "The Role of the Catholic Church in Zimbabwe: A Miscellany of Texts," ZCBC [1981?], mimeographed, 7; Astrow, *Zimbabwe*, p. 140. Samora Machel advised ZANU's Central Committee to omit the word "Marxism" from its election manifesto; see Smith, Simpson, and Davis, *Mugabe*, pp. 167–68.

16. See "ZANU(PF) Constitution," chap. 2, in *Spiegel*, 3 (August 1984), 13.

17. See "Two Months in Zimbabwe," *Zimbabwe Project News Bulletin*, No. 8 (June–July 1981), under date of May 12; "Industrial Democracy and Workers' Education," ibid., No. 13 (January 1982), 10; "Co-operatives: Problems, Policies, Resources," ibid., No. 27 (May 1983), 9; this publication will henceforth be cited as "*Bulletin*." See also "Socialism in Zimbabwe: An Address Delivered by the Prime Minister, Comrade R. G. Mugabe to a Meeting of the the Justice and Peace Commission," February 6, 1982, Catholic Commission for Justice and Peace, *Newsletter*, No. 2 (March 1982), Appendix I, p. 7, mimeographed; "Muzenda Urges Churches to Promote Socialism," Zimbabwe Government Press Service, 203/82/DB, March 9, 1982, p. 3, mimeographed; "The Building of Socialism," *Herald* [Harare], July 10, 1984, cited in *Spiegel* 3 (August 1984), 27.

18. See Mugabe, "Socialism in Zimbabwe," p. 4; Randolph, "Role of the Catholic Church," 3–4, 8, 10; "Month in Zimbabwe," *Bulletin*, No. 27 (May 1983), May 6; "Month in Zimbabwe," *Bulletin*, No. 31 (October 1983), October 28; "Month in Zimbabwe," *Bulletin*, No. 32 (November 1983), November 16, 25. "Month in Zimbabwe" (and "Two Months") will henceforth be abbreviated as "Month."

19. See "President Urges Churches: Re-examine Your Stance," Zimbabwe Press Statement 153/81/SFS, March 2, 1981, p. 3, mimeographed; Randolph, "Role of Catholic Church," 8; "Zimbabwean Socialism," p. 104/13.

20. See "Parties," *Bulletin*, No. 11 (October 1961), 7–8; Resolution 1:3 of the ZANU Party Congress, in *Spiegel*, 3 (August 1984), 19; Articles 5(h) and 34(5) of "ZANU(PF) Constitution," in ibid., 13, 17.

21. See Astrow, *Zimbabwe*, pp. 140–44; "Mugabe Outlines Plans and Priorities," *Moto* (Gwelo), No. 22 (May 1980), 3; a press interview with Altaf Gaunar, *Herald* (Salisbury), August 18, 1980 (typescript in ZCBC files); "We Have No Plans to Nationalize—PM," *Sunday Mail* (Salisbury), January 11, 1981; Richard H. Randolph, "Report on Zimbabwe, 18 Apr. 80–24 Dec. 81," ZCBC, General Secretariat, MS/RR/82, February 10, 1982, mimeographed, p. 2.

22. See "ZANU(PF) Constitution," chap. III, art. 6(4)-(5), chaps. IV, V, VI; "Resolutions," 1:1, 1:3, 1:5, 1:6.

23. See "Zimbabwe," *Africa South 1989*, p. 1141; Astrow, *Zimbabwe*, p. 167; Smith, Simpson, and Davis, *Mugabe*, pp. 111–12.

24. See "Zimbabwe," *Africa South 1989*, p. 1155; Randolph, "Report on Zimbabwe", 9–10; "Independence Has Brought True Democracy—PM," Report of the Central Committee, *Spiegel*, 3 (August 1984), 9; "Month," *Bulletin*, No. 24 (February 1984), February 26; "Month," *Bulletin*, No. 27 (May 1983), May 6; "Month," *Bulletin*, No. 32 (November 1983), November 16; "CSSD: Reconstruction and Rehabilitation," *ZCBC News Sheet*, No. 102 (February 1982), pp. 102/6–7, mimeographed.

25. See "Independence Has Brought True Democracy," 9; Randolph, "Report on Zimbabwe," 10; "The Three-Year Plan," *Bulletin*, No. 22 (November–December 1982), 14–15.

26. See "Independence Has Brought Democracy," 8; "Resolutions," 6:1, 6:3, 6:6; "Land," *Bulletin*, No. 32 (November 1983), 11–15, 17–18; "Land," *Bulletin*, No. 33–34 (December 1983–January 1984), 28–29; "AFC Gives $45 m. in Loans to Farmers," *Herald*, January 17, 1985, in *Spiegel*, 4 (January 1985), 9; "Even Bigger Harvest," *Herald*, May 1986, in ibid., 5 (May 1986), 7; "Imbalance in Land Allocation," *Financial Gazette*, May 23, 1985, in ibid., 5 (May 1986), 3.

27. See Government of the Republic of Zimbabwe, *Growth with Equity: An Economic Policy Statement, February 1981* [CMD.R.2.4. 1981] (Salisbury: Government Printer, 1981), pp. 1, 3, 5, 10.

28. See Zimbabwe, *Report of the Commission of Inquiry into Incomes, Prices and Conditions of Service under the Chairmanship of Roger C. Riddell, to the President, June 1981* (Salisbury: Government Printer, [1981]), pp. 1 and passim.

29. See Astrow, *Zimbabwe*, pp. 172–73; Stoneman and Cliffe, *Zimbabwe*, pp. 32–33; "Land," *Bulletin*, No. 4 (March 1981), 14; "Month," *Bulletin*, No. 12 (November–December 1981), November 5, December 1, December 22; "Land," *Bulletin*, No. 32 (November 1983), 13, 15, 17; "Land," *Bulletin*, No. 33–34 (December 1983–January 1984), 21–28, 36. See also the following speeches published by the Ministry of Information and Tourism, Salisbury: "Prime Minister's New Year's Speech to the Nation," December 3, 1980, p. 5; "Prime Minister Opens Zimbabwe Conference on Reconstruction and Development, (ZIMCORD)," March 23, 1981, p. 7.

30. See *Growth with Equity*, paragraphs 54, 66; "New Wage Regulations," *Bulletin*, No. 13 (January 1982), 4–10; "Overtime Ban," *Bulletin*, No. 13 (January 1982), 18–19; "Labour, Retrenchment," *Bulletin*, No. 31 (October 1983), 17–25; "Contract Workers—A Story of Poverty and Despair to Sustain Profits," *Moto*, No. 43 (n.d.), 8–9; "Domestics Still the Urban Poor," ibid., 9, 12.

31. See *Growth with Equity*, paragraph 68; "Labour," *Bulletin*, No. 8 (June–July 1981), 20; "Strikes," *Bulletin*, No. 11 (October 1981), 9–11; "Industrial Democracy and Workers' Education," *Bulletin*, No. 13 (January 1982), 10–12; "Rail

Strike," *Bulletin*, No. 11 (October 1981), 13–15; "Labour," *Bulletin*, No. 30 (September 1983), 10–12; Astrow, *Zimbabwe*, pp. 175–81.

32. See *Growth with Equity*, paragraphs 42, 101, 114, 117, 122–24; "We Have No Plans to Nationalize—PM," *Sunday Herald*, January 11, 1981; "Month," *Bulletin*, No. 29 (August 1983), August 11; "Expand—P.M.," *Herald*, April 26, 1986, in *Spiegel*, 5 (April–May 1986), 1.

33. See "Parties," *Bulletin*, No. 11 (October 1981), 7–8; "Month," *Bulletin*, No. 29 (August 1983), August 17; "Month," *Bulletin*, No. 30 (September 1983), September 22; Randolph, "Report on Zimbabwe," 6–8; "3-Year Plan for Progress Spelt Out," *Herald*, April 16, 1982, p. 1; "PM Addresses Women's Conference," *Herald*, March 24, 1984, in *Spiegel*, 3 (April 1984), 21.

34. See Astrow, *Zimbabwe*, pp. 169, 172; Randolph, "Report on Zimbabwe," 5–8; "Month," *Bulletin*, No. 16–17 (April–June 1982), June 24.

35. See Astrow, *Zimbabwe,* pp. 168–71, 223; "Month," *Bulletin*, No. 13 (January 1982), January 13; "Month," *Bulletin*, No. 28 (June–July 1983), July 13; "Security," *Bulletin*, No. 21 (October 1983), 18–21.

36. See "Army," *Bulletin*, No. 10 (August–September 1981), 18–19; "Month," *Bulletin*, No. 32 (November 1983), November 21.

37. See "Month," *Bulletin*, No. 24 (February 1983), February 2, 17; "Month," *Bulletin*, No. 25 (March 1983), March 3, 7, 8, 10; "Month," *Bulletin*, No. 28 (June–July 1983), June 8, 17, July 6; "Month," *Bulletin*, No. 31 (October 1983), October 7; "Month," *Bulletin*, No. 33–34 (December 1983–January 1984), December 25; "Land," *Bulletin*, No. 33–34 (December 1983–January 1984), 17–19; Astrow, *Zimbabwe*, pp. 171–72, 222–23; "Opposition in Zimbabwe Reports Kidnappings," *The New York Times*, March 8, 1985, p. A-3; "U.S. Group Accuses Zimbabwe of Repression," ibid., May 22, 1986, p. A-16.

38. See "Zimbabwe," *Africa South 1989*, pp. 1142 43; "Smith's Party Runs Strongly in Zimbabwe," *The New York Times*, June 29, 1985, p. 26; "Zimbabwe Vote Gives Mugabe 63 of 79 Seats," ibid., July 7, 1985, p. 1; "Zimbabwe after Vote," ibid., July 8, 1985, p. A-3; "Talks Aimed at Unity Stall," ibid., February 25, 1986: p. A-16; "Nkomo Says Sole Ambition Now Is Peace," ibid., March 2, 1986, p. 19; "Rival Zimbabwe Parties Agree to Merge," ibid., December 23, 1987, p. A-3; "Unity Talks," *Herald*, April 17, 1986, in *Spiegel*, 5 (April 1986), 6; "Full Text of the Crucial Document," *Moto*, No. 63 (March 1988), 9, being the text of the unity agreement between ZANU and ZAPU, signed December 22, 1987.

39. See "Zimbabwe," *Africa South 1989*, pp. 1141–44; "Prime Minister Opens Zimbabwe Conference on Reconstruction and Development, March 23, 1981," pp. 6, 9.

40. See Richard L. Sklar, "Reds and Rights: Zimbabwe's Experiment," *Issue*, 14 (1985), 29–31.

41. See ibid., 32.

42. See, Astrow, *Zimbabwe*, pp. 181, 195n257; also, e.g., "Month," *Bulletin*, No. 33–34 (December 1983–January 1984), December 8.

43. See A. J. Dachs and W. F. Rea, *The Catholic Church and Zimbabwe, 1879–1979* (Gwelo: Mambo Press, 1979), pp. 13–46, 54–56, 79-84, 95–101, 132–39.

44. See ibid., pp. 107–15.

45. See Randolph, "Report on Zimbabwe," Tables 1–5.

46. See Dachs and Rea, *Catholic Church and Zimbabwe*, pp. 93–94, 123–24, 192–94.

47. See Linden, *Catholic Church and the Struggle for Zimbabwe*, pp. 51–56.

48. See ibid., pp. 63–66.

49. See ibid., pp. 89–91; Catholic Bishops of Rhodesia, *A Plea for Peace* (London: Geoffrey Chapman, 1966).

50. See Linden, *Catholic Church and the Struggle for Zimbabwe*, pp. 112–13.

51. See ibid., pp. 191–93.

52. See Rhodesia Catholic Bishops' Conference, *The Road to Peace* (Gwelo: Mambo Press [1976]), pp. 6–7, 32.

53. See Dachs and Rea, *Catholic Church and Zimbabwe*, pp. 201, 219–20.

54. See Linden, *Catholic Church and the Struggle for Zimbabwe*, p. 76.

55. See ibid., pp. 105–107, 169–70, 200–201; Dachs and Rea, *Catholic Church and Zimbabwe*, pp. 11, 209, 215–16. See also Rhodesian Catholic Bishops' Conference, Commission for Christian Formation and Worship, *Social Teaching of the Catholic Church* (Gwelo: Mambo Press, 1979); the titles of the seven studies are: (1) *Man's Social Nature and Human Rights*; note the introductory remarks, pp. xi–xv; (2) *The Development and Liberation of Peoples*; (3) *Social Freedom and Social Harmony*; (4) *The Political Responsibility of Christians*; (5) *Social Justice*; (6) *The International Community*; (7) *Christ Is the Soul of Human History*.

56. The authors and titles of these booklets are as follows: (1) Roger Riddell, *Alternatives to Poverty*; (2) Roger Riddell, *The Land Question*; (3) Duncan G. Clarke, *The Unemployment Crisis*; (4) Colin Stoneman, *Skilled Labour and Future Needs*; (5) Rob Davies, *The Informal Sector: A Solution to Unemployment*; (6) Michael Bratton, *Beyond Community Development*; (7) John Gilmurry, Roger Riddell, and David Saunders, *The Struggle for Health*; (8) Vincent Tickner, *The Food Problem*; (9) Roger Riddell, *Education for Employment*. They were all published, between 1978 and 1980, by the Mambo Press, Gwelo, in association with the Catholic Institute for International Relations, London, and the Justice and Peace Commission of the Rhodesian Bishops' Conference.

57. See Dachs and Rea, *Catholic Church and Zimbabwe*, pp. 194–95; Linden, Catholic Church and the Struggle for Zimbabwe, pp. 174–75; interview with Fr. John Dove, Director of Silveira House, Chishawasha, March 1982.

58. See Dachs and Rea, *Catholic Church and Zimbabwe*, p. 195; interview with Fr. E. W. Rogers, Principal of the School of Social Work, Salisbury, April 1982.

59. See Dachs and Rea, *Catholic Church and Zimbabwe*, pp. 215, 218–19; Linden, *Catholic Church and the Struggle for Zimbabwe*, pp. 163-66, 186-91, 196–97, 208–209, 212–13, 232, 249–50, 253–58, 267–68, 274–75; Diana Auret, *Reaching for Justice: The Catholic Commission for Justice and Peace Looks Back at the Past*

*Twenty Years, 1972–1992* (Gweru: Mambo Press, in association with the Catholic Commission for Justice and Peace in Zimbabwe, 1992), pp. 24–28.

60. See Astrow, *Zimbabwe*, pp. 41–42, 47, 99; Linden, *Catholic Church and the Struggle for Zimbabwe*, pp. 218, 241–44 and note 24, 246–48, 261, 271–72; Dachs and Rea, *Catholic Church and Zimbabwe*, pp. 217–18; Smith, Simpson, and Davis, *Mugabe*, pp. 110–11; interview with a confidential informant, March 1982; interview with Fr. Dieter Scholz, onetime member of the Justice and Peace Commission, March 1982.

61. *Plea for Peace* as cited in Linden, *Catholic Church and the Struggle for Zimbabwe*, p. 91.

62. See *Road to Peace*, pp. 16, 18–19.

63. Interviews with Frs. Dove and Rogers; the series *From Rhodesia to Zimbabwe*, passim; Auret, *Reaching for Justice*, pp. 170–75.

64. See "Report of the NCOP Symposium on the Church and the New Order, Driefontein 17–19 May 1977," Pastoral Service Supplement 20, Pastoral Centre, Emerald Hill, Salisbury, June 1977, passim, mimeographed. "NCOP" means "National Council of Priests."

65. See Linden, *Catholic Church and the Struggle for Zimbabwe*, pp. 241, 243–44 and note 24, 278–79; "Zimbabwean Socialism," p. 104/11.

66. Interviews with Frs. Scholz and Dove; with Fr. Kenneth Spence, program organizer for the priests of the South Deanery, Salisbury, March 1982; Fr. Roland Von Nidda, parish assistant in Harare township, April 1982; Fr. Timothy Page, director of the National Pastoral Centre, April 1982. See Smith, Simpson and Davis, *Mugabe*, pp. 38–39.

67. See "Mugabe Outlines Plans and Priorities," 3; Mugabe, "Socialism in Zimbabwe," 1; "Mugabe Seeks Co-operation," Speech to Church Representatives, April 30, 1980, 2–5, mimeographed, ZCBC Secretariat files; "Mugabe Speech at First Assembly of the Inter-Regional Meeting of Bishops of Southern Africa. Aug. 22, 1984," 2–3, mimeographed, ZCBC files (henceforth cited as "Mugabe to IMBISA"); Randolph, "Report on Zimbabwe," 12.

68. See "Mugabe Outlines Plans and Priorities," 3; Mugabe, "Socialism in Zimbabwe," 2–3, 8–9; "Mugabe to IMBISA," 2; "Muzenda Urges Churches to Promote Socialism," 3; "Zimbabwean Socialism," pp. 104/14–15.

69. See, for example, "President Calls for New Role by the Church," *Herald*, September 3, 1980; "President Addresses Seventh Day Adventists," November 11, 1980, passim (Press Statement 714/80/JEP, Department of Information, Salisbury), mimeographed; "President Urges Churches: Re-examine Your Stance," 2–3.

70. See T. Sithole, "An Inclusive Interview with Comrade Banana," *Zimbabwe News*, 17 (May 1986) in *Spiegel*, 5 (May 1986), 9–10. A "Comment," *Moto*, No. 42 (February 1986), 1, points to a danger in Banana's emphasis, that the Church will be too closely identified with the regime.

71. See "Speech of Simbi Mubako, Minister of Justice and Constitutional

Affairs, to the South Deanery Pastoral Committee, Feb. 21, 1981," mimeographed, ZCBC Secretariat files; Report of an interview with President Banana by Tim Chogodo in *Herald*, January 27, 1982; "Keep Off Politics, PM Tells Clergy," *Sunday Mail*, January 31, 1982; "Mugabe to IMBISA," 4.

72. See Mugabe, "Socialism in Zimbabwe," 9.

73. Interviews with Frs. Scholz, Dove, Von Nidda, Page; with Fr. Richard Randolph, Secretary-General of the ZCBC Secretariat, April 1982; Fr. David Harold-Barry, staff of Silveira House, Chishawasha, March 1982; Fr. Clemens Freyer, parish priest at Alaska, April 1982; Clement Mundhoro, Executive Director of the Commission for Justice and Peace, April 1982; and a person well acquainted with affairs at the University of Zimbabwe.

74. See Randolph, "Report on Zimbabwe," 9; "CSSD: Reconstruction and Rehabilitation," p. 102/6; "Month," *Bulletin*, No. 27 (May 1983), May 29; "Month," *Bulletin*, No. 30 (September 1983), September 17; "Resolutions," 3:14; speech by Dr. Dzingai Mutumbuka, Minister of Education and Culture at Mrewa Center, as reported in *Herald*, February 15, 1982, ZCBC Secretariat files. Interview with Fr. Page.

75. See Randolph, "Report on Zimbabwe," 10; "Month," *Bulletin*, No. 27 (May 1983), May 9; Britain-Zimbabwe Society, "Twenty-First Review of the Zimbabwean Press, March 1st to April 18th, 1986," p. 11, mimeographed, citing an editorial in the *Herald*, April 12, 1986; this source will henceforth be cited as "Press Review."

76. See "Politics Undermining the Church," *Herald*, December 9, 1980; "CMRS Annual Meeting, Salisbury, 30 Nov. 1981," *CMRS News Sheet*, No. 102 (February 1982), pp. 102/16–17; "CMRS" means "Conference of Major Religious Superiors (Men)." Oral response of George Rutanyire, Deputy Minister for Youth, to a question during a conference at Silveira House, March 31, 1982.

77. See Zimbabwe Catholic Bishops' Conference, *Welcome Zimbabwe: A Statement of the Roman Catholic Bishops of Zimbabwe* (April 17, 1980), pp. 1–2, 4-paged printed leaflet.

78. See Richard H. Randolph, "The Catholic Church in the New Zimbabwe," December 15, 1980, ZCBC General Secretariat, passim, mimeographed, ZCBC Secretariat files.

79. See "Zimbabwe Bishops Urge Reconciliation, Inculturation of the Gospel Message," *International Fides Press Service*, May 6, 1981, p. NE243.

80. See *Our Way Forward: Pastoral Statement*, issued by the Zimbabwe Catholic Bishops' Conference for the First Sunday of Advent, November 28, 1982 (Gweru: Mambo Press, 1982), pp. 5–6, 8–12.

81. See *Socialism and the Gospel of Christ: Pastoral Statement*, issued by the Zimbabwe Catholic Bishops' Conference, January 1, 1984 (Gweru: Mambo Press, 1984), pp. 1–2, 4–6.

82. See "The Government, the Church and the Troubles," *Bulletin*, No. 24 (February 1983), 17–18; Auret, *Reaching for Justice*, pp. 150–52.

83. See "The Governments, the Church, and the Troubles," 18–19.

84. See ibid., 19–20.

85. See ibid., 21. Auret, *Reaching for Justice*, pp. 154–56, gives an account of subsequent events: renewals of violence, new Justice and Peace inquiries, an apparently halfhearted government investigation, and the gradual ebbing of open conflict.

86. Interviews with Fr. Scholz, Fr. Spence, Fr. Harold-Barry.

87. See letter of Bishop Lamont, *Herald*, January 29, 1981; Randolph, "Report on Zimbabwe," 21. Bishop Lamont was replying to a letter to the newspaper by A. K. H. Weinrich (Sr. Mary Aquina, O.P.) on January 25, in which she urged the churches to be more responsive to President Banana's appeals for help with reconstruction.

88. See "The Role of the Church in Revolutionary Politics," in ZANU(PF), *Society and Church* (N.p.: Jongwe Press, n.d.), pp. 5-8. The pamphlet also contains versions in Shona and Ndebele.

89. See Oskar Wermter, "Church and Party," *Moto*, No. 54 (n.d.), 24.

90. Interview with Fr. Spence. And see, for example, Bernard Chidzero, "The Dynamics of Leadership—The Zimbabwe Context," to Salisbury Archdiocesan Committee, May 25, 1981, Committee Minutes, mimeographed; "Muzenda Urges Church to Promote Socialism," to National Assembly of Diocesan Priests, March 9, 1982, mimeographed; Chidzero, "Opening Address to the Annual General Meeting of the Conference of Major Superiors of Women Religious of Zimbabwe, Feb. 26, 1982," as reported in the Minutes of the Conference's Executive Committee, March 19, 1982, mimeographed; Mugabe, "Socialism in Zimbabwe." The ZCBC Secretariat has assembled a file (untitled) of these and similar items indicative of the government's perspective on religion.

91. See "What the Nations Contribute," *Bulletin*, No. 6 (April 1981), 4; "CSSD: Reconstruction and Rehabilitation (Summary of Addendum, 17 October 1981, to Progress Report)," *ZCBC News Sheet*, No. 102 (February 1982), pp. 102/5–8.

92. Interview with Fr. Spence.

93. Interview with Fr. Dove. See "Silveira House Centre for Leadership and Development in Zimbabwe," 4–6, mimeographed description of the Center and its function; "Silveira House 'Musandiapamwe' C. A. Agricultural Project Zimbabwe," (1982), 1–3, the Centre's mimeographed explanation of a project; Silveira House's comprehensive *Annual Report, 1981*, mimeographed.

94. Confidential informant, July 1986.

95. Interview with Fr. Rogers.

96. See "The Zimbabwe Project," *Bulletin*, No. 11 (October 1981), 3–5; "Cooperatives," *Bulletin*, No. 20 (September 1982), 8–21; "Co-operatives," *Bulletin*, No. 27 (May 1983), 15–24. Interviews with Judith Acton, Director of the Zimbabwe Project, April 1982; with Fr. Dove; Fr. Von Nidda.

97. See Auret, *Reaching for Justice*, pp. 215–16.

98. See "NCYC: Catholic Youth League Council of Zimbabwe Formed," *ZCBC News Sheet*, No. 102 (February 1982), pp. 102/10–12; "CWOZ: Meeting of Catholic Women's Organizations, Salisbury, 19 Sept. 1981," ibid., pp. 102/14–15. Interviews with Frs. Page, Randolph. Confidential informant, July 1986.

99. Interviews with Fr. Oscar Niederberger, Rector of the National Seminary, and Fr. Anthony O'Flynn, seminary professor, April 1982; Mother Rocca, Director of Wadzenai Training Centre for sisters, April 1982; Fr. Henry Wardale, Provincial Superior of the Jesuits in Zimbabwe, March 1982; Fr. Page, Fr. Randolph, Clement Mundhoro.

100. See, for example, "When Is a Strike Lawful and Morally Justified," *The Light*, 23 (March 1982), and a piece in Shona, on Social Teaching, in the same issue.

# 8

# Marxism and the Church in Zambia

ZAMBIA, LIKE ZIMBABWE, had been a British colony. In fact, it shared Zimbabwe's history for some years when Zambia was Northern Rhodesia and was part of the Central African Federation. Zambia, however, won its independence without armed struggle. And here the Church's response to Marxism came to be centered upon a single, narrowly defined issue: an education syllabus.

## GEOGRAPHICAL AND HISTORICAL BACKGROUND

Zambia is just north of Zimbabwe in South Central Africa. Its other neighbors are Tanzania, Malawi, Mozambique, Botswana, Namibia, Angola, and Zaïre. Its area is 291,000 square miles. Situated on a plateau, it has a moderate climate and rainfall that is usually adequate. Commercial farming flourishes in the south and east. Some areas are suitable for grazing. Water power is well developed. Although varied mineral deposits are substantial, only copper is exploited. No oil has been discovered. Because the country is landlocked, its exports and imports move to and from the sea by road or railroad through Zimbabwe and then South Africa or Mozambique, or through Tanzania, Angola, or Zaïre.[1]

The country's population in 1987 totaled 7.2 million, of whom more than 99 percent were indigenous Africans. Among these were 73 ethnic groups. People were moving into the cities more rapidly than elsewhere in Africa, so that by 1980 the population was 41 percent urban. Europeans numbered about 29,000 and Asians 16,000 (in 1974).[2]

Cecil Rhodes's British South Africa Company (BSAC) penetrated north of the Zambezi River in the 1890s by negotiating concessions from local chiefs. The company then governed the area until 1924, when it turned it over to the British Colonial Office and the territory became the Protectorate of Northern Rhodesia. During the company's rule, mining proved less profitable than expected, but subsequently the discovery of extensive copper deposits transformed the economy. Mining companies drew large numbers of Africans into their work force. This brought major changes in social and cultural life, and began to awaken local political consciousness.[3]

## KAUNDA AND THE UNITED INDEPENDENCE PARTY

Because the colonial government had not permitted black workers to form trade unions, the workers established "welfare societies" instead, and they became the nucleus of a nationalist movement. In 1948 a federation of these societies became the Northern Rhodesia African National Congress (ANC). Kenneth Kaunda was one of its founding members.[4]

Kaunda was born in 1924. His father was a teacher and a Presbyterian minister; his mother was likewise a teacher. Kaunda followed their footsteps. Trained as a teacher, he served as headmaster in both Northern and Southern Rhodesia, then worked as a welfare officer for a mining company and as an interpreter for a wealthy white settler. Unhappy experiences with the color bar led him into politics. By 1958 he had become Secretary-General of the ANC, but left it to form a new organization that would become the United Independence Party (UNIP). The colonial government jailed him twice for relatively brief periods. In 1957 he visited India, where Mahatma Gandhi's philosophy of nonviolence so impressed him that he adopted it for his own party. UNIP pressed for a Northern Rhodesian constitution that would give blacks a legislative majority. To this end, Kaunda organized a boycott of territorial elections in 1959 and a campaign of passive resistance in 1961. Britain finally yielded, giving Northern Rhodesia complete internal autonomy in 1962. UNIP won a decisive majority in the elections of January 1964, and Kaunda became prime minister. In October of the same year, Britain granted the territory its independence under the name Zambia.[5]

## ZAMBIAN HUMANISM

The country's independence constitution combined features of the British and American systems. Kaunda was executive president, his party held a two-thirds majority in the legislature, and its members accepted his policies without question.[6]

Kaunda's ideology at the outset was, in fact if not in name, "African Socialism." It aimed to fashion modern political life on the pattern of the communalism and egalitarianism which were said to underlie Africa's precolonial societies. In 1967, however, he worked out a new ideology, possibly because his regime's accomplishments were disappointing. He called this "Zambian Humanism" and made it the official ideology of the party. Because some party members later gave it a Marxist coloration, it will be useful to indicate its lines in some detail.

Kaunda set out his ideas in two lengthy pamphlets published in 1967 and 1973: "Humanism in Zambia and a Guide to Its Implementation, Part I," and "Humanism in Zambia and a Guide to Its Implementation, Part II."[7] He referred frequently to these ideas, too, in speeches to party, government, and general public. Collections of his other writings also included elements of his thinking. Humanism consisted, first, of a social philosophy and, second, of commentary on the political institutions and policies necessary to make the philosophy operative. Kaunda did not explain his principles very carefully, paying little attention to metaphysics or logic. He relied instead, rather superficially, on history and anthropology. His emphasis was on moral norms and moral exhortation, often phrased in biblical terms.[8]

He rejected Communism as an ideology, objecting to its view of religion: "It is believed that a true Communist believes *not* in the Super-Being and the after-life. His religion is his ideology. On the other hand, a humanist believes in the Presence of a Super-Being—the source of all life."[9] He also rejected "the excesses of the ultra-left where man is . . . 'de-humanised'—and remains more as an instrument than the master of institutions."[10] Although at other points he used concepts like Marx's, he did not develop them in the same way as Marx had; his knowledge of Marxism appeared to be superficial.

While Kaunda took the existence of God as a basic principle, he focused on the creature rather than the creator. Man had a preeminent God-given dignity; he was an end in himself, so society had to be man-centered. Social, political, and economic arrangements must serve Man and promote personal growth. There must be no exploitation of man by man, no use of man as a means to an end, no discriminatory treatment of men, no racism. Human rights must be respected. Everyone must have the chance to participate in the social decisions that affected him. Kaunda claimed that this view was part of Africa's ancestral wisdom, a central feature of Africa's traditional way of life. Tradition also justified Humanism's main values. The practice of mutual aid and sharing marked village life. The community cared for *all* its members, the weak and the strong, the failed and the successful. It made no class distinctions; even the chief was only the first among equals. Land was not privately owned; the chief held it in trust for the community and allotted plots to members for their use. These, of course, were also gospel values, linked with Christianity and other world religions. The tragedy was that the societies that asserted them often failed to live up to them.[11]

Kaunda recognized that modernization was threatening the hold these values had on the Zambian people. The control of property was a central question. And in dealing with this, he severely criticized capitalism, which seemed to him the main enemy of humanist values. Capitalism stood for private ownership of productive property. It entailed employing workers for wages and thus of using them for the profit of the employer, exploiting them and extracting wealth from them. It encouraged individualism and competition instead of mutual concern and cooperation. It led to division in society, the creation of social classes. It sowed "the seeds of suspicion, fear, dissension, hatred and violence. It [was] devoid of . . . the need for love and humanity."[12] Capitalism alienated the worker because its autocratic style of management gave no say about production to the real producers. Owners and managers aimed to make their workers feel inferior and insecure, like strangers, in the workplace where they should feel at home.[13]

Sadly, too, capitalist attitudes were catching hold among an influential minority of Zambians, impeding the effort to create an equitable economy and a humanist way of life and leading to moral decadence. Zambians were living beyond their incomes and making up the difference through trickery, fraud, and prostitution. Well-off people were demanding higher pay and expensive perquisites regardless of the way their demands affected anyone else. Successful young people would not let their relatives live with them. The nation was making and importing large quantities of alcohol. Licentious conduct was widespread. People were adopting unseemly foreign styles of dress. The importation of luxuries was eating up foreign exchange. And all this was weakening the moral fiber of independent Zambia.[14]

Kaunda contraposed socialism to capitalism and made it an integral part of his Humanism. Its essence was that private individuals could not own the major instruments of production; the state held these in trust for the community as in the communalism and mutual help of traditional society. He cited only one difference between his socialism and "scientific socialism": the latter was atheistic, aimed only at material well-being, "bread alone." True, other socialists saw socialism as an end in itself. But humanists saw it as a means to an end: socialism would ensure the use of instruments of production for the interests of all; it would secure equitable distribution of society's benefits; it would bring society to its humanistic goals.[15]

Still, Zambia could not become socialist overnight; it could change only gradually. It needed large amounts of capital for development, so it had to allow a role for foreign investors. It also had to respect property that people had obtained before independence. Even emphatically socialist countries gave some scope to private enterprise. Zambia would encourage its citizens' initiative, but under conditions that would prevent man from exploiting man.[16]

Socialism, moreover, was only one stage on the road to the full achievement of Humanism. Chapter 9 of "Humanism II" listed "six important stages in man's development . . . to the time when Man will reach the stage of perfection." These were Creation of Man or Pre–historic age; Primitive Society; Slavery; Feudalism; Capitalism; and Socialism. "Thereafter the next stage is *Humanism.* Here Man is doing unto others as he would have them do unto him." It had taken millions of years "to get to the highest point so far obtained by Man. This is . . . the point of state capitalism flowing into the stage of socialism." Zambia was just emerging from a capitalist to a state-controlled economy. It would move from there to a socialist, or common-ownership, economy. Then the process would go on until Man reached the stage of perfection when the economy, like everything else, would be run by the force of love. Man would be loving the Lord his God with all his heart, soul, mind, and strength. The prophecy would be fulfilled: "Thy Kingdom come, Thy will be done on earth as it is in Heaven."[17]

The State's evolution would parallel that of the economy. Man needed the State because of his present imperfection. Elements of the animal in him blocked his progress. He needed authority backed by coercion to create a framework of order and justice. Although the State was entrenched in violence, it was useful because man had not yet worked out anything better. It had grown from the village-state to the nation-state and would grow to the world-state. In the humanist view, however, more had to be done. Man had to overcome the beast in himself and rid himself of selfishness. He would finally succeed, and then there would be no need of armies, prisons, and the police. "The State, no longer useful for man, would be buried in the past."[18]

Although Kaunda's description of history's movement had some similarities to Marx's, it was clearly not the same. His stages of social development were different. He did not use historical or economic analysis to show that the stages followed a systematic pattern. And he gave God a place in his theory. It was God who initiated history by creating the universe and making man preeminent in it. And man's Humanist destiny lay precisely in fulfilling God's great design.[19] Kaunda came closer to Marx when he described the end-product of social evolution. The process would end in Utopia: a stateless, classless society, free of coercion, in which men and women would live in harmony, selflessly serving the commonweal; each would contribute according to his ability and receive according to his needs. "Humanism II" acknowledged that both theories "believe in and work for the transcendance of the State . . . so that *man* will, in the final stage of development, be himself again . . . a *man* born free of, and living and dying free from, the *animal* in him."[20]

One other critical ingredient of Kaunda's Humanism was its call for citizen participation. He wanted the people to be more directly involved in decision making than they were through parliamentary representation. This would be "participatory democracy," giving effect to the slogan "power to the people." The public would "control, hour by hour, week by week and year by year, local as well as national affairs, and ultimately international affairs." He would implement this ideal by decentralizing the institutions of government and party. In the rural areas the village would be the basic unit; in the cities it would be a small grouping of houses or party members. These units would be gathered into a pyramid of intermediary institutions reaching upward to the centers of power.[21]

To arrange broad participation in economic decision making as well, Kaunda wanted to establish cooperatives in the rural areas and give employees a voice in industrial and commercial ventures. Workers would have a say about how much capital would be raised for their enterprise and about how to produce and distribute whatever they made. Workers and "progressive managers and directors" would keep the new managerial elite from exploiting their employees. They would be concerned, too, for the well–being of the peasants. They would use their productive resources to bring about balanced development in all parts of the country. Kaunda, however, did not at this time propose any concrete way to implement this program. He only suggested studying methods which were used in other countries.[22]

## UNIP as Political Party

After independence, as was said earlier, Zambia's legislature was controlled by UNIP, the political party Kaunda led. Before outlining the party's policies, it will be useful to say something about its structure and how it conceived its own role.

Several parties held seats in the first parliament after independence. But in Kaunda's view partisan politics endangered national unity as appeals to sectional and ethnic loyalties aggravated bitterness and encouraged violence; so the country needed a one-party system. Early on, he expected the electorate to rally around UNIP and change Zambia into a *de facto* one–party state. But two elections failed to produce this result, and in December 1972 government made it so *de jure*.[23] Although UNIP remained a mass movement rather than a vanguard party, its relationship to government was much like that of "the party" in Marxist states. Its 1978 constitution described it as "the militant organization of revolutionary peasants, workers and intellectuals" which would "exercise supreme authority over all state organs" and as "the supreme organization and the guiding political force in the land."[24] The party, then, was superior to government; it would determine the policy that the government would implement. The country's 1973 constitution incorporated UNIP's self-understanding. It institutionalized the one-party state, established UNIP's supremacy within the state, and integrated its structures with those of government: "The [Party's] Central Committee shall formulate the policy of the government. . . . Where a decision of the Central Committee is in conflict with a decision of the Cabinet, the decision of the Central Committee shall prevail." This constitution, too, included the party's (1971) constitution as an appendix, to serve as a basis for settling questions that required constitutional interpretation.[25]

The party's constitution empowered the General Conference "to formulate and revise party policies and programs," but the conference met only briefly every five years. The National Council was "the highest policy-making body of the party in the interval between General Conferences," but likewise met infrequently and only for a few days at a time. Real power, therefore, lay with the party's president and the twenty-five members of the Central Committee. They ran party business from day to day and set the agenda and controlled the flow of information to the conference and council. Rank-and-file party members played little or no role in choosing the members of any of these bodies. It was the members of the conference who chose the Central Committee and the party president. But all electoral choices were absolutely restricted to candidates approved by the National Council and virtually restricted to candidates approved by the Central Committee. Candidates for parliament also needed the committee's endorsement, and the committee designated the sole candidate in the country's presidential elections. Yet Kaunda insisted that UNIP was "synonymous with the people and their aspirations." "UNIP's political line is the line of the masses."[26]

Party discipline, moreover, limited members' free expression. Although they could comment freely on party shortcomings at party meetings, they had a duty "to refrain from criticising publicly the party or any member thereof in relation to its or his activities in the party." Kaunda himself agreed that democracy must respect and accommodate minority views, so there must be freedom of discussion. But there must also be obedience in implementation: "the minority have an obligation to accept the decision of the majority." He complained that people in parliament were criticizing party and government "as if they were not members of the party." Their assertions were distorted, fanciful, and malicious. He had ordered party and government leaders to stop making public statements about the working of parliament and would see that disciplinary procedures against offenders were tightened. In the National Council, once a decision had been made, members must accept it and defend it without question; decisions of the council's majority expressed the will of the people.[27]

### UNIP's POLICIES AND PROGRAMS

UNIP's main objective was to improve the material well-being of the black population, which the colonial government had gravely neglected. This entailed providing schools, medical services, housing, higher cash income, and amenities such as pipe-borne water. For the long term it entailed placing the national economy on firmer ground, especially by reducing its dependence on copper mining. The government accordingly worked out a succession of development plans, the first three of which covered the years from 1966 to 1984.[28]

Copper nevertheless remained central to the economy. Initially, its price and production were high. In the early 1970s it provided about 50 percent of of the Gross Domestic Product (GDP) and 95 percent of Zambia's foreign exchange. The government sought to capture for domestic use a higher share of the industry's profits—but to do this without driving away the multinational corporations or undermining confidence among other potential foreign investors. A constitutional amendment in 1969 authorized cancellation of the huge mining concessions and other prospecting rights which the colonial government had awarded to the Anglo-American Company and the Roan Selection Trust. Kaunda then negotiated leases with these companies on terms more favorable to Zambia. Government later brought together almost all the enterprises it controlled, more than ninety, under a holding company called the Zambia Industrial and Mining Corporation (ZIMCO); the prime minister chaired its board of directors. Kaunda, however, did not press Europeans to leave the country, because he knew he needed their expertise. Many whites stayed on, not only in the technical and managerial side of mining but also as public administrators and commercial farmers. Their number did decline, nevertheless, from seventy thousand at independence to twenty-nine thousand ten years later.[29]

In addition to strengthening its hand with the mining corporations, the UNIP government sought more control over the mineworkers' union and other trade unions. The mineworkers were particularly strong because their skills were so critical for the economy. Their pressure for wages and benefits accelerated the inflationary spiral. High wages widened the gap between the modern, urban sector and the traditional, rural sector, thus contributing to the rapid migration from country to city. UNIP's efforts at tighter control failed, however, and the unions retained their fundamental autonomy.[30]

Apart from the copper complex, the UNIP government took steps to stimulate indigenous entrepreneurship. In 1968 and 1972, Kaunda reserved retail and wholesale trading and some services to Zambian citizens. He offered financial incentives to foreigners who became partners to Zambians in other businesses. But to prevent the growth of an indigenous capitalism, he proposed quantitative limits above which government would take over an enterprise even if a Zambian owned it.[31]

Government took measures toward public ownership of land as well. In 1975 Kaunda converted freehold ownership into one hundred-year leaseholds. In the rural areas this mostly affected commercial farms; it seemed not to bestir any adverse reactions, perhaps because the leaseholds were so long-term. In urban and residential areas, national or local authorities were to take over certain categories of land and buildings, with compensation in some cases. This measure aimed to curb the sale or rental of property at exorbitant prices.[32]

UNIP's socioeconomic policies, unfortunately, did not work very well. The sharp drop in copper prices after 1970 and constraints arising from neighboring Rhodesia's UDI limited government's ability to finance development. Other problems lay in government's own failings.

It is true that UNIP's programs led to visible improvement on the educational front. Primary school enrollment increased by 60 percent between 1964 and 1968; secondary school enrollment more than doubled before 1973; the country's first university opened at Lusaka in 1966.[33] But agricultural programs lagged badly. Although the number of registered cooperative farms increased rapidly, few of them were still functioning in 1979. A project in 1980 to set up several large, mechanized, state farms apparently never got off the ground. The rural service centers that government planned never took shape. Arrangements for government to buy, pay for, and transport agricultural produce were poor; for one thing, the prices offered were too low.[34] The new managers of parastatal corporations enjoyed high salaries and expensive perquisites, thus accelerating the growth of social classes, contrary to Kaunda's intentions.[35] Many managers, too, used their positions for further enrichment through corrupt behavior. Kaunda pressed a reluctant party for several years to adopt a Leadership Code. But after it did so in 1972, the code was largely ignored in practice.[36]

In 1972 the UNIP government adopted a new national constitution that guaranteed a standard list of civil rights, including freedom of conscience and religion. But some rights could be suspended if the president declared a state of emergency, as the constitution allowed him to do for limited periods. The constitution provided for a Commission of Investigation which would function as an ombudsman, investigating charges of abusive conduct by party or government officials. It also guaranteed the independence of the judiciary by granting Supreme Court judges permanent tenure until age sixty-five; the president could remove them only for inability to do their work or for misconduct if these failings were confirmed by a special tribunal.[37]

In actual practice the government generally respected civil rights, although some of its actions raised questions. At different times, invoking a state of emergency, it restricted opposition political parties; in 1968 it forbade the ANC to organize in some localities; in 1972 it banned the newly organized United People's Party (UPP) and detained some of its leaders. In 1969 a public uproar followed the courts' release of two unarmed Portuguese soldiers who had crossed from Mozambique. Members of the Zambian Youth Service attacked the high court. Kaunda and the chief justice engaged in a bitter exchange and the justice resigned. Parliament then amended the constitution to allow the president to appoint relatively inexperienced lawyers (meaning "Africans") to judgeships that only whites had previously held.[38]

Although the UNIP government did not directly censor the media, it sometimes put them under heavy pressure. It took over radio and television. Early, it bought the *Central African Mail,* one of the country's two daily newspapers, and renamed it the *Zambian Mail.* The president, moreover, appointed the editor of the other paper, the *Times of Zambia,* even though it was privately owned. In 1972 he replaced the editor because the paper severely criticized governmental inefficiency and the behavior of important UNIP leaders. In 1977 he took over the *Times* on behalf of the party because it prematurely publicized a Zambian diplomatic initiative in the Rhodesian crisis, and took over the *Sunday Times* because it was snidely critical of his campaign against portrayals of sex and violence in films and other media.[39]

The UNIP government adopted the policy of nonalignment in foreign affairs. The country maintained its economic links with Britain. It was friendly to the United States and welcomed American economic aid. It established diplomatic relations with the Communist countries of Eastern Europe and with China. China built and financed, interest free, the Tazara railroad, which linked Zambia with the Tanzanian port of Dar es Salaam. Yugoslavia helped build the Kafue Dam. Bulgaria helped train the police.[40]

Zambia strongly supported the liberation movements in Mozambique, Rhodesia, Namibia, and South Africa. It permitted them to use its territory as a base for both civil and military operations. As intimated earlier, this support was costly. Most seriously, friction with the Smith regime hampered the export of copper and reduced the flow of imports vital to the economy. Rhodesian raiders, moreover, sometimes did heavy damage to the country's internal transportation facilities.[41]

All in all, then, Zambia's domestic and foreign policies showed no notably strong influence from the Communist bloc. Kaunda did not radicalize Zambian society. Although he explicitly advocated policies that could be called "socialist" and implemented some of them, his socialism was closer to Western than to Eastern European models. UNIP was a centralized party running a one-party state and showed some structural affinities with Marxist–Leninist models, but its style was not nearly so totalitarian. The government's record on civil rights was generally acceptable.

## Marxist Influence in Society

Yet Marxist influence was at work in some quarters. There were persuasive indications of concerted efforts to bring it to bear upon institutions and decisions.

At the University of Zambia some faculty members at least leaned toward Marxist views, and one channel for communicating these views to students was a course entitled "African Development Studies" (ADS), which for a long time was obligatory for all first-year students. Some student societies were centers of Marxist activism, most notably the Philosophy Society. Several short-lived student publications, carrying such titles as *Hammer, Grenade, Praxis,* and *The Dialectic,* showed strong Marxist inclinations. In the judgment of knowledgeable observers, only a small minority of students could be called hard-core Marxists, while a larger minority were sympathetic with them, but activists on the left often controlled the students' union, UNZASU, and used it to manipulate the entire student body.[42]

Such manipulation was at work, for example, in the demonstrations that led to closure of the university in 1982. The university had scheduled a ceremony to inaugurate a new Institute of Human Relations, and had invited an array of distinguished guests. UNZASU, which radical leftist students had previously taken over through a coup d'état, took the occasion to circulate a manifesto in scurrilous language protesting against the institute and its director. The university decided to expel several student leaders. UNZASU issued more circulars, more demonstrations followed, and authorities closed the university.[43] UNZASU's manifesto predicted that the new institute was going to conceal the real reason behind class conflict and put the workers to sleep. It would not accept that poverty in Zambia resulted from capitalist relations of production or that worker–peasant militancy was going to overthrow neocolonialism and establish the dictatorship of the proletariat.[44] According to another circular, there was "consistency in the manner of UNZASU's ideology, Marxism-Leninism," which guides its decision making. This complained, too, that ADS was no longer offered to science students, with the result that a student "in that school does not understand the essence of imperialism."[45] UNZASU observed also: "There have been misconceptions that we are sponsored by Soviet Russia in virtue of their provision to us of progressive literature. . . . This is not the case at all."[46] The fact was, however, that on the day of the institute's inauguration a truck from a foreign embassy unloaded in a campus parking lot a large stock of publications from the Soviet Union's Novosti Press.[47]

Indications of Marxist influence were also visible outside university circles. In late 1978, for example, Njeku Anamela, the publicity secretary of a newly formed organization called the Union of Working Class

Youths, announced that the union would train its members in scientific socialism.[48]

More important, UNIP's own leadership included people who were committed Marxists or at least had strong Marxist leanings. According to informed insiders, they were not numerous but they sometimes held strategic positions. Indications of their influence became strong during a lengthy debate between the Christian churches and the government about a proposal to teach scientific socialism in the schools.[49]

### History and Development of the Catholic Church in Zambia

Before discussing this episode, however, we will say something about the position of the Catholic Church in Zambia.

White Fathers from Nyasaland moved into the northeastern part of Northern Rhodesia around the turn of the twentieth century, establishing their first permanent mission in 1895. Jesuits from the Zambesi Mission set up their first station in the south in 1905; Polish Jesuits, expelled from Mozambique by the anticlerical Portuguese government, joined them in 1910. Irish Capuchins and Italian Franciscans took charge of the areas around Livingstone and Ndola in 1931. The White Sisters arrived in 1905 and other sisters came later. The missionaries initially organized farm settlements around their stations, but then adjusted to increasing urbanization as mining developed. Among other things, they paid more attention to schools. The Jesuits' Canisius College at Chikuni and a school of the Irish Sisters of Charity in Lusaka were among the country's first secondary schools. In the 1950s the Church began to expand its health care, and it also began to promote cooperatives and credit unions.[50]

Students first entered the major seminary in 1928, but the first ordination took place only in 1946. The Holy See appointed the first indigenous bishop in 1963. A congregation of local sisters was founded in 1927; local ordinaries then set up several other groups, and the missionary sisterhoods began to accept local young women. Catechists continued to carry a substantial share of the Church's pastoral work. Layfolk were also active in such organizations as Catholic Action during the 1930s, the Legion of Mary during the 1940s, and the Young Christian Workers during the 1950s. The national hierarchy was established in 1959. There were nine dioceses in 1985; indigenous bishops headed seven of these. There was a Zambia Episcopal Conference, with a National Catholic Secretariat as its executive agency. Catholics numbered about 1.9 million, 28.6 percent of the total population. There were about 500 priests, 160 brothers, and 700 sisters.[51]

Even though white racism existed in the Church during the colonial period, it was not as acute as in Southern Rhodesia. As the nationalist movement gained momentum, Irish and Polish missionaries who had their own experience of foreign oppression could be sympathetic; some of the Poles had been inmates in the Nazis' Dachau. Churchmen, then, were supportive of the campaign for independence. Archbishop Kozlowiecki of Lusaka wrote a pastoral letter on racial equality and social justice in 1959. The bishops sent a joint memorandum to the Prime Minister of the Central African Federation in the same year, calling attention to the discrepancy between the ideal and the practice of racial partnership. A Catholic periodical, *The Leader*, generally backed UNIP.[52]

The Church's relations with other Christian churches were good. Several mainline denominations set up a General Missionary Conference in 1914 which met periodically to discuss common problems, to coordinate joint projects such as biblical translation, and to represent the churches' views to the colonial government. It specifically aimed to "watch over the interests of the Native races." It accordingly intervened, with partial success, to end a poll tax, to limit the takeover of natives' lands, to reverse reductions of government funding for education, and to block the territory's incorporation into a single colony. Some of these churches merged, in 1965, into the United Church of Zambia (UCZ). In 1960 the membership of the mainline Protestant churches came to about 38 percent of the population. Most of these churches supported nationalist aspirations during the push for independence. The Catholic Church was a member of the Missionary Conference until 1935. Although it then withdrew on instructions from the Holy See, it continued to cooperate with the other churches. Thus it joined an ecumenical effort, in the 1960s, to communicate a Christian outlook through the media; one project was a weekly newspaper, the *National Mirror*. Catholic secondary schools used the ecumenical syllabus for religious education developed at Gaba in Uganda.[53]

Kaunda's government collided with two small religious groups in the 1960s. The Lumpa sect's failure to rally behind the nationalist cause in 1964 angered UNIP supporters. Subsequent clashes resulted in seven hundred deaths. The government sent troops to control the violence, proscribed the church, and detained its leader. The international Watchtower Movement (Jehovah's Witnesses) rejected all political authority; its children did not participate in patriotic ceremonies in schools; and the members refused to vote in a crucial referendum in 1969. Their attitude again angered UNIP's followers and led to violence. The government then deported alien officials of the movement.[54] But these measures were exceptional in Kaunda's dealings with the churches. His government did not interfere with the standard activities of the churches, including their running of schools and hospitals. By this time Kaunda himself had dropped his own church affiliation, but he remained a nondenominational Christian, still seasoning his public statements with religious references. The Catholic bishops, for their part, made no objection to Humanism, to socialism as the road to Humanism, to the one-party state, to the nationalization of enterprises, or to government actions touching civil rights.

## UNIP's Proposal for Political Education

In 1975, however, the bishops learned about a syllabus for "political education" which government planned to introduce into the schools and extramural educational programs. This provided, in grades 1 through 4, for "stories about how the Europeans came with the Bible in one hand and a gun in the other." Grades 5 through 7 would receive instruction on "the differences between humanism and religion." University courses would deal with "present-day options of capitalism or scientific socialism" and bourgeois-*vs.*-Marxist-Leninist strategies of accumulating surplus value. Education for the masses would include discussion of "the missionaries and the Church as fore-runners of imperialism and colonialism in Zambia." An appended reading list contained a generous selection of books published by Progress Publishers and the Novosti Press in Moscow.[55]

By 1978 the government had focused the syllabus more sharply on "scientific socialism," and was coming closer to introducing it in the schools. In December, the Ministry of Education instructed the heads of secondary schools and teacher-training colleges to send one teacher, who had to be a member of UNIP, to a six-month course on political education at the President's Training College.[56] Several similar but not identical versions of the syllabus for this course, along with notes on its content, appeared at about the same time. Some sections treated the standard fare of any civics program, but other sections were clearly oriented toward Marxism. A section on "philosophy" explained Marxist metaphysics and epistemology, dialectical materialism, base and superstructure, class and class relations. Another section treated the party's role in promoting revolutionary ideas and dealt with utopian socialism, scientific socialism, and "imperialism, the highest stage of capitalism." And a section on "political economy" covered modes of production, capitalist accumulation, and the Zambian economy as an appendage of the international capitalist system.[57]

When the bishops first learned of the school syllabus in political education, they did not react. But an incident in January 1979 made them uneasy. UNIP's Secretary-General, a Catholic named Mainza Chona, was addressing a Catholic celebration of World Peace Day. He spoke about taking the road to Humanism through scientific socialism. Some scientific socialists, he said, were not atheists; socialism was not uniform in all countries; and Kaunda repeatedly stressed Christian beliefs as the foundation of Humanism. So religion would continue to play an important part in Zambia's national life.[58]

### THE CHURCH'S RESPONSE TO THE SYLLABUS

The bishops apparently decided at this point that there was need to deal with Marxist influence in public life, but there is little documentation on how they approached this task. A small committee of clergy and laity did meet, in March, with Archbishop Milingo at Lusaka. They concluded that Marxism would undermine Humanism and threaten civil liberties, and recommended that the Church work out a program to teach Catholics their obligations.[59] A few months later, at Monze, Church personnel held a seminar on scientific socialism. Several members of UNIP's research bureau attended one session, and one of them gave an explanation of scientific socialist theory along with a Marxist analysis of what was wrong with Zambia's economy. At other sessions the participants suggested ways of dealing with Marxist influence. These included more effective witness through social action, improved formation of the clergy in social doctrine, and better instruction of Catholics on the problems that scientific socialism would raise.[60]

In August 1979 the Zambia Episcopal Conference, the Christian Council of Zambia, and the Zambia Evangelical Fellowship jointly published "The Churches and Marxism: A Statement by the Religious Leaders of Zambia."[61] There was much talk, the statement began, about advancing to Humanism through scientific socialism. The proponents were assuring Christians that this would not entail introducing atheism or attacking religion. As was well known, however, scientific socialism normally treated religion as an enemy, and scientific socialist governments usually tried to wipe out belief in God and to obstruct the Church's work. Christian leaders felt bound to speak to their followers on this topic lest they seem to agree with what was being said.[62]

"Socialism" had many meanings. "Scientific socialism" meant the particular theory inspired by the writings of Marx and Lenin. According to this theory, the vanguard party acted only on behalf of the people, but in practice it exercised absolute control over the state, the means of production, and the lives of the people themselves. According to Marxists, too, belief in God was an obstacle to human development.[63]

Socialism, taken as a system that used public ownership of the means of production to make sure that the nation's wealth served all citizens fairly, was in harmony with Christian belief. So the socialist policies that Kaunda outlined in "Humanism" were acceptable. But *scientific* socialism did not respect the dignity and religious dimension of man and, therefore, had to be rejected. Likewise to be rejected was any form of capitalism that put profit before persons or ignored human dignity. According to the Church's teaching, the right of private property was always limited by the requirement that it be used for the benefit of all.[64]

The Church leaders cited Lenin's writings and the policies of Marxist governments in Russia, China, Mozambique, and Angola to show how Marxist doctrine and practice were hostile to religion. Marx expected religion to die of itself, but Lenin campaigned to kill it. In the view of both men, socialism was completely opposed even to belief in God. People in Zambia perhaps did not fully understand this aspect of taking the scientific socialist road to humanism.[65]

Humanism, too, was of many kinds. *Atheistic*, or *secular*, humanism insisted that God and the spiritual world did not exist; so men did not need to look to any deity in conducting their lives. *Christian* humanism, by contrast, taught that men and women should become fully human by following the teaching and example of Jesus. Zambian Humanism, while it declared that society should serve man, agreed that man himself was centered on God. It respected man's nature and God's place in man's own life. Kaunda explicitly rejected scientific socialism; it was different from Humanism. Zambian Humanism, moreover, was not the theory of one man but a distillation of the people's traditional wisdom. The very ones who accused Christianity of attacking traditional values were destroying those values by introducing atheism to Zambian society.[66]

The church leaders rejected scientific socialism not just because it denied God but because it rejected man as well. "We differ profoundly from Marxists in our understanding of the human person." They explained Christian humanism at length. It insisted that men and women had inviolable rights to what they needed materially and spiritually to develop as human persons. Marxism did not value human beings because of their intrinsic worth but because they could contribute to the development of "humanity." Marxists would suppress individual rights, then, because, for them, "humanity" held the place of God. But suppression deprived men and women of the thing that most belonged to human persons: their freedom to be responsible for their own lives.[67]

Marxists, moreover, misunderstood the origin of evil. In their view, it came ultimately from private ownership of the means of production; so they would do away with oppression by doing away with private ownership. Although it is true that evil can be built into dehumanizing social structures, the root of evil was in the human spirit: pride, selfishness, greed, and hunger for power. We will not eliminate it by changing structures but by changing our hearts—with God's help.[68]

Scientific socialism, according to some people, differed from Christianity only because it did not believe in God. *This* difference, however, made *all* the difference. Belief in God ran all through the Christian's understanding of man and his whole effort at human development, especially his respect for human rights. From the viewpoint of Marxists' atheism, by contrast, the Communist state could exercise absolute power and override all rights in order to bring about the classless society.[69]

True, Christians in the Western world were carrying on dialogue with Marxism. Admittedly also, some Marxist criticisms were valid. For example, Christians were often silent about social injustices in capitalist and colonialist societies, whereas Marxists spoke out and their speaking reawakened the Church's own concern for justice and the needs of the poor. But people should not call themselves "Christian Marxists" just because they wanted a social revolution to set up a just social order or because they found some truth in what Marx said.[70]

It might be possible to use some parts of Marxist analysis in our study of social change. Christians and Marxists could also cooperate in acting to end exploitation "if they held their ultimate beliefs in abeyance." They could also talk about understanding each other better and deciding on areas of common concern. But obstacles remained: for example, regardless of what Marxists said during the struggle, they often forgot respect for other people's ideas once they had achieved power.[71]

There was new pressure in Zambia, the church leaders continued, to put scientific socialism in place of humanist socialism. This did not come from the process of participatory democracy; it followed the theory of the vanguard party, wherein the party claimed to know what was good for the people whether they wanted it or not. The very manner of acting indicated that persons unknown were manipulating us along a Communist path. Their talk of participatory democracy could become a smoke-screen for dictatorial rule.[72]

The church leaders therefore had some questions to ask. Given that party leaders and "political educators" were taking courses in Marxism, who made the decision to give the party a Marxist ideology? Were the common man's views being sought and would they be listened to? Were even the leaders free to disagree with the new policy, or was their reeducation intended simply to "enlighten" them about the decision? Were the parents asked about the Young Pioneers' indoctrination in scientific socialism? Was scientific socialism to be taught in the schools? If so, to what extent would it interfere with teaching religion?[73]

The church leaders' concluding paragraphs warned their members. The adoption of scientific socialism threatened constitutional freedoms. People should expect pressure on religious freedom as happened wherever this doctrine was applied. Church members should take a stand before it was too late; Christians in UNIP should keep the party true to its own principles. We must not let anyone introduce an oppressive system because of our indifference or inactivity.[74]

Neither the government nor the party reacted in any dramatic way to the church leaders' statement. Kaunda seems only to have expressed a wish to discuss Humanism and development with the churches.[75] The statement had no visible impact on the supporters of Marxist tendencies. Government went ahead with its plans for ideological education.

In September 1981, Catholic educational experts made discreet inquiries about the political education program in several teacher-training colleges. They concluded that it was hostile to religion and that the bishops' conference should do something to counter its influence.[76] In October an article in the *National Mirror* expressed alarm over the training of teachers for political education and cited other recent events that showed Marxist leanings in party or government; it saw a threat to religious observance and human rights.[77] In March 1982, the National Council of Catholic Women arranged a seminar to discuss political education with Education Ministry officials. The women asked why government had not publicized its plans much earlier and why it had not given opportunity for a public debate on the issue.[78]

A few days later, however, a much more significant meeting took place. Following up his earlier desire for a discussion with the churches, Kaunda himself invited Christian and non-Christian religious leaders to a seminar on "Humanism and Development," March 18–19, at Lusaka. Participating were representatives of twelve mainline Christian churches, the Salvation Army, the Quakers, the Seventh Day Adventists, the Bahai Faith, the Hindu Association, the Christian Council of Zambia, the Zambia Evangelical Fellowship, and such church-affiliated organizations as the Bible Society, the Young Men's and Young Women's Christian Associations, the National Council of the [Catholic] Laity, and the two [Catholic] religious superiors' conferences.[79]

The president addressed the seminar's opening and closing, and also distributed a paper entitled "The Attainment of Humanism through Socialism."[80] He opened by inviting the participants to examine "the role of all religious groups in the nation's efforts to build a Humanist state through Socialism." He reviewed his own writings on Humanism and then commented on the church leaders' 1979 statement. Here he showed more sympathy with Marxism than he previously had. Scientific socialism, he said, might well have matched the scientific and technological achievements of capitalism if it had the same amount of time (that is, since the industrial revolution). Look at the USSR's accomplishments in the relatively brief period since 1917. Yes, Marxist-Leninists did regard religion as the opium of the masses. But he could understand this; even in Northern Rhodesia the Bible had lulled the masses to sleep while exploiters captured power. Although he personally agreed that belief in God should influence men's conduct for the better, civilized behavior was not a monopoly of believers. Whatever people might say about Stalin, the two world wars "were started and supported by those who went to Church every Sunday." Ian Smith in Zimbabwe and racists in Angola killed innocent people by the thousands. "If we were to raise . . . the subject of allies, we could find much, much more in common between Humanism and Communism than we have with Capitalism." He appreciated the church leaders' concern that Marxism-Leninism should take over in Zambia. Still, scientific socialism existed; they agreed in their statement that Marxist analysis could be a useful tool for examining social change. Zambians, therefore, should study this ideology.[81]

The president went on to answer, one by one, the questions the church leaders posed in their statement. The party did *not* intend to establish a Marxist-Leninist state; UNIP had *not* adopted Marxist ideology. If the party were to take such a decision, it *would* seek the common man's views and party leaders *would* be free to disagree. The party did *not* establish the Young Pioneers to indoctrinate young people with scientific socialism; this is why it did not consult parents about it. "Scientific socialism as such" was *not* being taught in primary and secondary schools. But the party did intend "to have this subject taught . . . as part of political education." It would *not* replace religious education.[82]

In the paper he circulated, Kaunda proposed to discuss why socialism was necessary for Humanism, what exploitation meant, and how a Humanist looked at Marxism-Leninism. His comments on the first point largely repeated material from his earlier writings. Socialism was a system of common ownership in which the mass of the people controlled the economy. We needed this in order to curb capitalist acquisitiveness and exploitation. So socialism was a necessary stage on the road to Humanism.[83]

He explained "exploitation" mainly by homey and vastly oversimplified examples of how "small commodity production," "merchant capital," and "industrial capital" worked. Basically he followed Marx's view that the capitalist accumulated his wealth by taking to himself surplus value which rightfully belonged to the "producer." This process separated and alienated the worker from workplace, tools, product, and the capitalist himself. These views reflected some major themes of the Political Education syllabus.[84]

On his third point, Kaunda stated that history has been moving toward the ideal society for man. But international capitalism, on the one hand, and poverty, on the other, stood between man and the goals God had set for him. As man struggled to end these evils, he found that there were always two groups: those who oppress (the "haves") and those who fight oppression (the "have–nots"). Both the Humanist and the Communist fought against poverty and international oppression. The Humanist believed that man would go forward through the God-given power of creative thought; the Communist also believed that man would go forward but did not believe that creation was God's work. The capitalist talked about fighting poverty but would not do anything that would destroy capitalism; while he accepted God's existence, he was far from doing God's will in the way he organized society. As believers in man's perfectibility, Marxists were allies of Humanists. Yes, there were differences. People said that Stalin killed millions of people. But Stalin "was beleaguered by the capitalists who wanted to destroy . . . the first revolutionary state in the world." Exploiters in Russia were cooperating with them and this was civil war. Anyhow, those who blamed Stalin did the same thing in their colonies and elsewhere. "Stalin was trying to defend his own system from outside interference." Another difference was that Communism was godless; but the right to practice religious faith was enshrined in the Soviet Union's constitution. These two differences

should not keep Zambians from studying Marxism-Leninism as a subject. We should understand this powerful force just as capitalism and
other "isms."[85]

Kaunda's paper, like his opening speech, echoed Marxist-Leninist
thinking much more than his earlier writings had. It also showed aston-
ishing ignorance or naïveté about the historical background of the two
world wars, the Russian revolution, Soviet religious persecution, and the
enormity of Stalin's crimes against his own people.

After the president's opening speech, each of ten discussion groups
dealt with one of ten questions related to the seminar's theme, and each
group reported back to the plenary session. The reports often made identical points; they were critical of capitalism and resented charges that the
church was an agent of capitalism. Zambia's failings were basically
moral: corruption in high places, irresponsibility among workers, privileged access of insiders to scarce goods and services, and so forth. The
church should be prophetic: awakening consciences, denouncing injustices, teaching the meaning of Humanism, and motivating people to live
by Humanist ideals.[86]

Even though only one question was about Marxism, seven groups
dealt with this topic. Marxism-Leninism was coming to dominate Zambian Humanism. It was atheistic. It was undermining Humanism's foundation, namely, belief in God. Half the Political Education Syllabus was
about Marxism. The syllabus took the wrong approach. If there were
good points in scientific socialism, there were good points in capitalism
also. Our teaching should not aim at inducing students to accept either
one; we should point out the shortcomings of both.[87]

We should give Humanism a chance to succeed without tying it to
another ideology. So far, Zambia had been more successful than many
other African countries. Changing the social structure was not going to
ensure fairer distribution of material goods; political leaders in socialist
countries were much better off than the peasants. The basic difficulty
was in men's hearts. The introduction of scientific socialism without
consulting the people was itself exploitative. Why had government failed
to seek the public's input on this issue? The discussants welcomed Kaunda's assurance that no decision had been made to adopt scientific socialism as the country's ideology, but they would welcome even more an
assurance that no such decision would be made in the future. The dialogue begun at the seminar should continue.[88]

One group acknowledged that Marxist-Leninists were involved with
the liberation of the oppressed in other countries. But their methods were

coercive. They dictated what every person must do. They allowed no freedom of expression. They made people act like robots. They did not achieve the very thing that appealed so much to Kaunda: equality. They destroyed man in the name of man and thus produced the very opposite of humanization.[89]

In his closing speech the president seemed not to comprehend this barrage of criticism. He acknowledged that his effort to explain the party's viewpoint was not entirely successful, but he somehow believed that he had put to rest the religious leaders' concern about teaching scientific socialism in the schools. The country, he assured them, would continue to respect religion. But it must accept a new approach to organizing the production and distribution of wealth, namely, "socialism leading to Humanism." Although the economy was now "mixed," he would ultimately organize it on the basis of cooperative or common ownership. Some people thought this method was too slow. But the alternative was dictatorship, which he rejected because it was oppressive and did not accord with the centrality of man. He would stand by participatory democracy. The exchange of views at the seminar was itself an exercise of democracy. The party and the government would study the participants' observations.[90]

After the seminar, Catholic Church personnel met once more at Monze on April 17 and again went over the issues. They emphasized the need to speak in positive rather than negative terms and not to be apologists for capitalism. They should rouse the faithful to concern about scientific socialism and the syllabus through publications and group discussions. They should inform and organize Catholic parents and teachers. They should promote developmental education among Catholics. They should do their own homework on social doctrine.[91]

A General Synod of the United Church of Zambia met April 19–22. It prepared a sixteen-page paper "to inform our Church's members about scientific socialism." This was a well-organized, thoughtful presentation in relatively simple language. It reviewed, accurately but critically, the main ideas and programs of scientific socialism and their implementation in socialist countries. It explained the issues on which the Church and UNIP agreed and disagreed. It recalled the oppressive practices of Marxist-Leninist governments. It expressed fear that ulterior motives lay behind the government's plan to teach scientific socialism in the schools.[92]

The Zambia Episcopal Conference, the Christian Council of Zambia, and the Zambia Evangelical Fellowship published another joint document on May 11, "A Letter from the Leaders of the Church in Zambia to Their Members about the President's Seminar on Humanism and Development." It was a four-page leaflet, again in simple language. The church leaders wanted to share the seminar's results with their people. They noted the highlights of Kaunda's opening speech and summarized the discussion groups' reports. They urged their members to study again their own statement of 1979.[93]

## THE CHURCH'S ONGOING RESPONSE

Public discussion then subsided. But the Church continued its involvement in health care, education, and the improvement of agriculture. Some of its programs—the Delta Program, for example—made a particular effort to enlist local people in the group decision making that was part of self-development. The moral theology program at the major seminary continued to give substantial attention to the Church's social, political, and economic teaching.[94]

The Catholic Secretariat's Social Education Department sought to give Catholics a better understanding of social doctrine and to foster more active concern for justice and development. The department organized Zambia's participation in the SECAM project described in Chapter 4. In 1983 it published, in English and the major vernacular languages, the booklet *Justice and Evangelization in Africa*, which reproduced the SECAM bishops' exhortation, explained the project, and listed points to be discussed at meetings of the faithful. It also circulated a version of the points that raised a number of questions: How is social justice promoted in your area? What are the typical injustices? What about human rights and their violation? How do Church leaders and the faithful promote human rights by their actions? How are human rights promoted or violated in the Church itself? After it launched the program, the secretariat kept in touch with its progress, partly by having its own representative make personal contact with local groups all over the country.[95]

Independently of the SECAM project, Catholic agencies put out various popular publications about social theory and practice. The Mission Press at Ndola published a series of pamphlets under the general title "Christian Reflection." These dealt with such topics as "Justice," "Humanism," "Development," "Education," and "Service." Directed to well-educated readers in responsible positions, they aimed to give a more mature understanding of Christian principles than the schools had given, to help readers reflect on personal and community problems, and to assist the integration of faith into everyday life.[96] The booklet on "Justice," for example, explained the Church's duty to speak out on justice, especially for the powerless poor, and commented on corrupt practices in getting and using wealth. The booklet on "Education" discussed, among other things, the issue of political education, the shortcomings of the syllabus, and better approaches to such education.[97] Youthcare published *Speak Out*, a bimonthly for young people. This carried stories, editorials, contests, comics, and sports news, but also treated social topics: An issue in 1986 included an editorial about the cost of living, the rich–poor gap and the practice of auctioning foreign exchange.[98] The Workers' Pastoral Center at Kitwe published *Workers' Challenge*, an eight-page tabloid newspaper for the Young Christian Workers (YCW) of the Copperbelt. Workers wrote part of the paper, some of which was in the vernacular. A long feature in 1984 gave an informed explanation of Africa's economic crisis. Short pieces commented on concrete problems that touched the workers directly: for example, faulty water supply and sanitation, and political patronage in the allocation of housing. The paper stressed that workers should organize themselves to act on their grievances, and it reported successful uses of this tactic.[99]

In secondary schools and university, members of the Young Christian Students (YCS) movement likewise began paying attention to public issues. They were critical but balanced in their appraisal of Marxism. They were also more disposed than typical student activists to *do* things for marginalized people rather than merely *protest* social inequities.[100]

The bishops themselves returned to social issues in some of their instructions to the faithful. Their Lenten letter of 1986 called for conversion at the personal level and especially for self-denial by the haves in order to assist the have-nots. It called, too, for conversion on the level of the wider society, the breaking of unjust fetters. Here it cited the soaring prices of basic commodities, the sudden introduction of steep school fees, high unemployment, inadequate wage structure, and the lack of effective social welfare to help families overwhelmed by these hardships.[101]

The Episcopal Conference joined the Christian Council and the Evangelical Fellowship in yet another common statement in February 1987, "Christian Liberation, Justice, and Development." It was partly a response to Kaunda's request, in November 1985, for the churches to suggest ways of dealing with the country's grave economic difficulties. The churches favored Zambian Humanism, the statement said, but shortcomings in its implementation imposed serious inequities on the people, especially on peasants and ordinary workers. Although the problems arose partly from the international situation and the structures set up by colonialism, Zambians shared responsibility. The statement suggested specific adjustments in economic policies to favor poorer folk. It stressed the protection of human rights and the need for democratic participation. It supported socialist political structures but rejected both scientific socialism and the practical materialism that pervaded capitalism. Political education was valuable but should not become indoctrination. The program should present the positive and negative sides of different ideologies—something that could not be done by teachers trained only in Communist countries. The churches could not approve the teaching of any political philosophy which undermined belief in God and threatened people's practice of religion. Apart from its direct comments on politics and economics, the statement reminded church members that Jesus had come to liberate mankind from sin and oppression. Christian principles called for more than private piety; they imposed a moral obligation to stay clear of corrupt practices and a duty to work for justice and social development.[102]

## IMPACT OF THE CHURCH'S RESPONSE

After the somewhat climactic seminar of 1982, UNIP kept the project for political education on its agenda but seemed in no hurry to implement it. The party also continued to favor linkages of its youth movement with those of Communist states, but insisted that it did not establish the Young Pioneers as a vehicle for introducing scientific socialism into Zambia.[103] The public policies of UNIP and government continued along the same line as previously, social democratic rather than scientific socialist. The party did not adopt a Leninist philosophy or style. Civil rights remained as they had been. There were no moves toward drastic nationalization of land or of enterprises. Unfortunately, too, earlier failings persisted. Management of state enterprises was inefficient, leading to losses where there should have been profits, and corruption in high places was rife. Meanwhile copper prices remained low, resulting in scarcity of foreign exchange, and Zambia still carried a huge burden of foreign indebtedness. Ironically, in fact, government retreated from some of its socialist policies in order to deal with the economic crisis. First it accepted the IMF's "free market" conditionalities for assistance, ending government subsidies for basic commodities and eliminating price controls. This program imposed great hardship on people and ultimately produced a grave political crisis. Food riots broke out in Kitwe and

Ndola in December 1986. At least eleven people died in these disorders.[104] The president then changed course again. In May 1987 he formally abandoned the IMF program and announced that he was choosing "another way" to economic recovery, a way that in fact leaned heavily toward protectionism.[105]

During this period, Zambia's policies toward religion also continued along earlier lines. Government did not interfere with the churches or their schools or their medical institutions. Kaunda even asked the churches for help when, in October 1985, he announced an ecumenical week of prayer seeking God's assistance for dealing with the economic crisis. It was his request for suggestions at this time that led to the church leaders' joint statement of 1987.[106]

The focal issue for the churches, however, was the Marxist thrust in political education. The seminar had some positive results. The president denied unequivocally that the party had adopted Marxist ideology. He explicitly rejected dictatorial government and reaffirmed his commitment to democratic participation. He also stated plainly that the schools would continue to teach religion and that Zambia would maintain its respect for religious liberty. But he stated plainly, too, that the political education program would go on.[107]

Powerful pressures for the program and for its Marxist bias continued in the party. A striking instance of this was a book published by an influential party member in 1987. The author, Henry S. Meebelo, was Director of UNIP's Research Bureau from 1974 to 1979, and Minister of Education and Culture in 1981. At other times he was Minister of National Development and Planning and Minister of Decentralization. In his book, *Zambian Humanism and Scientific Socialism: A Comparative Study*, Meebelo acknowledged differences between Zambian Humanism and scientific socialism, but he contended that their similarities were more numerous and more significant. He intimated that the introduction of Marxist policies would overcome shortcomings in Humanism and bring it to full bloom. For the policies to work, however, it would be necessary to raise the citizenry's consciousness. So the political education program was essential.[108]

Meebelo paid special attention to the issue of religion. He recognized, one suspects, that the churches' challenge to Marxizing tendencies in UNIP was a serious obstacle to his proposals. He agreed, in the book, that the religious basis of Zambian Humanism clearly set it apart from Marxism-Leninism; but he argued that the religious perspective could be preserved in the new political framework he was setting forth.[109]

The fact that the book's foreword was written by Alexander Grey Zulu, UNIP's Secretary-General, indicated the weight that Meebelo's ideas carried in the party's higher echelons. Zulu wrote: "The basic trend of thought . . . is essentially that Zambian Humanism and scientific socialism are but one and the same thing except perhaps for minor variations given rise by history or tact. For instance, the accommodation of God in Zambian Humanism is one such variation to Scientific Socialism as espoused by Marxists."[110] It was especially unsettling that, in the opinion of a high party official, Humanism's religious perspective seemed only a minor deviation from scientific socialist ideology. By implication, God was not central to Humanism; he was merely "accommodated." And the use of the word "tact" suggested that the accommodation might be only a transitory device for placating religious opposition.

In this political atmosphere, then, the pressures of the Catholic and other churches on government to abandon or substantially modify its plans for political education had little visible impact. Despite Kaunda's declaration at the seminar that the program would go on, however, it can probably be said that the churches' challenge did slow down the program's implementation. The underlying significance of Meebelo's publishing venture may be that Marxist-leaning advocates were still pressing for their version of political education in 1987.

## Controversy and the Maturing of the Church

While the end result of the controversy over political education was inconclusive, the Church's response to government's flirtation with Marxism turned out to be a useful stimulus for the maturing of its social involvement. In this respect the response partly represented ongoing development of features already firmly established in the Church. Long before the Political Education Syllabus became an issue, the Church's social concern had led it to oppose colonial government policies that bore inequitably on the country's African population and to support Africans' calls for independence. Earlier, too, the Church had established friendly working relationships with the Protestant churches. And since at least the 1930s, it had encouraged its members to participate in several active lay movements. Promoters of the syllabus, therefore, could not credibly argue that the Church's opposition to it was an improper intervention of the sacred in the secular. The cooperative connection with the Christian Council and the Evangelical Fellowship eased the way for the drafting of a uniquely comprehensive ecumenical critique of Marxist theory and practice. And the lay participants' queries about the syllabus at the president's seminar made it clear that the bishops did not stand alone in their opposition to the Political Education program. After the seminar, moreover, development of these three features continued. The Church publicly addressed other social issues. It did this, sometimes, in ecumenical statements with other churches. And it expanded its efforts both to inform the laity about the syllabus and about the wider ranges of its social teaching and to involve them in organized social action.

But the response to the Political Education Syllabus also reflected newer tendencies in the Church at large, particularly tendencies advanced by Vatican II. The Church's approach to the issue of the syllabus was not hasty or alarmist. The bishops took four years before reacting publicly to the syllabus. They began with an exercise in self-education— specifically, the seminar in which their own personnel sought a more thorough understanding of Marxism. They also took steps to ascertain whether the program was, in fact, harmful in the schools. They then moved not toward confronting government but toward more active participation in social development and toward more effective education of the faithful about social theory and social obligations. Their critique of Marxist ideas was eirenic and positive. It focused as much on Marxism's threat to human rights as on its threat to religion and the Church. It did not reject socialism as such, and it explicitly refrained from endorsing capitalism. After the president's seminar, the Church systematically expanded its positive efforts and gave them more permanent shape. It established new publications to reach readers at popular as well as elite levels. It gave new life to old lay organizations and established new ones dealing with social structures and social life. And it utilized the preparation for SECAM's Conference on Justice and Peace as a vehicle not only for reinforcing Catholics' concern for justice in secular society but also for turning that concern inward, focusing it on the practice of justice within the Church itself.

The Church did not necessarily move at the same pace toward maturity in other aspects of its functioning—for example, inculturating liturgy and catechesis. But its challenge to the Political Education Syllabus and the developments that followed the challenge evidenced a Church coming of age: a young Church undertaking new and significant initiatives to fulfill the responsibilities of the "Church as servant."

NOTES

1. See "Zambia," *Africa South of the Sahara 1989* (London: Europa Publications, 1988), pp. 1112–14. This source will henceforth be cited as: " 'Zambia,' *Africa South 1989*."

2. See ibid., pp. 1113, 1117, 1124.

3. See ibid., p. 1113.

4. See ibid., pp. 1113–14.

5. See "Kaunda, Kenneth (David)," *Current Biography, 1966* (New York: H. W. Wilson, 1966), pp. 207–209.

6. See ibid., p. 209; William Tordoff and Robert Molteno, "Parliament," in William Tordoff, ed., *Politics in Zambia* (Berkeley: University of California Press, 1974), p. 236. This book will henceforth be cited as: "Tordoff, *Politics*."

7. See K. D. Kaunda, "Humanism in Zambia and a Guide to Its Implementation, Part I" (Lusaka: Zambia Information Service, n.d.); Kenneth D. Kaunda, "Humanism in Zambia and a Guide to Its Implementation, Part II" (Lusaka: Division of National Guidance, n.d.). These will cited as "Humanism I" and "Humanism II."

8. See, for example, Kaunda, "Humanism I," 5–8; "Humanism II," 117–25.

9. See Kaunda, "Humanism II," 8.

10. See Kaunda, "Humanism I," 8. See also an earlier comment of Kaunda's to the effect that Communism appealed to subject peoples as an instrument of liberation, but not to peoples who were already independent. It was true, however, that even small numbers of Communists could be very troublesome. They always tried to make bad situations worse. Ideological subservience was a form of colonial domination which could carve up Africa as effectively as European imperialism had done in the nineteenth century; see Kenneth Kaunda, *A Humanist in Africa: Letters to Colin M. Morris* (London: Longmans, 1966), pp. 119–21.

11. See Kaunda, "Humanism I," 3, 5–7, 12, 14; "Humanism II," xiii, 1–2, 24, 34, 119–23.

12. See Kaunda, "Humanism II," 104.

13. See ibid., pp. 5, 13, 45–46, 76, 103–104, 109–10, 119.

14. See ibid., pp. 111–15.

15. See ibid., pp. 6–7, 48, 53.

16. See Kaunda, "Humanism I," 14, 16, 31; "Humanism II," 52–53, 78, 80, 87–88; Kenneth D. Kaunda, *Towards Complete Independence* (Lusaka: Zambia Information Services, [1969]), pp. 41–42, 59–60.

17. See Kaunda, "Humanism II," 51–53.

18. See ibid., 14–17.

19. See ibid., 19, 51, 69–70, 127–29.

20. See ibid., 8, 16–17, 53.

21. See ibid., xv, 9–10, 23–24, 33–41, 49, 62, 101, 130.

22. See Kaunda, "Humanism I," 27, 31, 33, 35; "Humanism II," 97–100, 105, 107.

23. See William Tordoff and Robert Molteno, "Introduction," in Tordoff, *Politics*, pp. 34–35; Thomas Rasmussen, "The Popular Basis of Anti-Colonial Protest," in ibid., pp. 59–61; William Tordoff and Ian Scott, "Political Parties: Structures and Policies," in ibid., pp. 108, 152–53.

24. See Constitution of the United National Independence Party (N.p.: [1978]), articles 1(2), 5; also article 7.

25. See Republic of Zambia, *Constitution of Zambia, Chapter 1 of the Laws of Zambia* (Lusaka: Government Printer n.d.), article 47C; compare Article 45 of UNIP's 1978 constitution. The cited edition of the national constitution includes the full text of the Party's 1971 constitution; a note printed at the head of this section says: "The Constitution of the United National Independent Party is annexed to the Constitution of Zambia by virtue of Article 4(3) thereof." (Although this edition carries no date of publication, the text incorporates amendments to the national constitution made in 1976).

26. See UNIP Constitution 1978, articles 44(1)(2)(5), 46, 47(1)(2), 49(1), 53(3)(4), 50(1)(3)(4)(5), 54, 56. The 1971 UNIP Constitutiion had virtually identical provisions, differently numbered. See also Constitution of Zambia, articles 38(3), 67(i), 75(1)(3)(5); K. D. Kaunda, The *"Watershed" Speech* (Lusaka: Zambia Information Services, [1975]), pp. 4, 6.

27. See UNIP's 1971 Constitution, articles 6 (1)(h), 6(2)(b); also Annexure A, Standing Orders, Articles 5(2)(m); K. D. Kaunda, "You Hold the Key to the Success of Participatory Democracy" (N.p., 1972), pp. 17–18; idem, *"Watershed,"* pp. 20–23.

28. See Tordoff and Molteno, "Introduction," in Tordoff, *Politics*, p. 14; Tordoff and Scott, "Political Parties," in ibid., p. 144; "Zambia." *Africa South 1989*, p. 1121.

29. See Andrudha Gupta, "Trade Unionism and Politics in the Copperbelt," in Tordoff, *Politics*, p. 290; Kaunda, *Towards Complete Independence*, pp. 29–39; "Zambia," *Africa South 1989*, p. 1118; William Tordoff, "Conclusion," in William Tordoff, ed., *Administration in Zambia* (Manchester: Manchester University Press, 1980), pp. 265–66. This book will henceforth be cited as: "Tordoff, *Administration*."

30. See Gupta, "Trade Unionism and Politics," in Tardoff, *Politics*, pp. 290–92, 297–304, 315–17.

31. See Kaunda, *Towards Complete Independence*, pp. 8–13, 58–59; Robert Molteno and William Tordoff, "Conclusion: Independent Zambia: Achievements and Prospects," in Tordoff, *Politics*, p. 366.

32. See Kaunda, *"Watershed,"* pp. 43–48.

33. See Tordoff and Molteno, "Introduction," in Tordoff, *Politics*, p. 23; Robert Molteno, "Cleavage and Conflict: A Study in Sectionalism," in ibid., p. 103; Molteno and Tordoff, "Conclusion," in ibid., p. 366.

34. See Ottaway and Ottaway, *Afro-Communism*, pp. 41–42; "Zambia," *Africa South 1989*, p. 1122.

35. See Ottaway and Ottaway, *Afro-Communism*, pp. 37–39; Sheridan Johns, "The Parastatal Sector," in Tordoff, *Administration*, p. 124.

36. See Kaunda, *Towards Complete Independence*, pp. 62–63; *"Watershed,"* pp. 11–16; Molteno and Tordoff, "Conclusion," in Tordoff, *Politics*, pp. 367–68, 390, 391; William Tordoff, "Introduction," in Tordoff, *Administration*, p. 40n149; Constitution of Zambia, articles 32–36.

37. See Constitution of Zambia, articles 13–30, 108(1), 113(2)–(4), 117–119.

38. See Tordoff and Molteno, "Introduction," in Tordof, *Politics*, pp. 27, 33; Molteno, "Cleavage," in ibid., p. 57; Tordoff and Scott, "Political Parties," in ibid., pp. 108, 115; Tordoff and Molteno, "Parliament," in ibid., p. 234; Molteno and Tordoff, "Conclusion," in ibid., pp. 368–69.

39. See Tordoff and Molteno, "Introduction," in Tordoff, *Politics*, p. 20; Molteno and Tordoff, "Conclusion," in ibid., pp. 369, 378; Kaunda, *"Watershed,"* pp. 29–32, 35.

40. See Tordoff and Molteno, "Introduction," in Tordoff, *Politics*, p. 32; Richard L. Sklar, "Zambia's Response to the Rhodesian Unilateral Declaration of Independence," in ibid., pp. 335, 345; interview with confidential informant.

41. See Tordoff and Molteno, "Introduction," in Tordoff, *Politics*, pp. 13, 34, 36; Sklar, "Zambia's Response," in ibid., pp. 356–59; Molteno and Tordoff, "Conclusion," in ibid., pp. 367–68; "Zambia," *Africa South 1989*, pp. 1114, 1115, 1122.

42. Interviews with alumnus of the University, and with several undergraduates, members of staff, and informed observers. Henry S. Meebelo, *Zambian Humanism and Scientific Socialism: A Comparative Study* (Lusaka: Government Printer, 1987) lists the student publications in his bibliography, pp. 374–79, and cites them, passim, in his book.

43. Interviews with an undergraduate of the university, an informed observer, and several members of staff. See the following mimeographed circulars; University of Zambia Students' Union, "UNZASU Day, 9th February (1982). Revolutionary Day of the University of Zambia Students. Programme." "From UNZASU Executive to UNZA Community, 23 February 1982. *Re* On the Decadent Banalities of the Shemunaist Clique and Its Inhuman Relations." UNZASU circular, "Minutes of the Emergency Meeting Called by the Principal of the Lusaka Campus of the University of Zambia with the Executive Committee of UNZASU on Tuesday, 2nd March 1982." See also "Mwanza Mum over UNZA Rumpus," *Zambia Daily Mail*, March 22, 1982, p. 1; "UNZA Students Turned Away in Opening Mix–up," *Times of Zambia*, April 5, 1982, p. 1; "UNZA Closure Looms," *Mail*, April 14, 1982, p. 1; "What Next UNZA?" *Times*, April 19, 1982, p. 1; "UNZA Tones Down Action," *Mail*, April 20, 1982, p. 1; "UNZA Closed Down," *Times*, April 22, 1982, p. 1. Confidential informants provided copies of the UNZASU circulars and of related newspaper clippings.

44. See "On the Decadent Banalities of the Shemunaist Clique."

45. See mimeographed circular from UNZASU Executive, "UNZASU Stand vis-à-vis the Institute of Human Relations," March 2, 1982.

46. See mimeographed "Circular from UNZASU Executive to Student Body, March 18, 1982, Subject: Academic Freedom at Stake. Institute of Human Relations Boils. Which Way UNZASU?"

47. Interviews with a university staff–member and an informed observer.

48. See Fanwell Chembo, "Zambian Youths to Learn Scientific Socialism," *National Mirror*, November 1978, p. 2; "Scientific Socialism Defended," ibid., January 1979, p. 5.

49. Interviews with two university staff–members and three informed observers.

50. See Dachs and Rea, *Catholic Church in Zimbabwe*, p. 75; John Weller and Jane Linden, *Mainstream Christianity to 1980 in Malawi, Zambia, and Zimbabwe* (Gweru: Mambo Press, 1984), pp. 153–59, 160–71.

51. See Weller and Linden, *Mainstream Christianity*, pp. 159–61, 164; *Annuario pontificio per l'anno 1965* (Vatican City: Tipographia Vaticana, 1965), p. 554; *Catholic Almanac, 1988*, p. 366.

52. See Weller and Linden, *Mainstream Christianity*, pp. 163–64.

53. See ibid., pp. 141–53, 157, 180–81, 191–200. The Gaba series is entitled *Christian Religious Education for Secondary Schools: A Study of Life Themes* (London: Geoffrey Chapman, 1974). See also *Christian Living Today: Teachers' Handbook* (London: Geoffrey Chapman, 1978). Although it includes treatments of justice in society, service in society, and Christian involvement in the world, it does not include any systematic explanation of specifically Catholic doctrine, perhaps because it is intended to be ecumenical.

54. See Tordoff and Molteno, "Introduction," in Tordoff, *Politics*, p. 12; Molteno, "Cleavage," in ibid., pp. 85–86; Sklar, "Zambia's Response," in ibid., pp. 359n85.

55. See United Independence Party, *Syllabus on Political Education in Zambia*, produced by the Office of the Secretary-General of the Party (Lusaka: Freedom House, [1975]), pp. 3, 10, 14–20, 26, 28, 39–54.

56. See "A Letter from F. K. Chelu for Permanent Secretary, Ministry of Education to All Chief Education Officers, Heads of Secondary Schools, Principals of Colleges, 20th December 1978," mimeographed, in files of a confidential informant.

57. See, for example, "President's Citizenship College, Political Education Unit, Certificate Course in Political Education, 23 Weeks (19th July–14th December 1979)," mimeographed. This outlines a course for UNIP officials; the course for school teachers presumably followed the same lines. See also Ministry of Education and Culture, *Political Education Syllabus for Political Educators* prepared by the Office of the Secretary-General of the Party (Lusaka: Freedom House, [1981]), bound and mimeographed. A confidential informant provided copies of these documents.

58. See "Marxism Panic," *National Mirror*, February 1979, p. 1; "Mixed Economy a Transitional Period," ibid., p. 6.

59. See "Consultation Meeting on Scientific Socialism Held on 20th March 1979, at Archbishop's Residence," typed, files of the Catholic Secretariat, Lusaka.

60. See manuscript jottings on the meeting by Fr. Richard Cremins, files of the Catholic Secretariat. UNIP's speaker, Timothy Kandeke, had been educated in Poland and had written *Fundamentals of Zambian Humanism* (Lusaka: NEC-ZAM, 1977).

61. See "The Churches and Marxism: A Statement of Religious Leaders in Zambia," *Catholic Mind*, 78 (May 1980), 9–23.

62. See ibid., 10.

63. See ibid., 10–12.

64. See ibid., 11–12.

65. See ibid., 12–14.

66. See ibid., 14–16.

67. See ibid., 16–18.

68. See ibid., 19.

69. See ibid., 19–20.

70. See ibid., 20–21.

71. See ibid., 21–22.

72. See ibid., 22.

73. See ibid., 22–23.

74. See ibid., 23.

75. See "Church Warns of Marxist Threat," *Times*, September 17, 1979, p. 2; " 'Rebel' Church Leaders under Fire," ibid., October 27, 1979, p. 2; "Seminar of His Excellency the President with Church Leaders on Humanism and Development. Introductory Remarks of the Chairman, Mr. Philip Simuchoba," [March 1982], p. 3, mimeographed. The Seminar's documents are in the files of the Catholic Secretariat, Lusaka.

76. Confidential informant.

77. See "Marxism Scores," *National Mirror*, October 9–22, 1981, p. 1.

78. See "Notes on the Seminar Held at Evelyn Hone College on Saturday 13 March at 1430 Hours," pp. 4–5, mimeographed, Catholic Secretariat files.

79. See "Introductory Remarks by the Chairman," pp. 3–4.

80. See "Speech of His Excellency the President, Dr. K. D. Kaunda, to the Seminar of Religious Leaders Held at Mulungushi Hall, Lusaka, from 18th to 19th March, 1982," mimeographed; "The Official Closing of the Church Leaders' Humanism Seminar by President Kaunda at Mulungushi Hall," mimeographed; "The Attainment of Humanism through Socialism," mimeographed.

81. See Kaunda, "Speech to the Seminar," 3–13.

82. See ibid., 14–15.

83. See Kaunda, "Attainment," 4, 6–7.

84. See ibid., 11(b)–17.

85. See ibid., 18–20, 22–23.

86. See "Church Leaders' Humanism Seminar Held at Mulungushi Hall from 18th to 19th March 1982. Group Deliberations, Resolutions," mimeographed, 12 pages but the pages are numbered separately for each group. See especially the reports of Groups 1, 3, 4, 5, 7, 8, 9, 10.

87. See ibid., reports of Groups 3, 5, 7, 8, 9, 10.

88. See ibid., reports of Groups 1, 2, 3, 4, 5, 7, 8, 10.

89. See ibid., report of Group 2.

90. See Kaunda, "Closing Speech," 1–2, 4.

91. See manuscript jottings at the Monze meeting by Fr. Richard Cremins, files of the Catholic Secretariat, Lusaka.

92. See United Church of Zambia, General Synod Meeting, April 19–27, 1982, "A Paper Written to Inform Our Church Members about Scientific Socialism," passim, printed 16-page leaflet.

93. See "Letter from the Leaders of the Church in Zambia to Their Members about the President's Seminar on Humanism and Development," passim, printed 4-page leaflet.

94. Interviews with Fr. Richard Cremins, Secretary-General of the Zambia Catholic Secretariat, and with Fr. Peter Lwaminda, Rector of St. Dominic's Major Seminary, May 1992. See *Academic Calendar, 1981–1982, St. Dominic's Major Seminary*, description of the course on "Special Moral Theology."

95. *Justice and Evangelization in Africa* (Lusaka: Catholic Secretariat [1983]); see Father T. G. Mpundu, "Introduction," pp. 3–4; Appendix III, "Some Points as a Guide for Discussion," ibid., pp. 34–36; "Questionnaire of SECAM (Bishops of Africa and Madagascar) on Preparation for Pan-African Conference on Justice and Peace," circular SE/189, mimeographed. See also "Social 'Injustice' to Be Screened," *Sunday Times*, July 8, 1984, p. 1; "Church Launches Peace Drive," ibid.; "Social Education. Injustice Exposed," *Impact*, No. 109 (June 1985), 12–14. *Impact* is the mimeographed newsletter of the Zambia Catholic Secretariat. These papers and newspaper clippings are in the Catholic Secretariat files.

96. See the introductory statement, "Christian Reflection: A series of pamphlets for the informed Zambian," in *Christian Reflection: Justice* (Ndola: Mission Press, n.d.), p. 1; also the listing of other pamphlets in the series, ibid., p. 18.

97. See "The Need to Speak Out," ibid., p. 2; "Abuses," ibid., p. 8; "Political Education," *Christian Reflection: Education* (Ndola: Mission Press, n.d.), p. 11.

98. See "Editorial," *Speak Out* (March–April 1986), 1, and passim. The publisher was the Mission Press, Ndola.

99. See "20 Years of Uhuru," *Workers' Challenge*, November 1984, p. 1; "Africa in 'the' Crisis," ibid.; "Poor Sanitation," ibid., p. 3; "Editorial Comment," ibid., April 1985, p. 1; "Kapenta," ibid., p. 2; "Water Problems," ibid., p. 3.

100. Interview with Fr. Roy Thaden, Catholic chaplain at the University of Zambia, April 1982.

101. See *Reflections of the Catholic Bishops for the Season of Lent, 1986*, 1–2, printed 4-page leaflet (Lusaka: Teresianum Press, [1986]).

102. See Christian Council of Zambia, Evangelical Fellowship of Zambia, Zambia Episcopal Conference, *Christian Liberation, Justice, and Development* (Ndola: Mission Press, [1987]), pp. 4–7, 14–15, 26–41.

103. See "There's No Pressure, Says Minister," *Times*, August 15, 1986; "Kasongo on Youth Festival," *UNIP Youth*, July 1985, 14–15; "Party Chief Happy," ibid., 18; "KOMSOMOL Has Done a Lot," ibid., 19; "Two Youth Organizations Sign Accord," ibid., 21; "Kamilondo Visits GDR," ibid., 21; "Young Pioneers Role Explained," *Daily Mail*, July 12, 1986.

104. See "Introductory Remarks by His Excellency the President Dr. Kenneth David Kaunda to the Meeting of Principal Leaders of Church Organizations in Zambia Held at State House, Thursday, 31st October, 1985," 2, mimeographed; "Food Riots in Zambia; Borders Are Closed," *The New York Times*, December 10, 1986, p. A-2; "Zambia Halts Food Increases after Rioting and 11 Deaths," ibid., December 12, 1986, p. A-7.

105. See "Zambia Breaks Ties with IMF," *West Africa*, May 11, 1987, 924; Ad'Obe Obe, "Kaunda's May Day Call," ibid., May 25, 1987, 1006–1007.

106. See "Week of Prayer Coming," *Sunday Times*, October 27, 1985; Kaunda, "Introductory Remarks to Principal Leaders," 3–7; "Concluding Remarks by His Excellency the President, Dr. Kenneth David Kaunda, at the All Churches Service to End the Prayer Week for the Economic Welfare of the People of Zambia Held at the Cathedral of the Holy Cross on Sunday Afternoon, 17th December, 1985," 2–3, mimeographed.

107. See Kaunda, "Opening Speech," 14–15; "Closing Speech," 2.

108. Meebelo, *Zambian Humanism*; see for example, pp. 6, 7, 56, 64, 70–71, 95, 100–101, 153, 238, 368–69.

109. See, for example, ibid., pp. 6, 24, 26, 32, 44–47, 53–54, 56–57, 366–68.

110. See ibid., p. 1

# 9

# Comparisons, Contrasts, Reflections

THE FOUR PRECEDING CHAPTERS gave accounts of how the Church in four countries responded to rising Marxist influence in Africa and Madagascar during the 1970s and 1980s. It will be useful now to look at similarities and differences in the backgrounds of the cases and in the unfolding of the responses. Such an examination will help illuminate the ways in which the undertakings of these "young churches" contributed to their own growth toward maturity.

## THE COUNTRIES

In the context of Africa, the populations and areas of the four countries were substantial; their peoples each numbered upward of 7.2 million; each occupied 150,000 or more square miles of territory. Although the climates were not unduly hostile, neither drought nor excessive rainfall was uncommon. Natural resources were abundant and diverse. The colonial powers, however, had scarcely developed many of these. Instead they had established economies based on the exploitation and export of a very few primary products; in addition, they had prepared only scant numbers of indigenous people who could run major enterprises.

Mozambique's economy was the least developed of the four, and the massive flight of skilled European personnel had made its prospects even more problematic. Zimbabwe's prospects were most hopeful; during the years of UDI the settlers had shaped an unusually balanced economy, and after independence goodly numbers of them stayed on in managerial and technical positions. Madagascar and Zambia were much better off than Mozambique but not as well off as Zimbabwe. After a promising start, moreover, Zambia's economy quickly declined as world copper prices fell and neighboring Zimbabwe's independence struggle obstructed the flow of both exports and imports.

In the political order some facets of the four countries' backgrounds hindered their implementing Western democratic styles of government. Only small percentages of their respective populations were literate. For the most part, their citizenry had no experience of elections under the colonial powers. Nor did they have a voice in making public policy. People who had completed even secondary education were few; those who had the training and the experience for managing the business of large-scale governments were even fewer. On these counts, Mozambique was again the least well equipped. Rhodesia's settler regime had provided for the token participation of indigenous folk in politics and administration. Zambia had enjoyed several years of internal autonomy before independence. In Madagascar, Tsiranana's regime, authoritarian though it was, had used mechanisms of democracy for a decade before widespread discontent led to public disorder and a rapid succession of regimes.

Other circumstances complicated the four countries' establishment of smoothly functioning self-government. Ethnic loyalties spilled over into the structures and operations of political parties. Tribalism sometimes erupted, then, into violent conflict and sometimes led the dominant group to harass others. This was especially true in Zimbabwe. Parties' resort to thuggery—in Zimbabwe again and in Zambia—undermined the rationale and the credibility of elections. The MNR's guerrilla warfare in Mozambique severely limited government's ability to promote the common welfare in any way. In varying degrees among the several countries, politicians' financial corruption directly or indirectly drained the public treasury; this made even more difficult any sustained effort to satisfy people's rising expectations, and it aggravated public discontent.

## THE CHURCHES

The Catholic Church in all four countries kept a high profile. Its adherents numbered between 8.6 percent of the population in Zimbabwe (718,000) and 28.6 percent in Zambia (1,918,000). Its networks of schools and medical facilities made it very visible. For the most part, indigenous peoples regarded it with favor; many of them had benefited from its provision of education and health care. Evidence of racism among missionaries, however, offended and alienated some local folk—including indigenous clergy. The Church's public image was less favorable in Mozambique than in the other three countries because the Concordat and the Missionary Statute linked it so closely with the exceptionally oppressive Portuguese colonial regime.

In the 1970s and 1980s the Church in each of these countries was only beginning the transition from "young Church" to "mature Church." Except in Madagascar, it was managed largely by missionary bishops assisted largely by missionary clergy and religious. It was understaffed. Because many priests were serving multiple "stations," their contact with parishioners was intermittent and superficial. Doctrinal and moral instruction of the faithful tended to be rudimentary. And Church authorities could not readily make personnel available for such specialized tasks as theological research, religious publishing, and promoting social action. Relatively little attention could be given even to implementing the orientations of Vatican II.

The Malagasy Church had made more progress than the others. Larger proportions of its clergy and religious were indigenous. The laity were carrying assorted responsibilities. Theological and catechetical research was under way. A modest but effective Catholic press was operating. The bishops had been addressing social questions since the 1930s. The Church in Mozambique lagged furthest behind; its Portuguese bishops, apart from Vieira Pinto, seemed utterly insensitive to issues of social justice. It was true, however, that many other Church personnel were unhappy with the bishops' benightedness and were eager to promote a new agenda.

## THE ISSUES

As in other parts of Africa, the influence of Marxism came to the surface in the public life of the four countries in the 1970s and 1980s. The reasons were complex and differed from one country to another. In general it can be said, however, that some elements of the local elites came to regard Marxist-Leninist prescriptions as showing the way to overcome the countries' economic weaknesses and to ensure equitable benefits for their populations.

Mozambican Marxism was the most doctrinaire, the most radical, in its efforts to reshape social structures, and the most hostile to the Catholic Church. Mugabe's Marxism in Zimbabwe was doctrinaire in theory but much diluted in practice. The Marxist tendencies of Ratsiraka in Madagascar and of Kaunda in Zambia were ambiguous.

As things ultimately turned out, only Mozambique directly obstructed the Church's ministries. But the governments of all four countries stirred a certain uneasiness among Church leaders who feared that they would clamp down on religious and other human liberties as Marxist-Leninist governments commonly did. In the first instance, it was the Marxist-sounding pronouncements of political leaders that inspired the uneasiness. But in different degrees, the governments' structuring of political institutions and their style of operation reinforced the concerns of Church personnel.

Mozambique most clearly patterned its political structures on those of older Marxist-Leninist countries. It was a one-party state. Theoretically, FRELIMO was a vanguard party. The party centralized power in a small politburo at the top, and this was dominated by a single charismatic leader. It held primacy over the government. It used its regional branches and local cells to maintain control and discipline over its members at lower echelons and to monitor what was happening in society at large. A powerful secret police kept the citizenry under surveillance and dealt severely with dissenters. What amounted to a ministry of religious affairs supervised the churches. FRELIMO made a practice of promoting Mozambican exchanges with foreign Communist parties and of supporting involvement with Communist international organizations.

The party structures of ZANU-PF in Zimbabwe and UNIP in Zambia were similar to those of FRELIMO, although it is not clear that they consciously followed the Marxist-Leninist model. Mugabe sought to establish a one-party state *de jure* but settled for one *de facto*. Kaunda succeeded in making Zambia a one-party state *de jure*. In Zimbabwe the security police, the Criminal Investigation Organization (CIO), used highhanded methods to curb political opposition. The Army's Fifth Brigade was ruthless. Security forces in Zambia were more restrained. Neither government instituted formal censorship over the media, though Kaunda established rather effective control of public information by making the country's most widely circulated newspapers the property of the government or the party. UNIP promoted friendly exchanges with some foreign Communist parties.

In Madagascar, government and party structures were least like those of traditional Marxist-Leninist countries. Theoretically, Ratsiraka abolished political parties but he permitted "revolutionary associations," which were pretty much the same thing. He did not make AREMA, his own "association," a vanguard party; he did not set a politburo to rule over it; he did not make it a parallel government. But the governmental structure established by his constitution concentrated enormous power in the office of the president—which he himself held. His government exercised vigilant censorship of the mass media. The government's investigative agency, DGID, had a reputation for grave abuse of power. In foreign affairs, Ratsiraka, of set purpose, cultivated friendly relations with Communist nations; one consequence was to bring to Madagascar a goodly number of personnel from China, Korea, and other Marxist countries who were involved in technical assistance and cultural exchange.

The precise focus of the Church's encounter with Marxism varied from country to country. In Mozambique, FRELIMO deprived the Church of places of worship, restricted the clergy's freedom to move among their congregations, impeded the laity's access to their priests, and prohibited the functioning of the Church's lay societies. It forbade Church personnel to instruct or baptize young people and to admit them to training as priests or religious. Its immigration controls accelerated the attrition of foreign Church personnel. It harassed lay leaders. It assumed ownership of priests' residences and sisters' convents as well as of schools and medical facilities. It maintained indirect censorship of Church publications. It blocked the Church's access to domestic and foreign funding. It accused some priests and religious of managerial incompetence, financial embezzlement, and sexual immorality. These measures by FRELIMO seriously obstructed the Church's pursuit of its mission and, in the long run, threatened to reduce its numbers and its effective impact to insignificance.

In Madagascar there was no clear-cut encounter between the Church and Marxism. The government had resisted granting official recognition to private (that is, religious) schools long before Ratsiraka came to power, and its resistance had deeper roots in French laicism than in Marxist atheism. The Church was concerned, however, with indications that unidentified Marxist sympathizers in the educational bureaucracy were trying to undermine Catholic schools' viability and to propagandize through government schools. Such encounter as there was centered in Church personnel's perception of some leanings toward Marxist ideas in Ratsiraka's writings and behavior. They were apparently uneasy about an ultimate drift to typical Marxist-Leninist curbs on religious and other human freedoms, and about the damaging impact meanwhile of economic decline and increasing banditry on the citizens' well-being.

In Zimbabwe, the rise of Marxist influence was only one strand in the intricate web of social issues the Church had to face. The question of interracial justice began to attract serious attention in the late 1950s; UDI posed questions about the warrant for colonialism in the 1960s; and guerrilla action against Smith's regime prompted reflection about justifications for violence in the 1970s. Marxism became a serious concern

of the Church only when evidence of Communist influence in the nationalist movements began to appear. Especially disturbing was ZANU's
explicit adoption of Marxism-Leninism as its official ideology. Reports of
FRELIMO's attacks on the Church in neighboring Mozambique, where
ZANU was based, made this move more worrisome. In Zimbabwe as in
Madagascar, however, the Church's encounter with Marxism was not
defined by any particular issue. After the country finally achieved its
independence under ZANU's openly declared Marxist regime, the
Church's main conflict with the government centered on Mugabe's attempt to impose a one-party state by the use of ruthless force in Matabeleland. But such a conflict could have arisen just as readily with a rightist
dictatorship.

In Zambia the encounter between the Church and the government
was more sharply focused. It centered on government's plan to introduce
the Political Education Syllabus, with its clearly Marxist bias, into the
country's educational institutions at all levels. The Church saw the plan
as endangering the people's religious belief and their civil liberties.

## THE RESPONSES

The responses of the Church to Marxist influence in the four countries
were broadly parallel in structure but varied in their specific details.
They typically featured public statements by the bishops, private discussions between Church representatives and government, and programs to
improve Church members' understanding of social doctrine and to enlist
their involvement in bettering social conditions. The bishops' statements
took various forms. The most common was the joint pastoral letter—
which was formally addressed to the faithful but was readily accessible
to government and party officials and was equally intended for them.
Sometimes, also, bishops and other Catholic agencies or officials commented on social issues in press releases and interviews with journalists.
These statements were uniformly dispassionate and diplomatic in tone.
They showed none of the paranoid fixation with the "Red Menace"
which some critics often attribute to Catholic leaders. They were carefully reasoned. They were objective, giving due weight to Marxist
critiques of Western society's many structural injustices. Often they included criticism of capitalist as well as Marxist theory.

The bishops in Mozambique, in their joint pastoral letters and similar
documents, protested vigorously against the government's harassment of
the Church; they detailed the measures government had taken and

claimed a degree of legal autonomy for the Church. Early on, they argued this claim along the lines of Leo XIII's theory of "two spheres," but later shifted to the theory of religious liberty put forth by Vatican II in *Dignitatis Humanae*. Later also they showed increasing concern for the hardships FRELIMO was imposing on the people through its violations of civil liberties and its economic mismanagement. At the same time, following the lines of *Gaudium et Spes*, they affirmed Catholics' obligation to take part in national development. They did not engage in criticism of Marxist theory; on the other hand, they offered no support to Bishop Vieira Pinto's more open attitude toward Marxism. Because government restricted the availability of paper, ink, and printing presses, the Church's efforts to publish any additional material on its social teaching were of negligible significance. Once, in December 1978, the bishops tried to discuss their grievances directly with the national government at the latter's invitation. Small delegations of clergy and laity sometimes conferred with local officials about local applications of the national government's restrictions.

Beyond the bishops' verbal response to FRELIMO's Marxist policies, the Church took various initiatives to overcome the obstacles government placed in the way of its carrying on its sacral functions. As an especially important step, the Church began to promote small, virtually priestless, Christian communities for worship and related activities. Correspondingly, it accorded a wider leadership role to the laity in organizing and managing these communities. It developed formal and informal training programs to prepare them for this role. It began, too, to educate its clergy toward a less authoritarian style of dealing with the laity.

During the 1970s and 1980s, the bishops in Madagascar published a series of joint pastorals that were relevant to the Marxist leanings of Didier Ratsiraka even though they were not a direct response to his *Red Book*, his constitution, or his Charter of Socialist Enterprises. In fact, many of their publications preceded his. They also had their own positive purpose: namely, to instruct the faithful in light of the new social emphases of Vatican II. Cardinal Razafimahatrata's letter on the conduct of Christians in public life in effect extended this series. The letters said little in direct criticism of Marxism, and indicated the Church's openness in principle to socialism. They nevertheless made clear the bishops' concern about evidences of antireligious and Marxist leanings among some public officials and about ambiguous echoes of Marxist doctrine in Ratsiraka's writings. They were also disturbed by such phenomena as government's failure to check political corruption, revitalize the depressed economy, ensure respect for human rights, and curb violent crime. An alert Catholic press contributed to the ongoing social education of the faithful at different levels of sophistication, notably *ACM* for Church personnel and lay elite and *Lakroa* and *Isika* for simpler folk. *Lakroa* especially was able in subtle ways to correct Marxists' specious claims of virtue and success.

Although other undertakings of the Malagasy Church were operative in countering tendencies toward the acceptance of Marxism, this was not their purpose. Most of them were part of the Church's longstanding efforts to improve the material welfare of the poor and to advance the country's socioeconomic development. Examples included the programs of CAPR and FTMTK. Such undertakings contributed to easing the widespread hardships that Marxists, for their own purposes, customarily played upon in order to rouse and then to exploit public discontent.

Although the bishops of Zimbabwe included comments on Marxism in several of their earlier pastoral letters, their first extensive treatment of it appeared as part of the study document *The Road to Peace*—which they published in 1975, before ZANU came to power. This faulted mostly the Marxists' hostility toward religion and their autocratic governing style, but expressed sympathetic understanding of the theory's attractiveness to oppressed peoples. The bishops' fullest commentary on Marxism after ZANU took over appeared in *Socialism and the Gospel of Christ* in 1984. They accepted in principle the socialist path that Zimbabwe was following, but pointed out that the adoption of socialism did not necessarily imply, as many Marxists claimed, the adoption of atheism. Apart from the bishops, various Church agencies—Silveira House and the School of Social Work, for example—dealt with Marxism in the course of their instruction on social theory but did not approach it as controversy. Earlier on, in 1977, the Driefontein seminar on "The Church and the New Order" was a response to the perceived threat that a Marxist regime would adopt Mozambique's antireligious policies, but it apparently had no follow-up once ZANU actually achieved political control.

Subsequent to independence, the Church became more deeply involved than earlier in sponsoring and funding development projects—new initiatives as well as rehabilitation of war-damaged facilities. As in Madagascar, these ventures were intended not as direct responses to the rise of Marxist influence but as promotion of humane values.

In Zambia the bishops' main effort to instruct the faithful on Marxism and its implications took shape in "The Churches and Marxism," the statement they issued jointly with the Protestant leaders. This was wide-ranging and clear; its critique of Marxism was measured. While it instructed the faithful, it also protested indirectly to government over the plans to introduce the Political Education Syllabus in the schools. When government ignored the protest and continued with its plans, the *Mirror* again called the issue to public attention. Although convocation of the President's Seminar was Kaunda's initiative, the Church used the meeting to its advantage; and in this regard, the well-informed participation of the Catholic laity, along with the persuasive demonstration of interfaith agreement, at the seminar made a powerful contribution. Apart from informing its members about the results of the seminar the Church seems not to have taken any other significant steps specifically aimed at offsetting whatever Marxist influence lay behind the proposal for Political Education. Following the episode, however, Church personnel began a number of programs to awaken more interest among its own members in social concerns.

## THE OUTCOMES

When one studies the outcomes of the Church's response to Marxism two questions are of central interest: (a) how successful was the response in arresting Marxist influence and correcting the particular situations which concerned the Church? and (b) what effect did the response have on the Church itself, specifically on its maturing?

In Mozambique, FRELIMO did ultimately moderate its doctrinaire Marxism and shift to a more moderate stance. But the dominant influences behind this result were the sharp decline of the economy, the complications of droughts and floods, and the destabilizing tactics of the MNR. Among other things, however, the party recognized that peace with the Church would make for wider international acceptance of the regime, and so it allowed its antireligious policies to lapse. It could be said, then, that the Church's protests contributed in a small way by keeping an unwelcome international spotlight on Marxist religious oppression.

In responding to FRELIMO's Marxism, the bishops gave new attention to the Church's social doctrine. Over time, moreover, their public statements showed increasing appreciation of Vatican II's insights, and began to reach beyond defense of the Church's freedom to protest the government's violations of other civil liberties as well as the economic hardships its policies were imposing on the masses. The bishops were unable, however, to mount any systematic attempt at social animation of the faithful because of government restrictions on the press, on nongovernmental organizations, and on the Church's corporate involvement in development projects. The Church's progress toward maturity was more visible in the sacral than in the secular, social, domain. Especially noteworthy was the establishment of small Christian communities and the wider role accorded to the laity.

In Madagascar the Church had not been concerned with Ratsiraka's implementation of any specific marxizing policy and he did not make any specific concession. For the rest of his tenure, nevertheless, he did not lean more visibly toward Marxism. It is not unlikely that the bishops' expressions of concern made him cautious about provoking them to direct opposition. His fall from power in 1993 was related not to his ideology but to the prevalence of corruption, economic hardship, and uncontrolled banditry which the Church had continued to protest. His failure to cope with these issues fed the public discontent that ultimately brought his electoral defeat.

The Malagasy Church's response to Marxist leanings inside and outside government lay mainly in heightened attention to social issues. When Ratsiraka arrived on the scene, it was already addressing these issues more or less systematically in joint pastoral letters, trying specifically to convey the thinking of Vatican II to the faithful. By this time, the Church in Madagascar was already much further along the road to maturity than it was in the other three countries, and it now moved forward in the same direction. It carried on older development projects and undertook new ones. It continued work on such basically sacral tasks as the inculturation of catechesis.

In Zimbabwe, ZANU's generally diluted implementation of Marxism provoked serious challenge by the Church on only two closely linked issues: government's insistence on setting up a one-party state and its terroristic use of force in Matabeleland to achieve this purpose. Although the government ultimately ended the activities of the Fifth Brigade, it is not at all certain that the Church's objections had very much to do with this. For practical purposes Mugabe had established his one-party state, and he understood that the whole adventure was making the country less attractive to the foreign investors whose help he so badly needed. He reluctantly accepted dilution of ZANU's commitment to one-partyism and Marxist ideology only in 1990–1991 under pressure from party members who were disillusioned by the collapse of Communism almost everywhere else in the world.

The fact that the Church here had to address not one but several crises evoked a wider social concern and wider social vision than elsewhere. The bishops' pronouncements dealt not only with Marxism but also with interracial justice, self–government, and warfare. They established the Justice and Peace Commission. They initiated programs and produced teaching materials for the social education of both white and black Catholics. Catholic periodicals spoke to social issues. Silveira House and the School of Social Work offered practical social training. Several Church agencies involved themselves in organizing and funding postwar rehabilitation, and sometimes lent personnel for this kind of work.

In Zambia, Kaunda did not yield openly to the Church's pressure to put aside the Political Education Syllabus, but he seems to have delayed its implementation indefinitely. Meebelo's publication of his book on Humanism and socialism suggested that the influence of Marxist ideology persisted in high UNIP circles as late as 1987. On the other hand, student Marxists were apparently shedding their radicalism after they completed university and found employment.

The most marked consequence of the controversy for the Church was an intensified attention to social issues. This took concrete expression in several ways. Church leaders became more alive to other socioeconomic problems in the country. They became more outspoken about the adverse effects of government policies on citizens' well-being. The bishops assisted, in fact, in negotiating the conditions for the 1991 multiparty elections in which Kaunda met defeat. The major seminary treated the Church's social doctrine more extensively in its moral theology courses for the young men who were the priests of the future. The Catholic Secretariat added a Department of Social Education. Several Church agencies began putting out publications that provided information, analysis, and stimulus for social action—aimed at diverse readerships. The Church's preparation for SECAM's conference on justice and peace sought to reach all its parishes and included an effort to identify and correct injustices in its own structures and institutions. The Church's long tradition of ecumenical cooperation continued.

Generally speaking, then, even though the Churches' efforts did not effect any quick and dramatic reversals of Marxist influence, the indications are that they made governments cautious about implementing policies oriented in a Marxist direction—except in Mozambique. Within the Churches themselves, however, the encounters generated a thrust toward their own maturing. These formerly "missionary churches" took charge of their own functioning. They looked at their own circumstances, took account of their own distinctive postcolonial environment, and charted their own courses. Not all the effects were readily identifiable or measurable. The most visible was a heightened social consciousness. Church leaders spoke out on social issues. Church personnel sought in various ways to instruct and inform themselves and the faithful on the Church's social doctrine and its relationships with actual events—through newspapers and other publications, course outlines, study sessions, and discussion groups. The laity assumed a larger role in planning and action. Church agencies promoted active participation in socioeconomic development.

Generally speaking, too, the Church's efforts had less impact on its sacral than its social concerns. Even in this regard, however, development took place, notably in Mozambique. The Church's appointment there of layfolk as leaders and religious ministers of its small communities was a radical innovation.

## TOWARD THE FUTURE

It might fairly be asked what happened to the African Churches' progress toward maturity when Marxist influence faded away in the late 1980s. There is ample evidence that it continued. In the social field, for example, Church leaders in Mozambique were active in promoting peace between FRELIMO and the MNR. In Madagascar and Zambia they helped to relax Ratsiraka's and Kaunda's grip on power and to speed its passing to democratically elected successors. The Justice and Peace Commission in Zimbabwe maintained its vigil against governmental abuse of rights.

In the sacral field, the Churches had been laboring at renewal of their sanctifying mission independent of their concerns with Marxism. They continued this process. Among other things, they looked for more effective approaches to primary evangelization, instruction of adult church members, and outreach to youth; to making the Eucharist more generally and readily accessible, promoting Christian family life, and relating customary marriage to the Church's canonical norms; and to studying traditional religions carefully for a better understanding of inculturation. Some of these efforts broke new ground; some of them involved unforeseeable complexities that required discerning judgment. Taken together they made up an agenda identifiably African, yet quite different from the one they inherited from the missionaries. The very elaboration of the agenda was a demonstration of the Churches' maturing. Its implementation will take decades, its details may change as circumstances change, and, in a sense the agenda will never be finished—because the Church's work of touching people's minds and hearts must necessarily be extended with the coming of each new generation. The important points are that these initiatives came from these Churches themselves and that the Churches themselves assumed responsibility for their implementation.

# SOURCES CITED

## Books and Pamphlets

Abbot, Walter M., ed. *The Documents of Vatican II*. New York: America Press, 1966.

*Academic Calendar, 1981–1982. St. Dominic's Major Seminary*. Lusaka, Zambia.

"Accord missionaire entre le saint siège et la république portugaise (7-V-1940)." In *Angola*. Vol. 5. Ed. Antonio Brasio, C.S.Sp. Spiritana Monumenta Historica, Series Africana. Pittsburgh: Duquesne University Press. Pp. 678–87.

"Africa and the European Community: The Second Lomé Convention." In *Africa South of the Sahara, 1980–81*. London: Europa Publications, 1980. Pp. 57–68.

Albright, David E., ed. *Communism in Africa*. Bloomington: Indiana University Press, 1980.

*Annuario Pontificio per l'anno 1965*. Vatican City: Typografia Vaticana, 1965.

Archer, Robert. *Madagascar depuis 1972: La marche d'une révolution*. Paris: Éditions Harmattan, n.d.

Astrow, André. *Zimbabwe: A Revolution That Lost Its Way?* London: Zed Press, 1983.

Auret, Diana. *Reaching for Justice: The Catholic Commission for Justice and Peace Looks Back at the Past Twenty Years, 1972–1992*. Gweru: Mambo Press, in association with the Catholic Commission for Justice and Peace in Zimbabwe, 1992.

Blaustein, Albert P., and Gilbert A. Flanz. *Constitutions of the World*. Vol. 18. Dobbs Ferry, N.Y.: Oceana Publications, 1986.

Bociurkiw, Bohdan R., and John W. Strong, eds. *Religion and Atheism in the USSR and Eastern Europe*. Toronto: University of Toronto Press, 1975.

Bottomore, T. B., ed. *Karl Marx: Early Writings*. New York: McGraw-Hill, 1963.

Bottomore, T. B., and Maximilian Rubel, eds. *Karl Marx: Selected Writings on Sociology and Social Philosophy*. New York: McGraw-Hill, 1964.

Bratton, Michael. *From Rhodesia to Zimbabwe*. VI. *Beyond Community Development*. Gwelo: Mambo Press, 1978.

Broun, Janice. *Conscience and Captivity: Religion in Eastern Europe*. Washington, D.C.: Ethics and Policy Center, 1988.

Brown, Mervyn. *Madagascar Rediscovered: A History from Early Times to Independence*. Hamden, Conn.: Archon Books, 1979.

Brzezinski, Zbigniew, ed. *Africa and the Communist World*. Stanford, Calif.: Stanford University Press, 1963.

Bureau d'études des programmes–Organ technique d'élaboration des programmes BEP-OTEP. *Civilisations du monde contemporain. Série histoire–géographie–instruction civique*. N.p.: Papagile de la Grande Île, 1975.

*Catholic Almanac, 1988*. Huntington, Ind.: Our Sunday Visitor Publishing Division, 1987.

Catholic Bishops of Rhodesia. *A Plea for Peace*. London: Geoffrey Chapman, 1966.

*La Charte de la révolution malgache tous azimuts, 26 août 1975*. Tananarive: Imprimerie d'Ouvrages Éducatifs, 1975.

Christian Council of Zambia, Evangelical Fellowship of Zambia, Zambia Episcopal Conference. *Christian Liberation, Justice, and Development*. Ndola: Mission Press [1987].

*Christian Living Today: Christian Religious Education for Secondary Schools, A Study of Life Themes*. 2 vols. London: Geoffrey Chapman, 1974.

*Christian Living Today: Teacher's Handbook*. London: Geoffrey Chapman, 1981.

*Christian Reflection: Education*. Ndola: Mission Press, n.d.

*Christian Reflection: Justice*. Ndola: Mission Press, n.d.

Christie, Iain. *Machel of Mozambique*. Harare: Zimbabwe Publishing House, 1988.

Clarke, Duncan G. *From Rhodesia to Zimbabwe. III. The Unemployment Crisis*. Gwelo: Mambo Press, 1978.

Conférence Épiscopale de Madagascar. *L'église et la développement à Madagascar*. Pastoral letter. March 26, 1972. [Fianarantsoa: Imprimerie St. Paul, 1972].

————. *Lettre des évêques de Madagascar sur l'église et la politique*. Pastoral letter. December 15, 1973. [Tananarive: Imprimerie Catholique, 1974.]

Conquest, Robert. *The Great Terror: A Reassessment*. New York: Oxford University Press, 1990.

————. *The Nation-Killers: The Soviet Deportation of Nationalities*. London: Macmillan, 1970.

————. *Religion in the USSR*. New York: Frederick A. Praeger, 1968.

————. *The Soviet Political System*. New York: Frederick A. Praeger, 1968.

*Constitution of the United National Independence Party*. N.p. [1978].

*Constitution of the United National Independence Party* [1971]. Printed as annex of Republic of Zambia's *Constitution*, cited below.

Covell, Maureen. *Madagascar: Politics, Economics and Society*. London: Frances Pinter, 1987.

Dachs, A. J., and W. F. Rea. *The Catholic Church and Zimbabwe, 1879–1979*. Gwelo: Mambo Press, 1979.

Davies, Rob. *From Rhodesia to Zimbabwe. V. A Solution to Unemployment*. Gwelo: Mambo Press, 1979.

DeGeorge, Richard. *Soviet Ethics and Morality*. Ann Arbor: University of Michigan Press, 1969.

Deschamps, Hubert Jules. "Madagascar." *Encyclopaedia Britannica*. 15th ed., 1974, Macropaedia, Vol. 11: 277–79.

Deutscher, Isaac. *Stalin: A Political Biography*. 2d ed. New York: Oxford University Press, 1974.

Dulles, Avery. *Models of the Church*. Garden City, N.Y.: Doubleday, 1974.

Fanon, Frantz. *Black Skin, White Masks*. Trans. Charles Lam Markmann. New York: Grove Press, 1965.

———. *The Wretched of the Earth*. Trans. Constance Farrington. New York: Grove Press, 1968.

Footman, David. *The Russian Revolutions*. London: Faber & Faber; New York: G. P. Putnam, 1962.

Gauze, René. *The Politics of Congo-Brazzaville*. Trans., ed., and suppl. Virginia Thompson and Richard Adloff. Stanford, Calif.: Hoover Institution, 1973.

Gilmurry, John, Roger Riddell, and David Sanders. *From Rhodesia to Zimbabwe*. VII. *The Struggle for Health*. Gwelo: Mambo Press, 1979.

Government of the Republic of Zimbabwe. *Growth with Equity: An Economic Policy Statement, February 1981*. [CMD.R.2.4.–1981]. Salisbury: Government Printer, 1981.

Greco, Joseph, ed. *Vingt-cinq ans de pastoral missionaire: Receuil des principales ordonnances et directives pastorales des réunions des évêques de Madagascar (1931–1957) et quelques décisions du saint siège*. Issy les Molineaux: Imprimerie St. Paul, 1958.

Guillaumin, Armand. *La séduction marxiste: Un prêtre médite Marx*. Bologna: E.M.I., 1987.

Hazard, John. *The Soviet System of Government*. 5th ed. Chicago: The University of Chicago Press, 1980.

Henderson, William C. *The Life of Friedrich Engels*. 2 vols. London: Frank Cass, 1976.

Hevi, Emmanuel John. *An African Student in China*. New York: Frederick A. Praeger, 1962.

Hill, Ronald J., and Peter Frank. *The Soviet Communist Party*. London: George Allen & Unwin, 1981.

Hunley, J. D. *The Life and Thought of Friedrich Engels*. New Haven, Conn.: Yale University Press, 1991.

Indrianala, Hugues. *Civilisation des pays capitalistes*. II. *États-Unis d'Amérique*. Fianarantsoa: Librairie Ambozontany [1982].

———. *Civilisation des pays capitalistes*. III. *Japon*. Fianarantsoa: Librairie Ambozontany [1982].

———. *Civilisation des pays du tiers monde*. I. *Présentation générale et approche critique*. Fianarantsoa: Librarie Ambozontany [1979].

———. *Civilisation des pays du tiers monde*. II. *Algérie*. Fianrantsoa: Librairie Ambozontany [1979].

———. *Civilisation des pays du tiers monde*. III. *Madagascar*. Fianarantsoa: Librairie Ambozontany [1980].

———. *Civilisation des pays du tiers monde*. IV. *Vietnam*. Fianarantsoa: Librairie Ambozontany [1980].

———. *Civilisation des pays socialistes*. I. *Fondements historiques et idéologiques*. Fianarantsoa: Éditions Ambozontany [1980].

———. *Civilisation des pays socialistes*. II. *Union soviétique*. Fianarantsoa: Librairie Ambozontany [1979].

———. *Civilisation des pays socialistes*. III. *Chine*. Fianarantsoa: Librairie Ambozontany [1979].

———. *Civilisation des pays socialistes*. IV. *Cuba*. Fianarantsoa: Librarire Ambozontany [1979].

———. *Le socialisme à l'épreuve du sous-développement*. Fianarantsoa: Éditions Ambozontany [1981].

Ismaligova, R. N., *Ethnic Problems of Tropical Africa: Can They Be Solved?* Moscow: Progress Publishers, 1978.

Jesuit Conference on Africa and Madagascar. *JECAM 1976: Jesuit Response to the Challenge of Mission in Africa and Madagascar Today*. Washington, D.C.: Jesuit Missions, 1976.

*Justice and Evangelization in Africa*. Lusaka: Catholic Secretariat [1983].

Kandeke, Timothy E. *Fundamentals of Zambian Humanism*. Lusaka: NECZAM, 1977.

Kaunda, Kenneth D. "Humanism in Zambia and a Guide to Its Implementation: Part I." [Lusaka: Zambian Information Service, n.d.].

———. "Humanism in Zambia and a Guide to Its Implementation: Part II." [Lusaka: Division of National Guidance, n.d.].

———. *A Humanist in Africa: Letters to Colin G. Morris*. London: Longmans, 1966.

———. *Towards Complete Independence*. Lusaka: Zambia Information Services, [1969].

———. *The "Watershed Speech."* Lusaka: Zambia Information Services [1975].

———. "You Hold the Key to the Success of Participatory Democracy." [Lusaka: Zambia Information Services, 1972].

"Kaunda, Kenneth (David)," in *Current Biography, 1966*. New York: H. W. Wilson, 1966.

Keller, Edmond J., and Donald Rothchild, eds. *Afro-Marxist Regimes: Ideology and Public Policy*. Boulder, Colo.: Lynne Rienner, 1987.

Khrushchev, Nikita S. *The Anatomy of Terror: Khrushchev's Revelations about Stalin's Regime*. Introduction by Nathaniel Weyl. Washington, D.C.: Public Affairs Press, 1956.

Kolakowski, Leszek. *Main Currents of Marxism*. 3 vols. Oxford: Clarendon, 1978.

Leaders of the Church in Zambia. *A Letter from the Leaders of the Church in Zambia to Their Members about the President's Seminar on Humanism and Development*. N.p.: n.d. (4-page leaflet).

"Législation missionaire portugaise (5-V-1941)." In Brasio, *Angola*, cited above s.v. "Accord missionaire." Vol. 5: 792–817.

Lenin, V. I. *Imperialism: The Highest Stage of Capitalism*. New York: International Publishers, 1939.

———. *On Religion*. 3d rev. ed. Moscow: Progress Publishers, 1969.

Linden, Ian. *The Catholic Church and the Struggle for Zimbabwe*. London: Longman, 1980.

Lupo, Pierre. *L'église et décolonisation à Madagascar*. Fianarantsoa: Éditions Ambozontany, 1974.

"Madagascar." In *Africa South of the Sahara, 1988*. London: Europa Publications, 1987. Pp. 609–30.

Magesa, Laurenti. *The Church and Liberation in Africa*. Spearhead Series No. 44. Eldoret, Kenya: Gaba Publications, 1976.

Marx, Karl. *Karl Marx: On Religion*. Ed. Saul K. Padover. New York: McGraw-Hill, 1974.

———. *Karl Marx: On Revolution*. Ed. Saul K. Padover. New York: McGraw-Hill, 1971.

Marx, Karl, and Friedrich Engels. *Collected Works*. Vol. 25. New York: International Publishers, 1987.

———. *The Communist Manifesto*. Introduction by A. J. P. Taylor. Harmondsworth, U.K.: Penguin, 1984.

———. *On Colonialism: Articles from the New York Daily Tribune and Other Writings*. New York: International Publishers, 1972.

———. *On Religion*. Rev. ed. Moscow: Progress Publishers, 1975.

McGovern, Arthur. *Marxism: An American Catholic Perspective*. Maryknoll, N.Y.: Orbis Books, 1980.

McLellan, David. *Karl Marx: His Life and Thought*. New York: Harper Colophon Books, 1977.

Meebelo, Henry S. *Zambian Humanism and Scientific Socialism: A Comparative Study*. [Lusaka: Government Printer], 1987.

"Mozambique." In *Africa South of the Sahara, 1980–81*. London: Europa Publications, 1980. Pp. 695–712.

"Mozambique." In *Africa South of the Sahara, 1988*. London: Europa Publications, 1987. Pp. 700–20.

Mugabe, Robert G. *Prime Minister's New Year Speech to the Nation, December 31, 1980*. Salisbury: Ministry of Information and Tourism, n.d.

———. *Prime Minister Opens Zimbabwe Conference on Reconstruction and Development (ZIMCORD), March 23, 1981*. Salisbury: Ministry of Information and Tourism, n.d.

"Mugabe, Robert (Gabriel)." in *Current Biography 1979*. New York: H. W. Wilson, 1979.

Munslow, Barry. *Mozambique: The Revolution and Its Origins*. New York: Longman, 1983.

Nollau, Gunther. *International Communism and World Revolution: History and Methods*. New York: Frederick A. Praeger, 1961.

O'Meara, Patrick. *Rhodesia: Social Conflict or Coexistence.* Ithaca, N.Y.: Cornell University Press, 1975.

Ottaway, David, and Marina Ottaway. *Afro-Communism.* New York: Africana Publishing, 1981.

Pattee, R. "Mozambique." *New Catholic Encyclopedia.* Vol. 10: 57–58.

Paul VI, Pope. *On Evangelization in the Modern World* [Apostolic Exhortation "Evangelii Nuntiandi," December 8, 1975]. Boston: Daughters of St. Paul Editions, n.d.

————. *On the Development of Peoples* [Encyclical Letter "Progressio Populorum," March 26, 1967]. Boston: Daughters of St. Paul Editions, n.d.

Peffer, R. G. *Marxism, Morality, and Social Justice.* Princeton, N.J.: Princeton University Press, 1988.

Powell, David E. *Anti-Religious Propaganda in the Soviet Union: A Study in Mass Persuasion.* Cambridge, Mass.: The MIT Press, 1975.

*Rapport de la rencontre pan-africaine sur la justice et paix. Roma, Lesotho, du 29 mai au 3 juin, 1988.* Mimeograph. [Available through the SECAM Secretariat, Accra, Ghana.]

Rasolo, André. *L'éxperience socialiste à Madagascar.* Thèse de 3e cycle d'études politiques, 1978. University of Aix-en-Provence, Marseilles.

Rasolo, Louis. *Finoana sy Fivoaran-karena.* Fianarantsoa: Transoprinty Rasindahy Paoly, [1979].

Repoblika Democratika Malagasy. *Charte des enterprises socialistes.* Antananarivo: Imprimerie Nationale, 1979.

————. *Lalampanorenana.* [Constitution]. Antananarivo: Transoprintim Pirenena, 1980.

Republic of Zambia. *Constitution of Zambia: Chapter 1 of the Laws of Zambia* [1973]. Lusaka: Government Printer [1976?].

Rhodesia Catholic Bishops' Conference. *The Road to Peace.* Gwelo: Mambo Press [1976].

Rhodesia Catholic Bishops' Conference, Commission for Christian Formation and Worship. *Social Teaching of the Catholic Church* (7 pamphlets, different titles). Salisbury: Pastoral Centre, 1979.

Riddell, Roger. *From Rhodesia to Zimbabwe.* I. *Alternatives to Poverty.* Gwelo: Mambo Press, 1978.

————. *From Rhodesia to Zimbabwe.* IX. *Education for Employment.* Gwelo: Mambo Press, 1980.

————. *From Rhodesia to Zimbabwe.* II. *The Land Question.* Gwelo: Mambo Press, 1978.

Rodney, Walter. *How Europe Underdeveloped Africa.* Washington, D.C.: Howard University Press, 1974.

Rosberg, Carl H., and Thomas M. Callaghy, eds. *Socialism in Sub-Saharan Africa: A New Assessment.* Berkeley: University of California Press, 1979.

Schapiro, Leonard. *Government and Politics in the Soviet Union.* New York: Vintage Books, 1967.

————. *The Russian Revolutions of 1917: The Origins of Modern Communism.* New York: Basic Books, 1984.

Schapiro, Leonard, and Peter Reddaway, eds. *Lenin: The Man, the Theorist, the Leader.* London: Pall Mall Press, 1967.

Schatten, Fritz. *Communism in Africa.* New York: Frederick A. Praeger, 1966.

Schram, Stuart R. *The Political Thought of Mao Tse-Tung.* Rev. ed. New York: Frederick A. Praeger, 1969.

*Seeking Gospel Justice in Africa.* Spearhead Series No. 69. Eldoret, Kenya: Gaba Publications, 1981.

Sheptulin, A. P. *Marxist-Leninist Philosophy.* Moscow: Progress Publishers, 1978.

Shirer, John L., ed. *China Facts and Figures Annual.* Vol. 6. Gulf Breeze, Fla.: Academic International Press, 1983.

————. *China Facts and Figures Annual.* Vol. 7. Gulf Breeze, Fla.: Academic International Press, 1984.

————. *USSR Facts and Figures Annual.* Vol. 8. Gulf Breeze, FL: Academic International Press, 1984.

Shub, David. *Lenin: A Biography.* Garden City, N.Y.: Doubleday, 1948.

Smith, David, and Colin Simpson, with Ian Davis. *Mugabe.* London: Sphere Books, 1981.

Solzhenitsyn, Alexandr. *The Gulag Archipelago, 1918–1936.* 2 vols. New York: Harper & Row, 1973.

Stalin, Joseph. *Foundations of Leninism.* New York: International Publishers, 1939.

Stoneman, Colin. *From Rhodesia to Zimbabwe. IV. Skilled Labour and Future Needs.* Gwelo: Mambo Press, 1978.

Stoneman, Colin, and Lionel Cliffe. *Zimbabwe.* London: Pinter Publishers, 1989.

Synod of Bishops. *The Synodal Document on Justice in the World, November 1971.* Boston: St. Paul Editions, n.d.

Szajkowski, Bogdan, ed. *Marxist Governments: A World Survey.* 3 vols. London: Macmillan, 1981.

Takidy, Emil. *Introduction à la philosophie politique.* Antananarivo: FOFIPA, 1980. Mimeographed.

Ticknor, Vincent. *From Rhodesia to Zimbabwe. VIII. The Food Problem.* Gwelo: Mambo Press, 1979.

Tordoff, William, ed. *Administration in Zambia.* Manchester: Manchester University Press, 1980.

————. *Politics in Zambia.* Berkeley: University of California Press, 1974.

Torp, Jens Erik, L. M. Denny, and Donald I. Ray. *Mozambique, São Tomé, and Principe.* New York: Pinter, 1989.

Tucker, Robert C. *Stalin as Revolutionary, 1879–1929.* New York: W. W. Norton, 1973.

Ulam, Adam B. *Stalin: The Man and His Era.* New York: Viking Press, 1973.

United Church of Zambia. General Synod Meeting—April 19–27, 1982. *Paper*

*Written to Inform Our Members About Scientific Socialism.* N.p.: [1982]. Pamphlet.

United National Independent Party. *Syllabus on Political Education in Zambia.* Produced by the Office of the Secretary-General of the Party. Lusaka: Freedom House [1975].

Vezeau, Roland. *L'Afrique face au communisme.* Paris: Éditions Edimpra, 1967.

Vines, Alex. *Renamo: Terrorism in Mozambique.* London: Center for Southern African Studies in association with James Currey, 1991.

Weller, John, and Jane Linden. *Mainstream Christianity to 1980 in Malawi, Zambia, and Zimbabwe.* Gweru: Mambo Press, 1984.

Wesson, Robert G. *Why Marxism? The Continuing Success of a Failed Theory.* New York: Basic Books, 1976.

"Zambia." In *Africa South of the Sahara, 1989.* London: Europa Publications, 1988. Pp. 1112–35.

Zambia Episcopal Conference. *Reflections of the Catholic Bishops for the Season of Lent 1986.* Lusaka: Teresianum Press, [1986]. Leaflet.

"Zimbabwe." In *Africa South of the Sahara, 1989.* London: Europa Publications, 1988. Pp. 1136–63.

Zimbabwe. *Report of the Commission of Inquiry into Incomes, Prices, and Conditions of Service, under the Chairmanship of Roger C. Riddell, to the President, June 1981.* Salisbury: Government Printer [1981].

Zimbabwe African National Union (Patriotic Front) [ZANU-PF]. "The Role of the Church in Revolutionary Politics." *Society and Church.* N.p.: Jongwe Press, n.d.

Zimbabwe Catholic Bishops' Conference. *Our Way Forward: Pastoral Statement.* Issued by the Zimbabwe Catholic Bishops' Conference for the First Sunday of Advent, November 28, 1982. Gweru: Mambo Press, 1982.

————. *Socialism and the Gospel of Christ: Pastoral Statement.* Issued by the Zimbabwe Catholic Bishops' Conference, January 1, 1984. Gweru: Mambo Press, 1984.

————. *Welcome, Zimbabwe: A Statement of the Roman Catholic Bishops of Zimbabwe.* April 17, 1980. (Leaflet).

PERIODICALS

"À Madagascar: Après six mois de crise." *Chine-Maduré-Madagascar* [Lille], No. 235 (December 1991–January 1992), 15.

"À Madagascar: Chronique d'une révolution." *Chine-Maduré-Madagascar*, No. 234 (September–November 1991), 13–15.

"À Madagascar: En attendant le référendum." *Chine-Maduré-Madagascar*, No. 236 (February–March 1992), 19–20.

"À Madagascar: vers le référendum." *Chine-Maduré-Madagascar*, No. 237 (April–May 1992), 15.

"À propos des massacres de Mozambique." *Documentation catholique*, 70 (October 7, 1973): 647.

"Uma alliança de quinhentos anos contra o povo moçambicano." *Noticias* [Maputo], July 28, 1979, 1.

Andriamihaja, René-Claude. "Avec les jésuites malgaches rédacteurs de LAKROA." *Chine-Maduré-Madagascar*, No. 213 (June–August 1987), 17–18.

————. "Lettre ouverte aux députés malgaches." *Chine-Maduré-Madagascar*, No. 201 (February–March 1985), 14–16.

"Appel aux communautés chrêtiennes en faveur de la paix." *Documentation catholique*, 80 (September 4–18, 1984). 857–59.

"Assemblée plénière 1984." *Aspects du christianisme à Madagascar* [Antananarivo], 19 (September–December 1984), 323–28.

"Assemblée plénière de la conférence épiscopale de Madagascar, nov. 19–27, 1974." *Aspects du christianisme à Madagascar*, 15 (January–February 1975), 14–15.

"Assemblée plénière ordinaire de la conférence épiscopale de Madagascar, 6–14 novembre 1991." *Aspects du christianisme à Madagascar*, n.s. 4 (April–June 1992), 274–75.

Aubert, Jean-Marie. "L'église catholique dans le nord de Madagascar: Inculturation et structures pastorales." *Aspects du christianisme à Madagascar*, N.S. 1 (July–September 1985), 101–45.

Broun, Janice. "The Muslim Challenge Within the Soviet Union." *America*, 148 (February 12, 1983), 3–9.

"O Caminho do povo e da Igreja." *Alem-mar* [Lisbon], 27 (February 1982), 11–14.

"Le Centre 'Foi et Justice.'" *Chine-Maduré-Madagascar*, No. 223 (June–August 1991), 20.

"The Church and Christians in Madagascar Today." *Pro Mundi Vita Dossiers* [Brussels], Africa Dossier 6 (July–August 1978).

"A Church in Crisis Weeps and Prays." *Time*, 124 (September 17, 1984), 75–76.

"The Church in Mozambique: The Colonial Inheritance. Minutes of a Discussion Between the Roman Catholic Bishops and the Government of Mozambique." *IDOC Documentation Service Bulletin* [Rome], Nos. 7, 8, 9 (July–September 1979), 1–67.

"Communiqué des évêques et des supérieurs d'instituts missionaires." *Documentation catholique*, 71 (May 5, 1974), 427.

"Communiqué du Sécrétariat du diocèse de Nampula." *Documentation catholique*, 71 (May 5, 1974), 418.

[Conférence Épiscopale de Madagascar.] "Déclaration des évêques de Madagascar." *Maduré-Madagascar* [Paris], No. 167 (April 1978), 289–91.

————. "Déclaration des évêques de Madagascar aux chrêtiens de leurs églises et à tous les hommes de bonne volunté." *Lakroan'i Madigasikara* [Antananarivo], February 12, 1982, 2–3.

————. "Lettre des évêques du Madagascar à tous les catholiques d'île." *Aspects du christianisme à Madagascar*, 14 (January–February 1973), 16–26.

————. "Le pouvoir au service de la société." *Documentation catholique*, 82 (August 4, 1985), 840–46.

————. "Le redressement de la nation." *Documentation catholique*, 85 (May 1, 1988), 452–60.

[Conferencia Episcopale de Moçambique]. "Christmas Message of the Bishops to the Church in Mozambique, December 1975." *IDOC Bulletin*, Nos. 41–42 (March–April 1976), 11–12.

————. "Communiqué de la Conférence Épiscopale." *Documentation catholique*, 71 (May 5, 1974), 428.

————. "Communiqué de la Conférence Épiscopale du Mozambique." *Documentation catholique*, 74 (June 19, 1977), 574–75.

————. "Communiqué du Sécretariat de la Conférence Épiscopale du Mozambique." *Documentation catholique*, 71 (May 5, 1974), 421.

————. "L'église dans un Mozambique indépendant." *Documentation catholique*, 71 (October 20, 1974), 873–78.

————. "Mozambique: 'La vie chrêtienne dans le moment actuel' (Lettre des évêques)." *Agence internationale fides information*, June 28, 1980: NF 376–85.

————. "Renouvellement et réconciliation de l'homme au Mozambique." *Documentation catholique*, 71 (May 5, 1974), 422–25. Excerpt from a pastoral letter.

"Considérations sur les evénements en cours à Madagascar." *Aspects du christianisme à Madagascar*, n.s. 4 (October–December 1992), 379–81.

Costalungo, Natale. "Marxismo e missione in Mozambico." *SEDOS Bulletin* [Rome], No. 82/18 (December 1, 1982), 344–51.

"Debate on Religion in Nanking." *Ateismo e dialogo*, 14 (September 1979), 130.

Dumortier, Diogène. "Madagascar au bord de la guerre civile: Une élection présidentielle laborieuse." *Chine-Maduré-Madagascar*, No. 240 (December 1992–January 1993), 23.

"L'église des territoires portugaises d'outre-mer." *Documentation catholique*, 71 (February 3, 1974), 111–16.

"Les élections législatives du 16 juin 93." *Chine-Maduré-Madagascar*, No. 243 (June–August 1993), 17.

Emmanuel, John. "Marxist Mozambique." *Tablet* [London], 234 (May 17, 1980), 472–74.

"Ethiopia: A Tale of Two Revolutions." *Pro Mundi Vita Dossiers*, Africa Dossier 5 (January–February 1978).

"Full Text of the Crucial Document." *Moto* [Harare], No. 63 (March 1988), 9.

Galico, Laurice. "The Catholic Church and Africa." *World Marxist Review*, 4 (April 1961), 34–40.

Gheddo, Piero. "L'ésperienza 'socialista' in Mozambico." *Monde e missione* [Milan], 108 (November 15, 1979), 587–612.

Gonçalves, Jaime, and P. Obinna Aguh. "Pan-African Justice and Peace Seminar, Held at Roma, Lesotho, 29 May–3 June 1988. Communiqué Issued on 3 June 1988." *AFER* [Eldoret, Kenya], 30 (August 1988), 218–25.

"Governmental Policy and the Church in the Portuguese Territories of Africa." *Pro Mundi Vita Bulletin* [Brussels], No. 44 (1972).

Gujiyu, Ren. "The Struggle to Develop a Marxist Science of Religion." *Ateismo e dialogo*, 14 (December 1979), 165–71.

Heijke, J. "Socialism and the Church in Africa." *Exchange*, 10 (December 1981), 36–39.

Henriksen, Thomas H. "Marxism and Mozambique." *African Affairs*, 77 (October 1978), 441–62.

"A igrega em Moçambique hoje: entre o colonialismo e a revolução." *Noticias*, July 27, 1979, 1.

"Uma igreja incapaz de encontrar o seu lugar na historia." *Noticias*, July 29, 1979, 3.

"Un impératif de conscience." *Documentation catholique*, 71 (May 5, 1974), 419–21.

"Inside Mozambique." *Tablet*, 232 (July 1, 1978), 824–25.

"Inter sanctam sedem et rem publicam Lusitanam conventiones." *Acta Apostolicae Sedis*, 32 (June 1, 1960), 217–44.

Kimble, Judy. "The Lesotho Coup." *West Africa*, February 3, 1986, 235–36.

Lobkowicz, Nicholas. "Karl Marx's Attitude Toward Religion." *Review of Politics*, 26 (July 1964), 319–52.

"Madagascar à l'heure de l'autocritique." *Chine-Madagascar* [Lille], No. 183 (June–July 1981), 20–21.

Magesa, Laurenti. "Instruction on the 'Theology of Liberation'; A Comment." *AFER*, 27 (February 1985), 2–8.

Malley, Simon. "À coeur ouvert avec Didier Ratsiraka." *Afrique-Asie*, No. 151 (December 26, 1977–January 7, 1978), 30–36.

"Manuel de doctrine sociale de l'église." Part I. *Aspects du christianisme à Madagascar*, 18 (March–April 1982), 225–37. Part II, *Aspects du christianisme à Madagascar*, 18 (May–June 1982), 257–89.

"Message du Conseil Chrétien des Églises de Madagascar." *Documentation catholique*, 79 (September 5–19, 1982), 836–38.

Mittelman, James H. "Marginalization and the International Division of Labor: Mozambique's Strategy of Opening the Market." *African Studies Review*, 34 (December 1991), 89–106.

"Moçambique: Uma igreja como as demais?" *Alem-mar*, 25 (October 1980), 27–30.

"Mozambique: A Church in a Socialist State in a Time of Radical Change." *Pro Mundi Vita Dossiers*, Africa Dossier, n.s. 3 (January–February 1977).

"Mozambique: Problems, Options, and the Response of the Church." *International Fides Press Service*, December 4, 1982, NE518–522.

"Mugabe Outlines Plans and Priorities." *Moto*, No. 22 (March 1980), 3.

"Nos espoirs déçus: La situation actuelle de Madagascar par un malgache." *Chine-Madagascar*, No. 181 (February–March 1981), 14–16.

"Note du ministère portugais d'outre-mer." *Documentation catholique*, 71 (May 5, 1974), 422.

"Nouvelles de Madagascar." *Chine-Maduré-Madagascar*, No. 242 (April–May 1993), 23.

"Nouvelles de Madagascar: du référendum aux élections." *Chine-Maduré-Madagascar*, No. 239 (September–October 1992), 23.

"Ou va l'enseignement à Madagascar?" *Chine-Madagascar*, No. 169 (October–November 1978), 17–20.

"O Papel da igreja católica em Moçambique." *Tempo* [Maputo], No. 447 (May 6, 1979), 25–40: No. 448 (May 13, 1979), 37–40.

Pleyber, Yves. "La force des pauvres en terre malgache." *Aspects du christianisme à Madagascar*, 18 (November–December 1981), 168–71.

"Prêtre et journaliste à Fianarantsoa: Une interview du Père René-Claude Andiramihaja." *Chine-Maduré-Madagascar*, No. 227 (April–May 1990), 12–14.

"Prise de position de l'archevêque de Lourenço Marquès." *Documentation catholique*, 71 (May 5, 1974), 425–27.

Rabemora, Félix. "Dix années de socialisme à Madagascar." *Chine-Maduré-Madagascar*, No. 204 (September–November 1985), 14–16; No. 205 (December 1985–January 1986), 14–17.

Ralibera, Rémy. "L'enseignement privé à Madagascar a désormais son statut." *Chine-Madagascar*, No. 174 (October–November 1979), 13–15.

———. "Madagascar 1986." *Chine-Maduré-Madagascar*, No. 209 (September–November 1986), 16–17.

Rasediniarivo. "Billet malgache: Sécurité, revitaillement, et justice." *Chine-Maduré-Madagascar*, No. 202 (April–May 1985), 16–17.

———. "L'école catholique à Madagascar aujourd'hui." *Maduré-Madagascar*, No. 168 (July 1978), 339–41.

Razafimahatrata, Victor. "L'engagement chrêtien dans la vie du pays." *Chine-Madagascar*, No. 179 (October–November 1980), 13–18.

Razafintsalama, Adolphe. "À Madagascar: Le FFKM, Conseil des Églises, re-unit les forces vives de la nation." *Chine-Maduré-Madagascar*, No. 230 (December 1990–January 1991), 13–15.

———. "Sous l'égide du F.F.K.M. les conséquences du Forum National." *Chine-Maduré-Madagascar*, No. 238 (June–August 1992), 12–14.

"Religião a submissão do homen." *Tempo*, No. 372 (November 20, 1977), 56–63.

Religious Leaders of Zambia. "The Churches and Marxism." *Catholic Mind*, 78 (May 1980), 9–23.

"Remous autour d'une lettre." *Maduré-Madagascar*, No. 169 (September 1978), 353–54.

"Rencontre national des prêtres." *Aspects du christianisme à Madagascar*. 17 (July–August 1979), 105–28, and (September–October 1979), 129–64.

"Resolução do trabalho ideologico do Partido sobre estilo e metodos do actuação." *Noticias*, July 6, 1981, 2–3.

"Roman Catholics and African Politics." *Pro Mundi Vita Dossiers*, Africa Dossier 7/8 (March 1979).

Saint-Jean, Raymond. "Problèmes et perspectives du Synode Nationale." *Aspects du christianisme à Madagascar*, 15 (September–October 1976), 347–68.

Sales, M. "Praxis marxiste et discernement chrêtien." *Aspects du christianisme à Madagascar*, 17 (November–December 1979), 165–83.

Sartre, Victor. "*Rerum Novarum* et les syndicalistes chrètiens à Madagascar." *Aspects du christianisme à Madagascar*, n.s. 4 (October–December 1991), 173–79.

*SEDOS Bulletin* 77/8 (May 1, 1977), 181–203. Appendix I.

Sklar, Richard L. "Reds and Rights: Zimbabwe's Experience." *Issue*, 14 (1985), 29–33.

Sorio, Ezio. "Depois da autocrítica o quê." *Alem-mar*, 26 (April 1981), 11–14.

*Speak Out* [Ndola, Zambia]. March–April 1986.

Spindler, Marc. "Évolution de la théologie à Madagascar." *Aspects du christianisme à Madagascar*, 19 (September–December 1984), 329–44.

"Synode nationale de l'église à Madagascar." *Aspects du christianisme à Madagascar*, 16 (January–February 1976), 209–37.

"Synode nationale de l'église à Madagascar." *Aspects du christianisme à Madagascar*, 16 (March–April 1976), 245–53.

Ugochukwu, Onyema. "The Lost Revolution." *West Africa*, February 25, 1985, 346–47.

*UNIP Youth* [Lusaka]. July 1985.

Vieira Pinto, Manuel. "The Church in Independent Mozambique." *IDOC Bulletin*, Nos. 41–42 (March–April 1976), 2–9.

———. "L'église et le temps." *Spiritus*, 66 (1977), 65–78.

———. "Répenser la guerre." *Documentation catholique*, 71 (May 5, 1974), 413–18.

Wermter, Oskar. "Church and Party." *Moto*, No. 54 (n.d.): 24.

"Zimbabwe: Bishops Urge Reconciliation, Inculturation of Gospel Message." *International Fides Press Service*, May 6, 1981, NE243.

## Mimeographed and Typed Documents

"Aide-memoire del'incontro SEDOS sulla presenza missionaria in Mozambico." October 14, 1983. SEDOS, Rome.

Banana, Canaan. "President Urges Churches: 'Re-Examine Your Stance.'" Zimbabwe, Department of Information, press statement 151/81/SFS, March 3, 1981.

———. "President Addresses Seventh Day Adventists." Zimbabwe, Department of Information, press statement 714/80/JEP, November 11, 1980.

Bispos de Moçambique. "Testemunhar a fé em liberdade: carta pastoral dos bispos de Moçambique." December 3, 1978. Maputo: Secretariado Geral CEM.

Catholic Relief Services of the United States Catholic Conference. "Rapport annuel d'activités, année 1981, République démocratique de Madagascar." [Antananarivo, 1982.]

Chelu, F. K. "A letter from F. K. Chelu for Permanent Secretary, Ministry of Education to All Chief Education Officers, Heads of Secondary Schools, Principals of Colleges, 20th December 1978." Files of confidential informant.

Chidzero, Bernard. "The Dynamics of Leadership—The Zimbabwe Context." to Salisbury Archdiocesan Committee, May 26, 1981. Committee Minutes. Files of ZCBC Secretariat, Harare.

———. "Opening Address to the Annual General Meeting of the Conference of Major Superiors of Women Religious, Feb. 26, 1982," as reported in the Minutes of the Conference Executive Committee, March 19, 1982. Files of ZCBC Secretariat, Harare.

Church Leaders' Humanism Seminar Held at Mulungushi Hall from 18th to 19th March, 1982. Group Deliberations, Resolutions. Files of Zambia Catholic Secretariat, Lusaka.

"CMRS Annual Meeting, Salisbury, 30 November 1981." ZCBC News Sheet, No. 102 (February 1982),: pp. 102/16–17. Files of ZCBC Secretariat, Harare.

Consultative Meeting on Scientific Socialism Held on 20th March 1979 at Archbishop's Residence. Files of Zambia Catholic Secretariat, Lusaka.

Cremins, Richard. Manuscript jottings on seminar of Catholic Church personnel on scientific socialism, Monze, [June or July] 1979. Files of Zambia Catholic Secretariat, Lusaka.

———. Manuscript jottings on meeting of Catholic Church personnel at Monze, April 17, 1982. Files of Zambia Catholic Secretariat, Lusaka.

Kaunda, Kenneth D. "The Attainment of Humanism through Socialism." Paper distributed at the Church Leaders' Humanism Seminar, March 1982, Lusaka. Files of Zambia Catholic Secretariat, Lusaka.

———. "Concluding Remarks of His Excellency the President, Dr. Kenneth David Kaunda, at the All Churches Service to End the Prayer Week for the Economic Welfare of the People of Zambia Held at the Cathedral of the Holy Cross on Sunday Afternoon, 17th December 1985." Files of Zambia Catholic Secretariat, Lusaka.

———. "Introductory Remarks by His Excellency the President, Dr. Kenneth David Kaunda to the Meeting of Principal Leaders of Church Organizations in Zambia Held at State House, 31st October 1985." Files of Zambia Catholic Secretariat, Lusaka.

———. "The Official Closing of the Church Leaders' Seminar by President Kaunda at Mulungushi Hall." Files of Zambia Catholic Secretariat, Lusaka.

———. "Speech by His Excellency the President, Dr. K. D. Kaunda, to the

Seminar of Religious Leaders at Mulungushi Hall, Lusaka, from 18th to 19th March 1982." Files of Zambia Catholic Secretariat, Lusaka.

Mubako, Simon. "Speech of Simon Mubako, Minister of Justice and Constitutional Affairs, to the South Deanery pastoral committee (Salisbury), February 21, 1981." Files of ZCBC Secretariat, Harare.

Mugabe, Robert G. "Mugabe Seeks Church Co-operation." Speech to Church Representatives, April 30, 1982. Files of ZCBC Secretariat, Harare.

———. "Mugabe Speech at the First Assembly of the Inter-Regional Meeting of Bishops of Southern Africa." August 22, 1984. Files of ZCBC Secretariat, Harare.

———. "Socialism in Zimbabwe: An Address Delivered by the Prime Minister, Comrade R. G. Mugabe, to a Meeting of the Justice and Peace Commission." February 6, 1982. Catholic Commission for Justice and Peace, *Newsletter* no. 2 (March 1982), Appendix I, p. 7. Files of the ZCBC Secretariat, Harare.

Muzenda, Simon. "Muzenda Urges Churches to Promote Socialism." Zimbabwe Government Press Service, 203/82/MM/DB. March 9, 1982. Address by Deputy Prime Minister to diocesan priests of Gwelo diocese at Ft. Victoria. Files of ZCBC Secretariat, Harare.

"Notes on the Seminar Held at Evelyn Hone College on Saturday 13 March 1982 at 1430 Hours." Files of Zambia Catholic Secretariat, Lusaka.

"President's Citizenship College, Political Education Unit, Certificate Course in Political Education, 23 Weeks (9th July–14th December 1979)." Files of confidential informant.

Randolph, Richard H. "The Catholic Church in the New Zimbabwe." December 15, 1980. Files of the ZCBC Secretariat.

———. "Report on Zimbabwe, 18 Apr. 80–24 Dec. 81." February 10, 1982. Files of ZCBC Secretariat, Harare.

———. "The Role of the Catholic Church in Zimbabwe: A Miscellany of Texts." [1981?]. Files of ZCBC Secretarat, Harare.

*Rapport général sur CM-BLASC.* Antananarivo, May 17, 1982. Files of the Secretariat of the Conférence Épiscopale de Madagascar, Antananarivo.

"Report on the NCOP Symposium on the Church in the New Order, Driefontein, 17–19 May 1977." Pastoral Service, Supplement 20. Pastoral Centre, Emerald Hill, Salisbury. June 1977.

SECAM. "Pan-African Conference on Justice and Peace, 1983–1988." Circular prepared by the Secretariat of SECAM. Files of Zambia Catholic Secretariat, Lusaka.

———. "Questionnaire of SECAM on Preparation for Pan-African Conference on Justice and Peace." Circular SE/189. Files of Zambia Catholic Secretariat, Lusaka.

Secretariat for Non-Believers. Circular letter from Cardinal König to Presidents of Episcopal Conferences, November 24, 1974, Prot. n. 003465/74; and enclosure, "Conclusions of the Plenary Assembly, March 12–15, 1974. Theme I:

Relationship between Christian Faith and Marxist Ideologies Today. Theme II: Evangelization of the World Today, Confronting Atheism and Secularization." Prot. n. 003340/74.

Silveira House, Chishawasha, Zimbabwe, Center for Leadership and Development. *Annual Report, 1981.*

"Silveira House Centre for Leadership and Development, Zimbabwe." [1982?]. Descriptive circular.

"Silveira House 'Musandirapamwe' C. A. Agricultural Project, Zimbabwe." [1982?]. Descriptive circular.

Simuchoba, Philip. "Seminar of His Excellency the President with Church Leaders on Humanism and Development. Introductory Remarks by the Chairman, Mr. Philip Simuchoba." March 1982. Files of the Zambia Catholic Secretariat, Lusaka.

University of Zambia Students' Union. "Circular from UNZASU Executive to Student Body, March 18, 1992. Subject: Academic Freedom at Stake. Institute of Human Relations Boils. Which Way UNZASU?" Files of confidential informant.

———. "From UNZASU Executive to UNZA Community. 23 February 1982. *Re*: On the Decadent Banalities of the Shemuhaist Clique and Its Inhuman Relations." Files of confidential informant.

———. "Minutes of the Emergency Meeting Called by the Principal of the Lusaka Campus of the University of Zambia with the Executive Committee of UNZASU on Tuesday, 2nd March 1982." Files of confidential informant.

———. "UNZASU Day, 9th February [1982]. Revolutionary Day of the University of Zambia Students. Programme." Files of confidential informant.

———. "UNZASU Stand vis-à-vis the Institute of Human Relations." March 2, 1982. Files of confidential informant.

Vieira Pinto, Manuel. "Ateismo e religião: Fé e revolução" (Pastoral letter, Christmas 1978). Files of confidential informant.

———. "A minha reflexão apos encontro e a reunião de trabalho com o Ministro Oscar Monteiro em 15 do mes corrente." July 15, 1981. Files of confidential informant.

———. Untitled report on the diocese of Nampula, December 1, 1980. Files of confidential informant.

Zambia, Minister of Education and Culture. *Political Education Syllabus for Political Educators*, prepared by the office of the Secretary-General of the Party. Lusaka: Freedom House, [1981]. Files of confidential informant.

"Zimbabwean Socialism." *Zimbabwe Catholic Bishops' Conference News Sheet*, No. 104 (1982), 104/10-18. Files of ZCBC Secretariat, Harare.

PRESS, INFORMATION, AND DOCUMENTATION SERVICES
(EXCLUSIVE OF ITEMS LISTED ABOVE)

*AACC News*, July 1979. (IDOC Documentation Center, Rome. File no. 33144.)

*AIM Information Bulletin* [Maputo], Nos. 61 (July 1981) and 64 (October 1981). Mozambique Information Agency, Maputo.

Britain-Zimbabwe Society. [Surrey, England.] "Twenty-First Review of the Zimbabwean Press, March 1st to April 18th, 1986."

*Documentation SEDOS*, July 14, 1975. (IDOC Documentation Center, Rome. File no. 03255).

*IDOC Bulletin* nos. 3–5 (January 1973), 25 (November 1974), 37 (November–December 1975), 41–42 (March–April 1976).

*IDOC Communication* nos. 72/200/002 (August 16, 1972). (IDOC Documentation Centre, Rome.)

*Impact* no. 109 (June 1985). (Newsletter of the Zambia Catholic Secretariat, Lusaka).

*Informations catholiques internationales*, July 1, 1976. (IDOC Documentation Center, Rome. File no. 08357).

*International Fides Press Service*, February 15, 1978; February 23, 1980.

*Service du Presse Protestante Romande*, May 7, 1979. (IDOC Documentation Center, Rome. File no. 32966).

*Zimbabwe Catholic Bishops' Conference News Sheet* [Salisbury], February 1982.

*Zimbabwe Pressespiegel* [Harare and Berlin], vols. 3 (April, August 1984), 4 (January 1985), 5 (April–May, June 1986).

*Zimbabwe Project News Bulletin* [Salisbury/Harare], nos. 4, 6, 8, 10–13, 16–17, 20–22, 24, 25, 27–34.

## NEWSPAPERS AND NEWS MAGAZINES

*Daily Herald* [Salisbury]. August 18, September 3, December 9, 1980; January 26, 29, 1981; January 27, February 15, April 16, 1982.

*Daily Sketch* [Ibadan]. September 9, 1983.

*Lakroan'i Madigasikara* [Antananarivo]. December 13, 1981; January 10, 17, February 7, March 14, 21, April 18, May 9, 16, 1982.

*The Light* [Salisbury]. March 1982.

*Madagascar Matin* [Antananarivo]. April 15, 23, 26, 28, May 4, 1982.

*Moto*, Nos. 42, 43.

*National Concord* [Lagos]. August 31, 1983.

*National Mirror* [Lusaka]. November 1978; January, February 1979; October 9–22, 1981.

*The New York Times*. March 8, June 29, July 7, 8, August 3, September 18, 20, 1985; February 25, March 2, May 22, December 10, 12, 1986; December 23, 1987; May 10, September 17, 19, 1988.

*Sunday Mail* [Salisbury]. January 11, 1981; January 31, 1982.

*Sunday Times of Zambia* [Lusaka]. July 8, 1984; October 27, 1985.

*Tablet* [London] 238 (October 6, 1984).

*Times of Zambia* [Lusaka]. September 17, October 27, 1979; April 5, 19, 20, 22, 1982; September 28, 1985; August 15, 1986.

*West Africa*. August 15, 1982; September 5, 26, 1983; May 11, 25, 1987.

*Worker's Challenge* [Kitwe, Zambia]. November 1984; April 1985.

*Zambia Daily Mail* [Lusaka]. March 22, April 14, 20, 1982; July 12, 1986.

INTERVIEWS
(EXCLUSIVE OF CONFIDENTIAL INFORMANTS)

Acton, Judith, April 1982
Allain, Fr. Pierre, May 1982
Andriamihaja, Fr. René-Claude, May 1982
Bethaz, Fr. Giustino, May 1982
Bisson, Fr. Roger, May 1982
Cremins, Fr. Richard, April 1982
Dove, Fr. John, March 1982
Freyer, Fr. Clemens, April 1982
Girard, Fr. Pierre, March 1982
Harold-Barry, Fr. David, March 1982
Lwaminda, Fr. Peter, May 1982
Mundhoro, Clement, April 1962
Niederberger, Fr. Oscar, April 1982
O'Flynn, Fr. Anthony, April 1982
Page, Fr. Timothy, April 1982
Ralibera, Fr. Rémy, May 1982
Randolph, Fr. Richard, April 1982
Rasolo, Fr. Louis, May 1982
Razafindrabe, Fr. Michel, May 1982
Rocca, Rev. Mother, April 1982
Rogers, Fr. E. W., April 1982
Scholz, Fr. Dieter, March 1982
Spence, Fr. Kenneth, March 1982
Von Nidda, Fr. Roland, April 1982
Wardale, Fr. Henry, April 1982

# INDEX

www.ingramcontent.com/pod-product-compliance
Lightning Source LLC
Chambersburg PA
CBHW072059020426
42334CB00017B/1569